ISBN 978-1-331-55376-2
PIBN 10205105

PREFACE

TO THE AMERICAN EDITION.

Many words are not required to recommend to the American Catholic public a life of the Angelical youth, St. Aloysius Gonzaga. In a country like this, where every thinking man feels that the education of the rising generation is one of the most important objects that can engage the attention of all, who, from whatever cause, may be interested in the preservation of good morals, Catholics turn instinctively to the blessed Saint, whom the Will of Heaven, expressed by the Vicar of Christ on earth, has designated as the especial protector of youth in these latter days. To him they entrust the young people for whom they know that they will be held responsible at the tribunal of the Most High; and it is through his intercession, after that of the Mother of God, that they hope that the Invisible Head of the Church will vouchsafe them the graces necessary to enable them to succeed in the arduous task of imparting a truly Christian education to those committed to their care.

The present volume is the first of a series of lives of holy persons, now publishing in England, edited by a gentleman fully competent for the important task. A few inaccuracies, which had been allowed to creep into the English edition, have been carefully corrected in this reprint. This correction has been rendered the more easy by the fact that the author himself had substantially acknowledged the justice of the remarks, which had been made by his critics.

It will be seen that the author has spared no pains to make his work perfect. On this account, his life of St. Aloysius has special claims on the Catholic public. An extraordinary hero of sanctity, Aloysius is, at the same time, an exemplar which each one may copy, albeit imperfectly, in the regulation of his daily actions. It thus becomes a matter of importance, to know all the details of his short and saintly career; and these are given in the present volume with an exactness, a grace, and an earnestness, which mark a labor of holy love.

That this publication may conduce to the greater glory of God, the object for which Aloysius ever labored, and the preservation of innocence among those of whom he is the special protector, is the sincere wish and prayer of the American publisher.

ADVERTISEMENT.

MORE ample details exist for the life of St. Aloysius Gonzaga than for almost any other saint perhaps in the calender. P. Virgilio Cepari, his principal biographer, lived in close intimacy with him at the Roman College for several years, and, having resolved to write his life, he communicated his design to P. Girolamo Piatti. This father, who, as being set over the novices sent to serve masses at the Gesù, had enjoyed much communication with Aloysius previously to P. Cepari's personal intercourse with the holy youth, had exacted from him an account of his life and vocation, as well as of the graces he received in the world; all which P. Piatti had secretly committed to paper. This manuscript he now handed over to P. Cepari, approving and encouraging his design. By the help of these materials, and with the addition of what he had himself noted or learned from others, Cepari concluded his first biography about two years before the saint's death, but showed it to a very limited number of persons, and that in strict confidence, fearing lest it should reach the ears of the subject himself.

After Aloysius's death, P. Cepari submitted the manuscript to P. Bellarmino, who strongly urged him to add to his narrative the last two years of the saint's life. But as he was at that time much occupied, he handed over his papers, with many fresh materials which he had collected, to P. Giovanni Antonio Valtrino, who had just come from Sicily for the purpose of compiling the chronicles of the Company, in order that he might complete the work or make any other use of it he pleased. This father had no personal knowledge of Aloysius, but when he heard the details of his wonderful sanctity at the Roman College, and witnessed the veneration of which he was the object, he felt pressed to give so edifying an example more rapid publication, and not wait to consign the recital to the chronicles which were in process of formation. Accordingly, he wrote a separate life, and this was the second manuscript biography of the saint which was circulated. As Cepari, Piatti, and Valtrino, however, had mainly relied upon Aloysius's own account extracted from him by obedience, or caught and noted down from his lips when led by some pious artifice to speak of himself, much, they were aware, must necessarily be deficient in the statement; for the holy youth's humility not only veiled from his own eye his sublime perfection, but made him solicitous to conceal it from others. As far as truth and obedience would permit, Aloysius had, no doubt,, diminished the merit of what he related, as well as omitted much which would have redounded to his praise. Saints' descriptions of themselves must always be open to similar charges. For this reason it was therefore extremely desirable to refer to other authentic sources, as well as for the purpose of insuring accuracy in regard to time, place, and circumstance. The information obtained from Castaglione, Mantua, and other places so swelled the materials in hand, that it soon became evident that the life must be re-written. But P. Valtrino's death taking place before he could take any further measure, the task again devolved upon P. Cepari, whom the General of the Company, Claudio Acquaviva, who was most desirous to see the work completed, enjoined to resume his labour.

P. Cepari received the charge as though it came direct from heaven. With indefatigable diligence he now sought out and inquired personally at the mouth of every one who from the cradle to the grave had been in relation with the holy youth. He first visited Florence, in order to obtain every minute detail of Aloysius's life in the world from his governor, Signor Pier Francesco del Turco, who had entered the household of Don Giovanni de' Medici when his saintly charge had joined the company. This gentleman was attached to the court of the Marquis of Castiglione at the time of Aloysius's birth, who was consigned to his care at a very tender age; and he held this office about the youth's person for eighteen years, quitting it only when he entered the doors of the Company's house at Rome. From Florence, Cepari passed into

Lombardy, and repaired to Castiglione, where he spent many days in collecting every particular from the mother of the saint, and from those who had served and attended upon him in the world; with the bishop's licence, and in order to give greater authenticity to his narrative, he also caused two long processes to be drawn up of his life and manners. From countries which he was unable to visit, such as Spain and France, he solicited and obtained letters from persons who had known or conversed with Aloysius; he interested himself also to have examinations instituted and processes formed with all the due solemnities, in various parts of Poland, and before the ecclesiastical tribunals of the patriarch of Venice, of the archbishops of Naples, Milan, Florence, Bologna, Siena, Turin, and also of the bishops of Mantua, Padua, Vicenza Brescia, Forli, Modena, Reggio, Parma, Piacenza, Mondovi, Ancona, Recanati, and Tivoli. More than once he himself went round all parts of Lombardy where he could hope to glean information or verify more fully the accuracy of any facts related. At last he took up his quarters at Brescia, on account of its proximity to Castiglione, and the facility thus offered for promptly clearing up doubts or solving questions which might arise. From the processes and from the written statements which he had procured, and which were also attested on oath, Cepari then composed his biography, which thus possesses guarantees for veracity and exactness which it would be scarcely possible to exceed; add to which that, previously to its publication, it was strictly examined and compared with the episcopal processes.

Notwithstanding, however, all his diligence, Cepari could only avail himself of what existed in the form of authentic documents previous to the date of the publication of his work in 1606. As yet, no ecclesiastical processes existed, except those drawn up by the authority of the bishops. But the increasing glory of the saint led to the formation of the first processes instituted by apostolic authority in the year 1608, under the pontificate of Paul V. The depositions then made contain, of course, much repetition of what was already embodied in Cepari's work, but they also furnish additional matter of great interest. The present biography is grounded upon Cepari's work, and the writer can by no means pretend to have exhausted his valuable materials; but reference has been made to the processes of 1608, as given by the Bollandists, and advantage taken of what might serve to illustrate the text or supply deficiencies. This has been done more especially with respect to the circumstances of the saint's death, for an account of which the father seems exclusively to have relied upon two letters written to him in the year 1604, at his express desire, by P. Fabrini, one of the witnesses of Aloysius's last moments. The two other persons present were P. Guelfucci and the infirmarian. Their depositions appear in the processes, and help to complete the narrative as well as to elucidate the order of the incidents.

A few notes had been collected by Cepari subsequently to the publication of his work, with a view to their future insertion. But no advantage had been taken of these memoranda until the recent edition of the Life by the Jesuit fathers at Rome, which also contains many valuable additions and carries on the narrative of all that relates to the saint's honour down to the present day. Some hitherto unpublished writings of St. Aloysius form an interesting appendage to the volume.

P. Cepari concludes his advertisement, addressed to the "pious reader," with these words, which the writer desires to adopt and appropriate:—"The defects in this history must be attributed to me; for the good it may do, may glory be rendered to God, whom may it please to give us grace to imitate the holy example of this youth, and to arrive, through his intercession, at that blessed end which he now enjoys with great glory in Heaven. And thou, most holy and most blessed Luigi, who in the happy abodes of Paradise art now receiving the reward of thy holy labours, and who in the mirror of the Divine Essence seest my imperfection, forgive me if I have presumed to write in unworthy language of thy heroic virtues, and obtain for me, from our common lord, grace to live religiously and virtuously; so that, favoured by thy aid and protection, I may one day come to enjoy thy company in eternal blessedness.'

CONTENTS.

PART I.

The Saint in the World.

CHAPTER I.

LEWIS GONZAGA'S BIRTH AND INFANCY.

CHAPTER II.

LEWIS'S EARLY BOYHOOD.

CHAPTER III.

LEWIS'S MODE OF LIFE AT CASTIGLIONE.

CHAPTER VII.

LEWIS JOINS THE COMPANY OF JESUS.

PART II.

The Saint in Religion.

CHAPTER I.

LEWIS'S ENTRY INTO THE NOVICIATE.

CHAPTER II.

THE PERFECT NOVICE.

CHAPTER III.

THE SAINT'S VISIT TO NAPLES, AND CLOSE OF HIS NOVICIATE.

CHAPTER IV.

THE FIRST YEARS OF HIS RELIGIOUS PROFESSION

CHAPTER V.

ALOYSIUS'S MISSION OF PEACE TO CASTIGLIONE.

CHAPTER VI.

ALOYSIUS'S CONDUCT IN THE AFFAIR OF HIS BROTHER'S MARRIAGE.

CHAPTER VII.

ALOYSIUS'S LIFE AT THE COLLEGE OF BRERA, AND RETURN TO ROME.

CHAPTER VIII.

ALOYSIUS'S LAST ILLNESS AND DEATH.

PART III.

The Saint in Heaven.

CHAPTER I.

TESTIMONIES TO ALOYSIUS'S SANCTITY. HIS BEATIFICATION.

PART I.

THE SAINT IN THE WORLD.

CHAPTER I.

LEWIS GONZAGA'S BIRTH AND INFANCY.

THE life of St. Aloysius is not an eventful one, if the outward vicissitudes of our earthly pilgrimage are to be taken as the measure of eventfulness. It was, moreover, a short life, and what men might call an incomplete life, even as respected the vocation to follow which he had made the sacrifice of all his worldly prospects. For he saw but the opening of his twenty-third summer, and died before attaining to the priesthood. But if we look to the interior life, the true life of all Christians—if we turn our eyes to that stage upon which the great drama of our existence is enacted—then the life of this youth becomes one of surpassing interest; and such is the light in which every devout Catholic has always regarded it. When acts of perfection, acts done for God, and not mere days and years, are considered as the measure of extension, then also does it expand into a long life; and if the entire fulfilment of the Divine purpose of grace towards the soul be taken into account, then, too, does it come before us as a complete life. To him may truly be applied the words of the wise man,—"*Consummatis in brevi, explevit tempora multa.*" "Being made perfect in a short space, he fulfilled a long time." (Wis. iv. 13.) It pleased God, who in him designed to furnish a perfect model to youth, to finish His work in a few days, and call away his servant to receive his crown before he had passed beyond the threshhold of a more advanced period of life; so that he should for ever be imaged forth to us in all the charm and grace of life's early spring, and as such be recommended as a more familiar pattern and patron of adolescence, no less than of boyhood.

The Gonzagas were amongst those princely families of Italy which have furnished rulers to its little independent states, and with which crowned heads have not disdained to seek alliance in marriage. The elder branch had reigned at Mantua for two centuries at the period to which our story refers, but even in the tenth century nobles of the same ancient stock had exercised sovereignty over many Lombard towns. The father of our saint, Ferrante Gonzaga, was by inheritance Marquis of Castiglione della Stiviere in Lombardy, and by birth, as were all the Gonzagas, a prince of the Holy Roman Empire. His mother was a Spanish lady of high extraction. The marquis had spent his life chiefly in camps, in the Imperial service, and his tastes and pursuits were in consequence thoroughly military. Secular ambition occupied a large place in his heart, and he does not appear to have turned his thoughts towards marriage until his first youth was passed. On the whole, judged by an ordinary standard, he appears to have been an estimable man and a good Catholic. If his tastes and views were in a large degree worldly, he was capable, to a certain extent, of appreciating something higher, and was evidently desirous of meeting with qualifications of a superior order in his future consort. We may argue thus much at least from his choice. The lady upon whom it fell deserves a somewhat more extended notice.

Philip II. at this time ruled Spain, and was also sovereign of the Low Countries, king of Naples, and duke of Milan. After the death of Mary Tudor, queen of England, his second wife, he married Elisabeth of Valois (usually called Isabella in Spanish history), the daughter of Henry II. of France and Catherine of Medicis. On leaving France the princess had brought with her as her lady of honour, Donna Marta Tana, daughter of the Baron de Santena, lord of Chieri in Piedmont, a nobleman of high lineage, possessing independent fiefs which owned vassalage to the Emperor alone, and of Donna Anna della Rovere, daughter of the duke of Urbino. They were attached to the household of Catherine of Medicis, and their daughter had thus grown up on terms of the most affectionate friendship and confidence with the young princess Elisabeth. Marta was worthy of the love and esteem in which she was held, and formed the chief consolation of her royal mistress in the not very enviable position she held in a court distracted by the moody jealousies of the heir to the throne, the unhappy Carlos, and his dissensions with his father.

The visit of the king's nephews, the Archdukes Rudolph and Ernest of Austria, sons of the Emperor Maximilian II. and Maria, the daughter of Charles V., was the occasion of the presence at Madrid of many German and Italian nobles who came in their train. Foremost amongst the latter ranked Don Ferrante Gonzaga, Marquis of Castiglione, himself, as we have seen, on his mother's side of noble Spanish extraction; and it was thus at the Court of Madrid that he became acquainted with the high merits of his future spouse, Donna Marta. Having resolved to seek her in marriage, his first step was to allow the project he entertained to reach the royal ears, and he was fortunate enough to find his views favourably regarded in that quarter. The queen herself undertook to become a suitor in his behalf. In one of those hours of privacy which formed Elisabeth's sweetest recreation, she gently and lovingly broke to her dear Marta her own and the king's desire for her union with Don Ferrante. There was nothing in the proposed alliance calculated to be very attractive in the eyes of a young maiden. True, it was, as the world would say, a very great match; for, although Donna Marta came of noble lineage, her proposed husband was a kind of petty sovereign in his own land. But, on the other hand, Marta was in the bloom of early youth, and Ferrante was hovering on the confines of middle age; and what was even of more importance than the discrepancy in years, there was that which existed in disposition between the pious, retiring, humble girl—for such, though reared in courts, was Marta de Santena—and the mail-coated baron, who esteemed the upholding of the honour and interests of his ancient and lordly family the great active business of life. Ferrante, indeed, was an honourable man, attached to his faith, and zealous in his own way for God's glory. Had it been otherwise, we may conceive that not all the favour of royalty could have led Marta to lend an ear to his proposals. As it was, she asked for time to reflect and refer the matter to God. For this end she caused many masses to be offered; to these she added her own fervent prayer for guidance together with abundant alms to the poor; she consulted also her spiritual director; and finally decided on accepting the offer which had been made to her.

Pius V. had granted a jubilee to the Christian world, which had just been published in Spain; and Marta, with her intended spouse, seized the opportunity to hallow their betrothal by uniting it with this devotion. Upon the morning of the feast of St. John the Baptist, in the year 1566, they communicated, in order to gain the Indulgence, and forthwith concluded the antenuptial contract. Philip richly endowed the affianced bride and presented her with costly jewels, to which his royal consort added magnificent presents in testimony of her own personal affection. But Marta's mind, so far from being dazzled with her brilliant prospects, was more than ever fixed upon God and holy things; and she herself in after years told P. Cepari that on the day of her betrothal she felt herself moved internally to devote her whole future life to the more perfect service of God. On the wedding-day we again find the marchese and his intended bride preparing themselves by confession and communion for the worthy reception of the sacrament of matrimony; and thus was this marriage concluded in a truly Catholic spirit. It has been noticed that it was the first marriage celebrated in Spain with all the formalities prescribed by the Council of Trent.

Having obtained the sovereign's assent, Gonzaga now left Spain for Italy, distinguished by many testimonies of royal favour, Philip having appointed him his chamberlain and conferred other honours and emoluments upon him. He was impatient to reach his own dominions and present his young wife to his vassals. They took up their residence in the rock castle of Castiglione, the ancestral abode of Ferrante's race. It adjoined the town, in which also the marchese possessed a palace. He had his own private chapel and chaplain within the fortress; nevertheless, the noble couple regularly attended all the services of religion in the parish church. As the sound of the bells summoned the faithful on the numerous festival days to the sacred offices, the lord and lady of the place descended with their household from the old feudal castle, while their vassals, moved at once by precept and example, congregated to meet them. Business, amusement, all was forsaken in an instant when the chime rang out; houses were closed, and young and old, high and low, rich and poor, descended together to the house of God. Faithful to her resolve, and freed from the trammels of a court, the marchesa added to her public devotions long hours of prayer in her private oratory, and the active exercise of works of mercy amongst her dependents. The constant subject of her petitions was a son whom God might deign to accept for His service. For this she besought the Lord with many tears. Often was she heard to say, that, for a mother, there could be no joy comparable to that of seeing her son wholly consecrated to God; but it was chiefly to God Himself, and to His saints, that she gave utterance to these aspirations; for the marchese was far from sharing her views and feelings in this respect. He, too, ardently desired a son as the complement of his happiness; but it was much more as the heir of his name, of his honours, and of his little states, than as an heir of glory, and of those high places in God's kingdom which are the prize of heroic sanctity. Not that the lord of Castiglione thought meanly or otherwise than reverently either of priests or monks, or of Christian perfection;

but the first-born of his house had a vocation ready marked out for him. What that vocation was in Gonzaga's estimation we have already seen.

It was the mother's pious aspirations, not the father's fond hopes, which were to be fulfilled; and the eldest son of this marriage may well be regarded as the special fruit of her prayers. The danger in which mother and child were placed at his birth was the cause of his being baptised ere scarce he had beheld the light of day. In the case of so great a saint we can hardly regard it as an accidental or unmeaning circumstance (were we ever warranted in characterizing any circumstances as such) that the rising of the Sun of justice in the soul of the infant should have scarce been preceded by the dawning of the material light on the bodily eye, and that it should thus have been rescued at the very earliest moment from the powers of darkness. It is also worthy of notice that the marchesa vowed to the Blessed Virgin, in the event of her safety, to make a pilgrimage to the Santa Casa of Loreto, and take her child with her. Thus early was this babe, afterwards so remarkable for his devotion to Mary, placed under her patronage, being, indeed, in a peculiar manner, the son of her intercessory love. It was on the 9th of March, 1568, that our saint was born. The first thing he received after his baptism was his mother's blessing, who made the sign of the cross over him; and he then lay so still and motionless that it seemed as if he were dead; an hour elapsed, when awaking as from deep slumber, he made one slight wail, but wept and complained no more as infants are wont to do; a sign, as men deemed it in after times, of his future meekness and the innate sweetness of his disposition.

The 20th of April saw the whole town of Castiglione astir, and arrayed in gay, festal trim; at intervals the boom of the castle artillery resounded along the Lombard plain; the courts of the ducal residence and the avenues leading to it were thronged with cavaliers and men-at-arms, while the whole road from the castle to the collegiate church of SS. Celsus and Nazarius was strewn with bright spring flowers. It was, indeed, a day of great rejoicing to Gonzaga's vassals, who loved their lord, and were happy under his mild rule, when his first-born was to be presented in church to receive the supplementary rites of baptism. The procession was one brilliant with all the splendour distinguishing the worldly rank of the infant's princely relatives, several of whom graced the ceremony with their presence; amongst them the Prince Prospero Gonzaga, cousin to Ferrante, represented the godfather, the duke of Mantua, head of this great family. The child received the name of his paternal grandfather, Aluigi. In the parish register might be seen (in Cepari's days at least) these words inscribed as by some divine prescience, for nothing of the sort is added in the case of his younger brothers :—" *Sit felix, carusque Deo, ter optimo terque maximo, et hominibus in æternum vivat.*" " May he be happy, and live for ever, dear to God and men." As the noble party left the church, largesse was abundantly distributed among the gazing populace. The Princes Ferrante and Prospero scattered silver pieces by handfuls, and the marchese's younger brothers, Orazio and Alfonso, imitated their liberality;

then followed the majordomo, with his beautiful basket full of sugary dainties, which he flung amidst the crowd, and for which the rising generation of Gonzaga's vassals, doubtless scrambled as eagerly as their elders for the coin. All was glitter, merriment, and joy, and loud cries of "Viva the Prince Aluigi! May he be happy above all!" followed the young heir of Castiglione, till the castle gates closed on the gay procession. Such was the wordly pomp which ushered Lewis Gonzaga into the world, for by that name we shall at present call him, as more familiar to English ears than his Italian appellation.*

This predestinated infant inspired respect, even while still in his swaddling bands, by the sweet serenity of his countenance; and his head lady-nurse, Camilla Maynardi, often told her mistress that when she took the little prince Aluigi in her arms she experienced a thrill of devotion, as if she carried an angel of heaven, not a child of earth. His mother let not a day pass without forming the sign of the cross with the babe's own hand, and was forever repeating to him in accents of reverence and tenderness the names of Jesus and Mary. She was abundantly repaid when she heard them lisped as the first utterances of his infant tongue. Lewis may be said to have begun to pray before he began to speak, as well as to exercise a compassionate charity towards the poor. He saw his mother give to all the destitute persons she met, and no sooner did he in the distance espy a ragged object than with the most expressive gestures he petitioned for something to be-

* We reserve the Latin name Aloysius, by which the Saint is known in the Universal Church, to be applied to him when he enters religion.

stow, and manifested the liveliest joy when the alms were placed in his little out-stretched hand. His mother watched incessantly for the first dawn of conscious reason, that she might bespeak its first act for God. She taught him the Our Father and the Hail Mary, when he could scarce form his words; and Lewis was never tired of repeating them after her. Often he might be heard stammering them to himself, and, bye and bye, when able to walk and run about, he would be missed, and, after diligent search, found behind some piece of furniture, or the tapestry of the apartment, on his knees, with hands joined in prayer, and eyes cast down to earth, praying like a little seraph. Marta's gratitude and delight were unbounded, and she indulged in the happiest prognostics of the future sanctity of her darling. But the marchese, who entertained quite other projects in Lewis's regard, was by no means charmed with the pacific temper of his boy. A second son had now been born to him. Ridolfo was a complete contrast to his elder brother; he was full of childish impetuosity, noisy and boisterous; and the marchese began almost to think that he ought to have come first into the world. Ridolfo, only two years old, was in the father's eyes quite a little man for spirit already, while Aluigi, his senior, looked as mild and placid as a girl. And so he resolved to take him out of the women's hands. Marta heard this announcement with dismay, and gently represented that Lewis, not being yet four years old, was scarcely of an age to be placed under a tutor. But Ferrante thought that, if left much longer with the women, he would be only good to make a churchman of. He was his eldest born, and must be trained to serve his sovereign and keep up the honour of his ancestors. Marta submissively held her peace; she never opposed the will of her husband.

On the 7th of October, 1571, the united squadrons of the Holy See, of the King of Spain, and of the Republic of Venice, under the command of the heroic Don John of Austria, had gained in the gulf of Lepanto that memorable victory which broke the maritime preponderance and destroyed the prestige of the Ottoman power. The day cost the enemy of the Christian faith 30,000 men, and 200 vessels; a remnant was rallied by one of their boldest commanders, an unhappy Calabrian, who, carried off by pirates in his youth, had turned renegade and, renouncing his family name as well as his religion, was styled Ouloudj Ali. Selim II. made him a capitan-pasha in reward for this service, and sent him to attack the Spanish possessions on the African coast; for Philip at that time held Tunis and some other minor towns. That monarch made preparations, however, for a vigorous defence, and proposed to the Marquis of Castiglione to take the command of a body of 3,000 Milanese destined for Tunis. Ferrante was over-joyed; he was a man of war, and his Catholic heart bounded moreover at the thought of grappling with the infidel. The 3,000 men were assembled at Casal, whither their leader purposed to repair, in order to manœuvre them for a month and get them into training for active service. It was a splendid opportunity to inoculate Lewis with military tastes; and so, disregarding the mother's fears,—for mothers' fears are matters of course, and the great Marquis was used to have his own way,—the father resolved to take the hope of his house with him. The anxious Marta may well have considered that it was exposing the child to unnecessary risks thus to introduce him to a rough camp at his tender age, for the purpose of witnessing martial exercises which he could not comprehend. But her husband judged otherwise: it was after this manner he himself had been reared· the boy would be amused and interested by what he saw, and he would be taught to play the soldier. In order to flatter and encourage the warlike spirit in his infant mind, Ferrante even caused a complete suit of armour to be made for him. Behold, then, the future saint armed *cap á pie*, at the age of four years, with cuirass, helmet, and flowing plume, sword, belt, and powder-flask. A lance completed the array of·the miniature soldier. His father beheld him with pride thus accoutered; while his mother, suppressing, however, all murmurs, embraced him with many tears, and with a heart full of anguish. It was a first parting, trial enough in itself; added to which was the fear of all the dangers to body and soul which her dear child might encounter, thrown among rude soldiers and bereft of the fostering care of tender and loving hands. She betook herself to her prayers, and commended him to God; while his father gave him in charge to Don Pier Francesco del Turco, a gentleman of his household, and one, be it observed who was in every way worthy of his new office. And so the party took their road to Casal Maggiore.

But Lewis was not only to play the warrior in his outward garb; his father, intent upon kindling martial ardour in his son's breast, designed him to take a personal share in what was going on, so far as his tender age permitted. Accordingly he had his charge of powder in his belt, and a small arquebuse was provided for him to load and fire off. Gunpowder was as exciting a toy, no doubt, to little boys in the 16th century as it is in the 19th, and Lewis's pacific temper was not proof against its attractions. All the stirring exercises with which he was surrounded formed, indeed, a new and strange scene to this child taken out of the nursery, and one calculated to lay hold on the imagination. The heir of Castiglione evinced at any rate that it was not spirit that he lacked; and even Don Ferrante might be content when he saw his little son assisting at the reviews, visor down and lance in hand, with all the serious gravity of a veteran, and, when his turn came to make some display, acquitting himself with an intelligence and dexterity which delighted both officers and soldiers. He was, however, not always so fortunate, and one day, when discharging his fire arm, the ammunition he had about him exploded in his face. Providence watched over the child, for his eyes were uninjured and the skin of his face only superficially burned.

As may be supposed, he was a great favourite of the camp, where he was permitted to run about with considerable freedom. After this accident he was not allowed to have any powder in his flask; but the little event seemed to have whetted his desire for handling that dangerous article, and those who surrounded him would not fail to add fuel to the new passion by praising him for the courage he had shown. For he was the soldiers' darling and pride; and the child naturally relished their applause and was anxious for a further opportunity of displaying his prowess. Accordingly one day while all were enjoying their siesta, he crept away and ran to the camp, where, slipping quietly between the lines of slumbering soldiers, he opened one of the men's cartridge boxes, took out a charge of powder and was off at once with his treasure to the castle. Here he loaded and discharged a little field-piece which stood upon the ramparts. At the sound of the detonation the slumberers start to their feet, all is confusion, mixed with some dismay; the prince himself fears that there may be mutiny amongst his troops, and a gentleman of his household is posted off to ascertain the cause of the alarm-signal. Don Ferrante meanwhile gravely dons the insignia of his rank and office to sit in judgment on offenders, when—behold! the messenger returns to say that it is only Prince Aluigi who has fired off a cannon for his amusement. A glow of pride and joy passed over the father's heart, and his first impulse would assuredly have led him to receive the boy with open arms, but he concealed his feelings, and, assuming a severe air, threatened to punish the delinquent for this rash act of insubordination. A universal appeal for pardon for the dear little offender instantly arose on all sides, "*Grazia, grazia,* pardon, pardon, for his highness, pardon for Prince Alguigi!" The happy father was of course, not implacable, and graciously extended his forgiveness. He was, in fact, far more tempted to reward than to punish. Lewis in after years acknowledged that it was by the special protection of Heaven that he escaped death on this occasion from the recoil of the gun, and said that for long afterwards he did not cease to reproach himself for having stolen the powder of one of the soldiers, and only consoled himself by the reflection that he knew the man would willingly have given it if he had asked him for it.

When the marchese embarked for Tunis with the troops, Lewis was sent back to Castiglione with his tutor and a gentleman of his suite. Del Turco took the opportunity upon the road to upbraid his little pupil for the habit he had acquired of using certain words unbecoming his high rank and likely to distress his lady-mother. The language of camps, as we all know, is not very choice, and often far from decorous; Lewis had mixed with the soldiers, and, in the innocence of his heart, had imitated his new friends, not only without knowledge of the import of his words, but without a suspicion that they had any evil meaning. The sweet child burst into tears, and promised that he would never use these expressions again. Lewis did not forget his engagement, for not only was he never again heard to utter a reprehensible word, but if others made use in his presence of any course or immodest terms, he would blush and cast his eyes to the ground, or turn away as if he did not hear; and, if he could not do this, he would manifest his displeasure in his looks. Nay more, he continued all his days to regard this childish inadvertence as the great sin of his life, and when he was in religion, would allege it as a proof of his early wickedness. What a life must that have been where such a pardonable error figured as the chief transgression! Possibly God allowed this speck, this shadow of a sin (as we may call it), that it might furnish to the tender conscience of the saint a subject of humiliation amidst the many graces and gifts with which he was hereafter to be crowned; as also to serve at the time to scare him back when he seemed to be advancing one step into the world. God would have Lewis all for Himself from the very first; and, by his own confession, his heart, at the age of seven years—the epoch at which theologians generally consider that a child arrives at the full use of reason—was altogether converted to God. We have, besides, the independent testimony of four of his confessors, who at different times heard his general confession, and one of whom, Cardinal Bellarmine, received that which he made at the point of death, that he never committed a mortal sin or lost the grace of his baptism; and this is a circumstance the more worthy of remark because by far the greater part of this saint's life was spent, not in the shade of the cloister, or in the midst of every spiritual help, but in the courts of princes, besieged as we shall see, by every effort that blind fondness could devise to turn him away from his high vocation.

Lewis, on his return from Cassal, related all his little imprudences and faults and perils to his mother; and she told him it was the Madonna della Santa Casa who had watched over and preserved him. Then she related to him the story of the Holy House of Loreto, and informed him of her own vow; which, however, had been commuted by Gregory XIII. at her husband's desire. We shall hereafter find the holy youth himself discharging the vow made for him by his pious mother. Marta also told her dear "angel," for she never spoke of him save by this appellation, how ardently she desired to consecrate one of her sons to God, and how much she regretted that Ridolph exhibited no signs of a future vocation. "It will be me, perhaps," said the little Lewis; and again, upon another occasion, he said with more confidence, "I believe that it will be me." "You are the eldest," she replied, "and your father would not readily consent to part with you." Well, indeed, did the watchful mother recognize in Lewis those signs which she missed in Ridolph, but well also did she know what an all but insuperable obstacle the marchese's will would present to the realization of her pious hopes in the person of their first-born.

Lewis, having learned from his mother that seven years was the age of reason, felt himself constrained on its attainment to lead a life of perfection and give every instant to God. He multiplied his prayers, and began to enter on that path of mortification which he trod till death. Daily he said the Office of Our Lady and recited the Penitential and Gradual Psalms upon his knees, on the bare floor, refusing the cushion of which he had hitherto made use, like the other menbers of his family. Nor would he intermit this practice when attacked by a quartan fever, under which he laboured for eighteen months, bearing his sufferings with angelic patience; only, when too much exhausted, he would call one of his mother's waiting women to join with and assist him in the repetition. Was he not seven years old, and bound to become a saint? Already, indeed, the vassals said to one another, "Prince Aluigi will be a great saint?" It would seem as if the devils themselves were forced to bear testimony to the child's marvellous holiness. A religious of the order of St. Francis, in great repute for sanctity, passing that way and making a short stay at a convent of his order, numbers resorted to him for spiritual advice or to beg his prayers; and, as he was reported to possess miraculous gifts, persons possessed by the evil spirit were brought to him that he might exorcise them. A large party from the castle being present on one of these occasions, an energumen, singling out from amongst the crowd the little heir of Castiglione, exclaimed, pointing to him, "Do you see him? do you see him? Yes that child will go to heaven and be raised to high glory." This saying therefore went abroad among the people, and confirmed throughout the fief the growing opinion of the sanctity of the "little angel," destined, as they believed to be their future lord.

CHAPTER II.

Lewis's Early Boyhood.

The war in Tunis being closed, after an obstinate struggle, by the surrender of the fort of Goletta in 1574, Don Ferrante sent back his troops to Italy, but he himself repaired, by the desire of Philip, to the court of Madrid, where he held the office of chamberlain, with which he had been invested at his marriage. Here he was detained two years. On his return to his family he was struck with the amazing progress which had taken place in the mind of his son Lewis, who exhibited a maturity of judgment and seriousness of deportment, as well as a firmness, prudence, and discretion, quite unusual at his age. The father felt much satisfaction at these early manifestations of superior capacity, which gave promise of future eminence in the heir of his house, and of singular fitness to succeed to the government of his dominions; nor would it appear that he even experienced any repugnance to the devout disposition and pious habits of the boy, viewed simply in themselves. To do the marchese justice, he appears to have had no aversion to great piety; no small matter in one who himself neither follows nor aims at any exalted standard. It was the possible results of such exceeding piety which alone he dreaded. Could sanctity be made compatible with the secular position which Lewis was destined to fill, it could not only be excused but even valued and admired. Lewis must be lord of Castiglione; if he were a saint besides, the marchese might have no objection; but a saint *instead* was not to be thought of. As yet probably the very idea of such a worldly calamity had never crossed his imagination, but he missed the martial airs and military tastes which had been engrafted on the boy when they parted at Casal; and since to be the accomplished knight and gallant soldier entered as an integral part into his conception of the character of a great feudal noble, the absence of such tokens distressed and disappointed him. He accordingly revolved in his mind some plan by which a new turn might be given to Lewis's disposition; and the marchesa soon perceived that fresh trials were in store for her.

At this time the plague broke out in different parts of Italy, and rumours of its approach to the neighbourhood of Castiglione induced the marchese to remove with his family to Monferrato. Here he was attacked by the gout, to the frequent recurrence of which painful disorder he seems to have been subject for the remainder of his life, and an almost continual victim to it during the latter portion. The physicians recommended him to try the baths of Lucca, and Ferrante determined to take with him both Lewis and Ridolph, designing on his return to leave them at Florence, at the court of the grand duke. The scheme had been in contemplation with him for some time, but was hastened by his visit to Lucca. At the little capital of northern Italy, the metropolis of arts, science, and élegant literature, his sons would get the advantage of professional instruction and learn to speak their native tongue in all its purity. The marchesa, who remained with her younger children, Carlo and Isabella, repressed with fortitude the rising emotions of her heart at this painful separation, yet she could not restrain her tears as she bade adieu to her angelic child, to whom she earnestly recommended the special care of his turbulent brother; charging him to keep Rodolph from imprudent and dangerous sports, and, above all, to remind him not to fail in his religious duties.

After taking the baths, the marchese journeyed to Florence; but, being unable to get admittance within the walls, on account of the strict precautions adopted in consequence of the plague, he accepted during his quarantine the hospitality of Giacopo del Turco, brother to his children's governor, who occupied a neighbouring villa.* Francesco de' Medici, the grand-duke, was related to the Gonzagas, and a cordial

* The room inhabited by Lewis was afterwards, by the permission of the Sovereign Pontiff, converted into a chapel, where mass might be celebrated. The stirrups which this child of nine years old made use of during his stay at this house were preserved as relics, and operated many miraculous cures after his death.

friendship had sprung up between him and the lord of Castiglione during their residence at the Spanish court. Since this period the ruler of Florence had given much scandal by the irregularity of his conduct; he retained nevertheless a high esteem for his relative and former friend, and gave him a princely reception. Soldiers lined the way on the marchese's entrance into the city, military music greeted his approach, cannon thundered from the wall, and the most distinguished grandees were sent to meet and conduct him, with his two little sons, to the ducal presence. The grand-duke himself offered to play the father to the boys, and give them apartments in his palace; but this honour Ferrante prudently declined, on the plea of the necessity of more retirement for study; and Francesco de' Medici assigned them a house in a street which, by a happy coincidence (as Cepari notices), bore the name of the "Strada Degli Angeli."* Here they were left under the charge of their governor, Del Turco, with the gentlemen of their suite and a suitable retinue of domestics, having for their preceptor in Latin, as well as in religious and moral duties, Giulio Bresciani of Cremona, a priest distinguished for his virtues and abilities.

It must be borne in mind that the Gonzagas kept up a princely state and etiquette. We must not conceive of these great nobles as living with the same

* Cosmo III., the grand-duke of Tuscany, placed an image of St. Aloysius over the door of this house, with an inscription on a marble tablet to commemorate the abode therein of the young Saint. Purchased afterwards by the Doctor Antonio Pistolesi, it received extensive internal embelishments, and a brief of the Sovereign Pontiff permitted mass to be celebrated within its walls.

easy freedom and unceremoniousness as do families of our own high aristocracy in modern times, not to say even princes of the blood-royal. If there was, as is true, less of that luxury which ministers to comfort in the sixteenth than in the nineteenth century, amongst those whose rank and fortune entitled and enabled them to surround themselves with all those adventitious advantages which were attainable, there was certainly more conventional state and grandeur. It is plain, for instance, from incidental remarks of the contemporary biographers, that the young Gonzagas never went out without attendance, and this, not for security only, but for honour, and that they were not expected so much as to pull on and off their own shoes and stockings.

Lewis Gonzaga was nine years old when he was left at Florence by his father, and he spent above two years in that city. This visit was to form a memorable epoch in his life. Whatever Lewis was appointed to do, he performed with the exactest diligence, regarding every work of obedience as work done for God. Accordingly, he pursued his study of Latin and the more perfect acquirement of his own tongue with the utmost assiduity. On festival days alone, according to his father's arrangement, the children went to pay their court to the grand-duke. Upon these occasions the two young princesses, Eleonora and Maria,* would invite them to come and take part in their

* Donna Eleonora was afterwards married to Vincenzo Gonzaga, the son and heir of the Duke of Mantua; and her sister Maria, at that time but five years of age, became Queen of France by her marriage with Henry IV, and mother of Henrietta, Queen of England, wife of the unfortunate Charles.

juvenile sports in the palace or garden; but Lewis would generally find some excuse for deserting the frolicsome party; he preferred amusing himself with erecting little altars—this indeed, was his favourite pastime—or he would begin talking to them of Divine things. Lewis, in truth, had already passed his childhood; along with the innocence of that age, or, rather, with the purity of an angel, he had the maturity of manhood in reason and judgment. Yet he whom God destined to be the model of youth, was singularly attractive to children, although he so widely differed from them in habits. The few with whom he was acquainted at Florence tenderly loved him, and he availed himself of their partiality to direct their hearts to God, and to the practice of the virtues becoming their age. Left to himself, Lewis knew but one recreation, converse with God; although, in obedience to his governor, he occasionally, during the early part of their stay, joined with his brother in some youthful sport, yet he had no relish for such diversions, and this disinclination waxed stronger as his devotion day by day became more intense. His governor assigned to him as his confessor, Padre Francesco della Torre, rector of the College of the Jesuits; and the first time he presented himself at the tribunal of penance, he was so overcome with reverence, shame, and confusion, that he fainted at the good father's feet, and had to be lifted up and carried home by his governor. Neither was this the result of an excess of sensibility; it was the genuine love of God and an intense horror of sin, and not mere childish timidity and sensitiveness, which had been the cause of his swooning. "God is so good, and I have offended Him so much!"

such was the thought which his delicate conscience suggested to him; and that thought overwhelmed him. This guileless child reckoned himself the greatest of sinners, and in the minister of God he beheld God Himself. He now with many tears begged for strength to make his general confession, and this he was able to accomplish with a spiritual consolation of which he never lost the recollection.

But not only did Lewis take himself minutely to task for all the offences or shadows of offence in his past life which he could call to mind, he now began to examine closely into the causes and very roots of his faults. By nature he was quick and impressionable, but he had never given way to his temperament, nor had he externally exhibited so much as a passing movement of irritation; but now he condemned himself for the inward disturbance he had sometimes experienced, and at once set himself to work to die to all these mere human emotions. So complete was the victory he soon achieved over all impressions of anger, that he seemed like one in whom the passion was utterly extinct. Lewis's meekness was, indeed, something so altogether perfect and supernatural, as to remind us, not so much of other saints, of whom, undoubtedly, meekness has been the constant characteristic, as of Him who said emphatically of Himself, "I am meek and humble of heart." The Sacred Humanity possesses, it need not be said, every perfection in an immeasurable degree, yet Jesus singled out this one attribute as His pre-eminent distinction; so, in its proportion, we may say that it stands forth in surpassing loveliness in this close follower of the Lamb of God. His gentleness and humility endeared him to all those about him. To his governor, and to every one who had authority over him, he was an example of perfect submission; and he exerted all the influence which his goodness and sweetness insured to him over his headstrong brother, to lead him to the practice of obedience and self-restraint. To the domestics and attendants, and all those upon whose services and respectful attention his position gave him a claim, he behaved with a lowliness which even drew remonstrances from their lips. They were zealous to fulfil his least command, yet he never asked for anything save in the tone of one begging a favour:—"Could you do so and so for me, if convenient;" or "I should wish for such a thing, if it would not be troublesome." Even his governor suggested that it was not necessary to ask his servants whether it would suit them to comply with his orders; yet Lewis could not bring himself to adopt a more imperative tone, having always before his mind, as he observed upon some occasion of this sort, that there was "no difference between the carcase of a prince and that of his servant." He had always been sparing of words, and careful to restrain his lips from any breach of the law of charity; yet, observing that by casual observations upon the conduct of others, such as are almost inevitable in conversation, he was led occasionally to commit what might be venial offences against that law, or, at least, was exposed to hear what might wound the purity of his conscience, he resolved henceforward, as far as possible, not only to withdraw himself from the society of those without, but even from much discourse with those who dwelt under the same roof. With this view, he sought solitude and retirement, and when he was in consequence taxed with melancholy and scrupulosity, he made no account of the accusation. He preferred having less whereof to accuse himself before God

Lewis, in after life, always looked upon the city of Florence with affection and reverence, styling her "the nurse of his devotion." It was here, indeed, that he took the first decisive step which began to sever him from the world. In the Church of the Annunziata was a miraculous image of our Lady, held in great veneration. Hither he often resorted to pour out his soul in fervent prayer to the Mother of God, for whom his devotion daily increased, and at length became so intense, that when thinking or speaking of her, he appeared as it were to dissolve in a rapture of love and tenderness. A little book upon the Mysteries of the Rosary, by P. Loarte, of the Company of Jesus, contributed to nourish in him these sentiments. Love burns to manifest and express itself in some act pleasing to the beloved; and so Lewis cast about in his mind what there was in his power to offer to his dear Mother that would be acceptable to her. One day, while perusing the above-mentioned work, it struck him that it would please the Queen of Virgins if he should consecrate to her by vow his own virginity. Acting on this inspiration, he repaired to the Annunziata, and there throwing himself at the feet of her miraculous image, he renounced all love of earthly creatures, and all the ties which might bind him to earth, by an irrevocable vow of chastity. He was then but ten years old. From this day Lewis never raised his eyes to the face of any woman; nay, he kept them habitually fixed on the ground, as the attendants who followed him as he passed through the streets have testified. His precautions long forestalled the age when his steadfastness was likely to be shaken or imperilled by permitting himself greater liberty; yet so pleasing, doubtless, was this jealous custody of his eyes to the Mother of God, in whose honour he had made this vow, that to the day of his death he was preserved, by a special grace, from any, the slightest temptations against the virtue of purity. So far did he carry his reserve that he shunned, not only all unnecessary intercourse with his nearest female relatives, but the very acquaintance of such as he could avoid. Even where no danger of sin or possibility of temptation existed, he wished as it would seem, to shun all that softens the heart towards creatures and predisposes it to engrossing affection, reserving all his tenderness for God. He afterwards made a sort of compact with his father that he would obey him in undertaking any transaction or business he desired save such as must be negociated with women; and to this condition the marchese, seeing his determination, assented. Lewis willingly allowed his surrounding circle to attribute this behaviour to other motives, and he accordingly received amongst his household the playful nickname of the woman-hater.

To those who have enjoyed the training and teaching of the Holy Church, we need scarcely observe that influences beneficial in the case of those who are living ordinary Christian lives, as having a softening effect on the hardness and selfishness of the heart, and thus helping to dispose it for the impressions of grace and lead it out of self to God, may be shunned as snares and hindrances by those who are treading higher paths, and whose whole hearts are fixed on the Sovereign Good, and aspire to unceasing intercourse with Infinite Love. As respects the custody of the senses, and the absolute renouncement of every human satisfaction, however innocent and lawful, we find, it is true, our saint carrying self-discipline and abnegation, not to excess (for in true sanctity there is no excess), but to sublime extremes; and it will perhaps occur even to the Catholic reader that there are other saints who have apparently held an opposite course, exhibiting, though ever in subordination to the supreme love of God, tender sentiments of affection for relatives and friends. There is, however, no radical difference in their respective conduct. By all alike creatures are either loved for and in God, or shunned and sacrificed for God. The Holy Ghost in the soul of each individual saint marks out for it the line it is to pursue. Lewis Gonzaga is remarkable in everything for a certain close perfection and exactness, a certain unsparing conformity to the highest rule, of which we may note many instances as we proceed. It was thus designed, perhaps, in order that he might in all things be the more striking pattern for youth, so prone, under every plausible pretext, to indulge their feelings and natural inclinations, and so little apt to see or suspect peril in any gratification not directly sinful

At the period at which our story has arrived, Lewis had no formed resolution of leaving the world, though such, without question, was his heart's aspiration: but he had firmly determined that, if in the world he did remain, it would only be to lead there the most holy and perfect life possible. Indeed his biographer, Cepari, considers that at the age of ten years this child had already reached a degree of perfection higher than that to which many a good religious barely attains after a long life of strenuous application and labour. As yet Lewis had no acquaintance with mental prayer, and had not received the gift of contemplation; but he gave himself diligently to the exercise of vocal prayer, including that which, though not uttered by the lips, takes the form of inward language. He was before long to receive the invitation of the Master of the Feast, "Friend, go up higher."

During the first year of the sojourn of the young Gonzagas at Florence, died the grand-duchess, Jane of Austria, mother of the young princesses. Lewis and his brother attended the funeral at the church of San Lorenzo, and a letter from the saint to his father, penned the ensuing day, has been preserved, and may interest the reader:—

"Illustrious Signor, my father,—Your illustrious lordship's letter of the 6th of this month had grieved me, learning from it as I did, that you were suffering from gout, attended with some fever, although both were abated considerably at the time you wrote. But another letter from the Signora my mother, dated the 8th, comforted me with the news that you were quite recovered. Thanks be rendered to the Divine Majesty!

"Yesterday we went to see the funeral of the grand-duchess. It was very fine, and lasted about three hours. The funeral procession was in the following order:—At the head was borne the banner of San Lorenzo, followed by the Cross, and accompanied by a hundred and fifty poor, dressed in mourning and bearing lighted torches. Then came all the religious, not of the town only, but of the neighbourhood for three miles round. There were eighteen different orders, and each brother carried a wax candle of a pound's weight. Then came the mourners with their customary trains. Then the priests, each also with a candle weighing a pound. After the clergy followed the pages, lords, and courtiers, all in black, with lighted torches. Then came the body under a canopy; it was borne by the titled lords, and the canopy was supported by the gentlemen of the city. The grand-duke followed in a mourning cloak and undress cap (*beretta alla civile*), with the rest of the court and his armed guard. After accompanying the body to S. Lorenzo, he retired to his palace.

"We continue our devotions and studies. We are well in health. I have nothing else to tell you, except that, to conclude, we kiss your hands, and those of the Signora our mother, of the Signorina our sister, and of our brother.—Your good son,

"Aluigi Gonzaga."

The Duke of Mantua having confided the government of Montferrato to his cousin, the Marquis of Castiglione, Don Ferrante removed his boys from Florence to Mantua, his object apparently being to knit closer the family tie between himself and the great head of his house, and insure its continuance by their respective heirs, through the familiar intercourse which would thus be early established between Lewis and Prince Vincenzo, the duke's eldest son, then about seventeen years of age. The two brothers arrived at the ducal capital in November, 1579, Lewis being at that time eleven years and eight months old; they were installed in the palace of San Sebastiano, the the property of the Marquis of Castiglione in that city. Here he continued his studies under P. Bresciani, which were, however, frequently broken in upon in a manner extremely distasteful to his inclinations; namely, by visits to the court, attendance on festive occasions, or recreative excursions with Prince Vincenzo. No youth ever longed for pleasure and amusement with the ardour with which Lewis sighed for retirement and ceaseless commune with God, varied, rather than interrupted, by pious discourse or spiritual reading. A court life, with all its inane grandeur and burdensome ceremonial and empty frivolity, was wearisome to his soul, though as yet only called to give to it but a few brief, occasional hours; what then must it have been to him in prospect! For bye and bye he would be required to buckle on his worldly harness or chain himself to the car which his father had dragged through life with a spirit and an energy worthy of a higher end. From this vision of his future his whole soul recoiled; like the dove he would seek the clefts of the rock—he would flee away and be at rest; and so the idea began now first to dawn on his mind of giving up his rights of primogeniture and all its attendant honours, riches and duties to his brother Ridolfo.

A few weeks after his arrival at Mantua, Lewis was attacked by a distressing and tedious malady, for which the physicians prescribed as a remedy the strictest abstinence in diet. Up to this time the child had been blessed with an excellent constitution; he was strong and well-grown, and presented nothing of that almost transparent pallor and emaciation which we associate with the image of the boy-saint. The blood coursed freely through his veins, and the ruddy bloom of youth was on his countenance. The severe regimen to which he was subjected, not only was freely accepted and borne with the most unmurmuring patience, but came to be loved by him from motives of devotion ; so that when, upon the entire removal of the disorder, the prohibition was withdrawn, Lewis continued to restrict himself to the same scanty fare. In vain did the doctors, and those who had the personal care of him, suggest that it was not only safe but advisable to return to a more generous diet; Lewis offered no opposition, he allowed them to talk, and said nothing in reply, but he ate not a mouthful the more. Under the supposition that he dreaded the return of his disorder, it was represented to him that he ran the more serious risk of radically damaging his constitution. Lewis cared not to remove the error, and his reply that he desired nothing more, and that he believed this spare diet to be good for him, only served to confirm his friends in their mistaken impression. But it was of his soul's welfare that the child spoke; what he desired and believed to be profitable for him was to suffer in union with his Lord. That this scanty nourishment, at an age when the process of growth demands support, had an injurious effect in producing and perpetuating the languor and enfeeblement of his physical powers, there can be little doubt; and it would seem strange that there was no interference on the part of those whose injunctions Lewis, the pattern of docility and obedience to his spiritual superiors, would certainly have respected. We can only suppose, then, that it was so expressly permitted by God, and that Lewis acted herein at the suggestion of His Holy Spirit. What serves to confirm this view is that, whereas St. Bernard condemned himself at the close of his life for excess in his earlier austerities, Lewis, when reminded of this circumstance by his fathers and brethren in religion, could never be persuaded to entertain any scruple in the matter; and this his firm persuasion he took occasion to repeat when about to receive the Viaticum, as we shall notice when we come to speak of his happy death. Youth demands vivid colouring in a picture in order to have its attention engaged and its admiration captivated; its ideas are simple and uncompounded; it is not the age for qualifications and reservations, which, if allowed to precede the simple love and desire of virtue in all its splendour, mar enthusiasm and quench fervour. To qualify and to moderate is the office of rulers and guides. Lewis was to stand forth as a model of consummate perfection to the young. Mere temperance would not have attracted their notice; temperance, indeed, is a matter altogether relative, for what may be moderation in one would be excess in another; but when they see this young saint of twelve years considering that he had made an unusually full meal if he partook of a single egg as his entire repast, they cannot fail to recognize one of youth's common faults, that of gluttony, condemned in the person of their patron; a fault which, be it noted, unless very glaring, passes with scant rebuke or discouragement from elders. For, not to advert to the too common leniency exhibited in this respect, it is a task requiring some little prudence to discern where the legitimate claims of the healthy appetite of children end, and where begin those irregular cravings of greediness, the indulgence of which, if not checked betimes, is sure to grow into a settled habit.

Lewis, at any rate, was allowed to pursue his strict regimen unthwarted, and the indefinite prolongation of his convalescence, so far from furnishing matter of regret to himself, was hailed as a boon; releasing him as it did from attendance at many of the court festivities and many a walk or excursion with the prince of Mantua. He was able, however, to resume his studies, though he seldom left the house. When he went out, it was to repair to some church or monastery; or he would go to the palace of his uncle, Prince Prospero Gonzaga, where his first visit was always to the chapel under his roof. He would then discourse with the prince, or those in his company, on divine things, and this with such insight, such depth, and such unction of piety, that all were amazed at beholding in a child so marvellous an understanding of spiritual things; an understanding which he could have acquired in the school and at the feet of Him alone who, at twelve years of age, astonished the elders and doctors of Israel by His wisdom. The remainder of his time he spent in solitude, praying, saying office, and reading the lives of Saints. His illness had confirmed in him the resolution of escaping from the trammels of his position, by resigning his paternal heritage to Ridolfo, and embracing the ecclesiastical state; but at present he discreetly kept his secret in his own bosom, only requesting his father to dispense him from court attendance and occupations, that he might give all his energies to study.

The winter season being past, the ducal family prepared to leave Mantua, as was their habit, in order to spend the summer months at one of their country residences. The marquis thought well also to remove his sons from the city to the fresher breezes of Castiglione; hoping, too, that in his native air Lewis would regain his pristine health and vigour. We may conceive with what joy the marchesa clasped her children in her arms; but oh! how changed was the blooming boy who had received her parting embrace three years before. The soft rounded outline of that cheek had departed, and gone for ever, indeed, were its roses, or gone only to re-appear in the more delicate and evanescent hue of a blush which the angelic modesty and humility of the child would cause to mantle at times on his face. But if all the rich colouring of natural beauty was effaced, beauty of a more unearthly and spiritual character had developed itself; and in the eyes of the Christian mother there was that to be discerned which brought joy and consolation surpassing all the common delights of mere maternal love. It is not to be supposed, however, but that Donna Marta would have gladly prevailed on her son to moderate his extreme abstinence, but Lewis persisted in his resolution; and so far was he from relaxing in his rigourous way of life, that any change he made was always in the form of addition to his austerities.

God was about to reward the fidelity of his young servant by revealing to him all the secrets of the interior life. Lewis had received no instruction in mental prayer; ever since he has devoted his whole soul to the adoration of his Lord, he had lain as a humble and fervent worshipper on the pavement of the outer courts of the temple. There he had offered the holocaust of his entire being, but the sanctuary was as yet veiled; he was now about to be admitted to adore in the Holy of Holies, that secret centre of the soul where God establishes His kingdom, and where He speaks an unutterable language to those chosen ones whom He draws within to worship before His face.* This child in years was to be introduced into the wine cellar of divine charity, and inebriated with that "wine of the elect which buds forth virgins."† His intellect being now illuminated with supernatural light, he was taught to contemplate the Divine perfections and meditate on the mysteries of redemption in a manner immeasurably more perfect than he could have learned from the best human instructor, or acquired by the most laborious personal efforts. Inundated with sweetness in this new region, this paradise so wonderfully opened to him, the boy spent well-nigh the whole day in prayer, tears pouring from his eyes like two rivers, which not only soaked the clothes he wore, but bathed the very floor of the room. He was thus only the more unwilling to leave his retirement as, in addition to the fear of losing the tenderness of his devotion, he now dreaded the alternative

* The oracle where God dwelt between the Cherubim in the old Temple, is called, in the literal Hebrew, the "face of the Lord," *e. g. Leviticus*, II. 10, "And fire coming out from the Lord (Heb. *face of the Lord*) destroyed them" (Nadab and Abihu). This interpretation throws a light upon the mystical imports of many passages in the Psalms, where the face of the Lord is spoken of; such, for instance, as, "Seek ye the face of the Lord. Thy face, Lord, will I seek;" which thus acquire a fuller and deeper significance.

† *Cant.* II. 4, *Zach.* IX. 17.

of being seen to weep and so betraying his inward emotion. But he could not conceal these things from his personal attendants. Desirous to observe how he demeaned himself during those long hours of prayer, they would often peep through chinks and cracks in the door, more numerous and convenient for the purpose probably in those days in the splendid mansions of the great, than they would now be found in any mean lodging-house, and there they would behold their young lord, prostrate before the crucifix, where for hours he would remain, or praying with his arms extended or crossed over his breast; and all the while, the perennial fount gave forth its stream from eyes riveted on the image of the Lord, and his bosom heaved with deep sobs and sighs. After a time he would become quite still; his spirit seemed to have passed into some other region; he was rapt in an ecstasy; his eyes were fixed, the lids remained motionless, he seemed scarce to breathe, and you might have thought you gazed on a statue. So abstracted, in fact, was he from his senses at these times, that his governor and servants might pass through his room making a considerable noise, and yet he saw and heard them not, nor was he in any way cognisant of their presence. Whispered from mouth to mouth these wonders became known abroad, and the unconscious child, who would have been overwhelmed with confusion at the bare idea of such exposure, was not only often seen thus engaged by his own family and their court, but even by strangers, whom friends within the castle would sometimes admit to the favour of seeing prince Aluigi at his prayers. Often also would members of the household stand to listen to the saintly child repeating

Ave Marias at each short flight of stairs, as he mounted to his room; for everywhere in the palace, in the street, in carriage, or on foot, Lewis was praying or meditating upon some divine mystery. A little book which at this time fell in his way, by Father Peter Canisius, of the Company of Jesus, containing points for meditation and directions concerning its method, was esteemed a treasure by him; for, though taught immediately by the Spirit of God, he was himself as desirous of instruction as if he had hitherto had no insight into the mysteries of contemplation. This book and the letters of Jesuit fathers from the Indies served not a little to draw his affection towards the Company, as he afterwards related; and his heart was inflamed with the desire to go forth himself and spend his life in labouring to convert the heathen.

Meanwhile he exercised a little Apostleship at home, going on all festival days to teach the children in the schools of Christian Doctrine, and in this office he manifested such exquisite gentleness and modesty coupled with such lowliness towards his vassals, especially the poorest, that the very sight of him inspired devotion. The parents and friends would gather round to share in the instructions and counsels given by one who, though not much, and indeed, not always the senior in years of his scholars, yet from his premature wisdom and angelic goodness, inspired both young and old with a reverence generally accorded only to age. If dissension arose between any members of his household, Lewis became the peace-maker; if blasphemous or other evil words were uttered, Lewis was at hand to reprove with a holy zeal for God's honour and for Christian purity; his admonitions being, however, always tempered with a benignant though austere gentleness. Such majesty and force had every word that came from his lips, though allied to a humility and meekness quite indescribable, that when his mother took him with her, on the occasion of a visit to Tortona, where she went to compliment the duchess of Lorraine,* on her passage through Tuscany with her daughter, the duchess of Brunswick, the courtiers of these princesses were no less impressed by the marvellous grace with which this young child spoke, than were his partial and obsequious dependants at home. And all this time he had not yet made his first communion! It was a saint who was first to give to Lewis the Bread of Angels.

CHAPTER III.

Lewis's Mode of Life at Castiglione.

In the July of this same year, 1580, the archbishop of Milan, having been appointed by Pope Gregory XIII. Apostolic visitor of the dioceses in his province, came to Castiglione. This prelate was no less a personage than the great Cardinal Charles Borromeo, the fame of whose sanctity had already spread far and wide. The news of his approach caused great excitement, and the noble family of Castiglione had hoped to entertain him in their castle; but St. Charles made a rule to decline all such invitations, taking up his quarters

*Claude, daughter of Henry II. and Catherine of Medicis, and sister consequently of Elisabeth of Valois, whom Donna Marta accompanied into Spain.

invariably under the roof of some of the clergy of the place where he tarried, and being always accompanied by a very slender retinue, in order not to be burdensome to them. At Castligione he made his stay at the residence of the arch-priest, in the close vicinity of the church, and here he preached to an immense crowd of people, amongst whom, in their reserved places, were Donna Marta and her "angel." Fruitful of grace are the words of saints; they seem to pass over the souls of men like a breath from Heaven, moving them as "the trees of the forest are moved by the wind." The whole congregation were dissolved in tears: what, then, may we conceive, passed in the mind of that child of grace, so alive to its slightest impression? No one probably had been more deeply disappointed than Lewis at losing the golden opportunity of entertaining a saint; but he would not altogether fail of reaping the benefit which he chiefly had in view, spiritual counsel from this great servant of God. He accordingly took courage, or rather—for it was not courage that ever failed him—he overcame his bashfulness, and presented himself to ask for a private interview with the cardinal, to whom he laid bare his whole soul and conscience.

A saint instinctively recognizes a saint. In Lewis, indeed, the marks of holiness were patent even to a less divinely illuminated eye than that of Borromeo. The holy cardinal marvelled, and blessed God who, in the midst of the thorns of the world and in the ungenial atmosphere of a court, had warmed and nourished into vigourous bloom this tender plant, without the fostering care of any human hand. When he discovered from his questions that this high degree of perfection had been attained by one who as yet had not partaken of the Bread of the Strong, his admiration at such close correspondence with grace exemplified in this marvellous boy must have been doubly heightened. He desired him to lose no time before making his first communion. It was a blessing for which Lewis ardently longed; and it would seem certainly more than matter of surprise that a delay of this kind should have been permitted in his case. Be this as it may, St. Charles exhorted him now to practice frequent communion, adding instructions with respect to its profitable reception; and amongst other counsels given by the holy archbishop, we recognize the zealous promoter of the decrees of Trent in his recommendation of the diligent study of the Catechism put forth by the Council. Those who were awaiting without their own turn for admission were meanwhile expressing one to another their suprise that the cardinal should spend so much of his time—and who did not know how jealously the great archbishop husbanded that precious time?—in conversing with a little boy. But the Saint valued the privilege of conversing with this stripling, in his eyes the sweetest marvel of grace he had ever beheld, as much (and that is not saying a little) as the child himself valued that of receiving the counsels and benediction of the mature servant of God. He desired himself to communicate this young angel; and no more touching sight can we conceive than that of our dear boy-saint receiving the Body of his Lord from the hands of the glorious St. Charles, whose praise is in all the Churches, and the splendour of whose charity has even won the commendation of the cold world without.

Lewis's mother could not remember, when questioned by Cepari, the precise date of this memorable act, but it must have been towards the end of July. One circumstance, however, the marchesa did most clearly recall to mind, namely, that from this day she noted the extraordinary increase in her son's devotion to the Holy Sacrament of the Altar. Thus every morning, when present at the Adorable Sacrifice, she observed that he burst into tears at the consecration, and that they continued to flow to the close of the mass, and wet the stones of the floor where he knelt. It was so to the close of his life. With what searching care Lewis habitually examined his conscience, and with what humility and contrition he made his confessions, we have the testimony of those who received them. The faults which he could discover in himself, as may be supposed, were those of omission rather than commission; but with him these seemed very grevions, for he never believed that his acts corresponded with the great light which God vouchsafed to him; and thus Lewis's confessions of sin became so many lessons of perfection to his confessors. His preparations for communion were made with corresponding diligence. On the days which preceded, all his thoughts were fixed on the Adorable Sacrament, all his words referred to It; to his approaching reception all his prayers and meditations were directed; and so frequent were these, that the household were in the habit of saying that he seemed to desire to hold conversation with the walls, for he was constantly discovered in the corner of some apartment on his knees. What passed between our Lord and this favoured soul in communion, God alone knows; Lewis seems never to have revealed the secret to any one; but all might witness the recollection and deep devotion with which he approached the Sacred Banquet, and the long thanksgiving which followed its reception.

All this while the marchese was at Casal, where the governors of Montferrato usually resided. The information which reached him of the state of debility in which his eldest son continued, a state prolonged by his own refusal to take sufficient nourishment, caused him much uneasiness: no one, it was evident, exerted the needful authority in this matter; he hoped to be more successful himself. Accordingly, towards the close of the summer, the marchesa received a summons to join her husband at Casal with her children. The orders of heads of families were reckoned to be very imperative in those times, and the marchesa was not one to derogate an iota from the respect habitually accorded to the expressed desires of husbands and fathers, or to allow herself any latitude of judgment or discretion on such occasions. She started therefore without even waiting for an escort, and although heavy rains had been falling for several days. To reach Casal, it was necessary to ford the Tesino, whose waters were now swollen to a furious torrent. Donna Marta, accompanied by two of her ladies, occupied the first vehicle; in the second carriage followed the heir, with his brother and their governor. Donna Marta's coachman boldly entered the stream, the frightful rapidity of the current being scarcely apparent to its full extent on the bank. However, the ponderous carriages of those days were calculated to resist a good deal of pressure, and the struggling horses brought them safe through to the opposite side. Lewis's driver followed the lead, but upon reaching the centre of the stream an ominous crack was heard in the body of the massive coach. The vehicle, unable to resist the force of the impetuous torrent, now broke violently in twain, the fore-part alone, containing Ridolfo, being dragged, not without labour and peril, to the shore, while the hinder part, in which Lewis and his governor were seated, being left at the mercy of the rushing current, began to drift rapidly down the river. A cry of terror arose from the waters, which was taken up by the spectators on the bank, and borne to the ears of the anxious mother and the occupants of the first carriage. Her children are in peril; she turns back: there is Ridolfo: he has safely reached the shore; but where is Lewis? where is her angel boy? Providence had watched over him; the carriage had floated without turning over, and was now arrested in its course by the trunk of a tree, which the tempest had swept into the river. A peasant, mounted on horseback, waves his hand and shouts encouragement to them from the bank. Don Francesco sees him, but the din of the elements prevents him from distinguishing a word: as for his saintly charge, he neither hears or sees anything. He is calmly praying, just as he so often prays in some secluded corner of his father's palace. He allows himself quietly to be taken in the peasant's arms, when with difficulty the man has reached the spot, and to be placed behind him on his horse. The countryman, after depositing the heir of Castiglione on dry land, returns for the governor, and performs the same service successfully for him also. The happy mother leads her children and the whole party to the little church of the adjoining village, there to thank God and His holy Mother for their rescue from death. But ill news travelled fast even in days when the locomotive and the telegraph were unknown; tidings borne from mouth to mouth have almost electric swiftness: the marchese has heard of the peril in which his sons are placed, and a horseman comes galloping up to ascertain the truth. He is despatched with the tranquillizing intelligence of their safety, and Don Ferrante has soon the happiness of pressing his children in his arms.

The marchese had hoped that under the paternal eye and authority Lewis would become docile to sanitary regulations, but there was one circumstance which he had not taken into account. Somehow or other none could bring themselves to compulsory interference with the boy. He seemed invested with a halo of sanctity, inspiring even his elders with a veneration which disarmed their resolution. By common consent he appeared to be left to take pretty much his own way in spiritual matters. Not but that Don Ferrante endeavoured to bring the power of paternal remonstrance to bear upon him, but even he, the lordly marquis, was himself under the influence of the spell, and his reluctant admiration for much which he regretted, tempered the exertion of his authority, and restrained him from forcible interference with his son's way of life. The very meekness of the boy's respectful refusals, which were made rather in the guise of humble and tender appeals to be spared what he dreaded, put to flight all his father's stern resolves. On his arrival at Casal, the marchese's first attempt was to engage him to join in diversions and sports, in the hopes of distracting his mind from his devotional exercises.

Lewis, however, studiously avoided every place of public resort; much more did he shun all banquets, plays, and similar entertainments; indeed he not only shunned, but resolutely declined to be present at them. The marchese would at times exhibit displeasure at this pertinacious love of retirement, but there he allowed the matter to rest. Once, however, when his term of government was near its expiration, and he was about to repair to Milan, in order to attend a grand review of cavalry at which all the high nobility of the country were to be present, he insisted upon his son's bearing him company; and Lewis, marking his father's determination, felt it incumbent on him to submit. It was a grand sight, that review. When we remember the splendour of dress displayed by the upper classes of those days, and the taste for grandeur and magnificence which generally distinguished the 16th century; and when to these brilliant features, we add the crowd of spectators, from the middle and lower classes, all in their festive attire, at a period when the rolling stone of uniformity had not begun to pass over everything, mercilessly effacing differences and crushing all that imparts originality, picturesqueness, and variety to such a spectacle, we may conceive that the scene offered no small attractions to a boy not quite thirteen years of age. The marchesino must of course occupy one of the best places; all were solicitous that he should have a good view of what must possess so lively an interest in the eyes of youth. Poor boy! They little knew that his sole desire was to mortify those eyes, and not to suffer them to drink in pleasure from any earthly object. In vain did he excuse himself, on the plea of his youth, from occupying a prominent position: he had excellent sight, and did not need to be seated in a front rank; his modest objections were overruled, and he was placed in an advantageous situation for witnessing the display. Then he had recourse to another expedient; he turned away his eyes or cast them down—the attitude in which the saint is so familiar to us—and would witness as little of the world's pomp and pageantry as he could help.

And what all this time were Lewis's recreations? for no one, young or old, really lives, or can well live, without some recreation. Lewis's recreations, we have seen, were those neither of boys nor of ordinary grown men, but he *had* his recreations, in which he took as much or more delight than others in their games and shows. When the rest of the family accepted some invitation abroad, Lewis would find his entertainment at home in the society of some one or two grave men, learned and pious, who would come and discourse with the boy of letters or holy things; or if he went out to refresh his spirit, it would be to visit a venerated sanctuary of Our Lady in that neighbourhood, known as the Madonna di Crea, or to enjoy the conversation of the Barnabite Fathers of San Paolo Decollato. From these holy monks, whose convent he much frequented, and where he often confessed and communicated, he derived much light in the ways of God. Each day that he left their company to return to his secular home, it was with an ever-deepening impression of the peace, the unruffled serenity, which dwelt within the shelter of convent walls; specially did he admire the happiness which beamed in the faces of the fathers, so foreign to the look of care which hangs more or less about the countenances of the men of the world, and their thorough contempt of all temporal interests, from which they had divorced themselves forever. And then, with what holy envy did he consider the even flow of a life in which prayer and psalmody daily ascended at stated hours, the ravishing calm of months and years spent where no sound which recalled the world without came to trouble the deep silence and quiet of the sacred precincts. "See, Lewis," he said to himself (as he afterwards related to Cepari and others), "how excellent is the religious state! These fathers are free from all worldly ties, and far removed from all occasions of sin. That time which secular persons squander in running after transitory goods, or vain amusements, they wholly employ in the meritorious acquisition of true riches, heavenly treasure; and they are secure of not losing the fruit of their labours. Religious are the really reasonable people; for they do not allow themselves to be tyrannized over by their senses or passions. They are not ambitious of honour, and they do not prize worldly possessions, they are not goaded by emulation, they are not envious of the good of others, they are satisfied with serving God, *cui servire regnare est* (whom to serve is to reign). And then, what wonder if they be always joyons, and fear neither death, judgment, nor hell, since they live with their conscience pure from sin—nay more, day and night are making fresh gains, and are for ever occupied in holy works with God or for God! it is this testimony of a good conscience which preserves them in that peace and interior tranquillity whence flows the outward serenity of their countenances.

This well-grounded hope which they possess of heavenly goods, this abiding remembrance of Whom it is they serve, and in Whose court they stand, to what soul would not they bring consolation? And what are you doing? What think you? why could not you, too, make choice of such a state? See the great promises which God has made to it. See what opportunities would be yours of attending without disturbance to your devotions. If, giving up the marquisate to Ridolfo, your younger brother, as you have already determined to do, you nevertheless remain with him, you will, perhaps, have to witness many things which will not please you. If you keep silence, then remorse of conscience will follow; if you speak out, then you will be thought troublesome, or you will not be listened to: and even if you enter the priesthood, and become an ecclesiastic, you will not obtain your object; rather, while taking on yourself a higher obligation to a perfect life than is laid upon seculars, you will remain exposed to the same perils which encompass them—nay, in a manner, be subject to greater temptations than beset married persons: while, any how, you will not escape from human respect; for, living in the world, you will have to take account of it, and now satisfy this great man, and now accommodate that other. If you entirely avoid women, and, in particular, your own female relatives, it will be noticed as a singularity; if you converse familiarly with them, what becomes of the resolution you have made? If you accept prelacies in the Church, then you will be plunged into the vortex of worldly affairs, even more than in your present state of life; if you refuse them, your relatives will be dissatisfied with you, and disesteem you, and will say that you dishonour your kindred, and will press you in a thousand ways to accept these distinctions. Whereas if you become a religious, at one blow you remove all these impediments; you close the door against every peril, you liberate yourself from all human respect, and you place yourself in a condition to be able to enjoy perfect quiet and to serve God with all perfection."

These and such like considerations Lewis inwardly revolved, and remained in so great a state of abstraction for some days, that those about him clearly perceived that something unusual was working in his mind; yet no one ventured to question him. At last, after assiduous prayer and many communions offered to obtain light in so momentous an affair, Lewis became convinced that he was divinely called to the religious state. Well aware that at present he was too young to carry out his intention, he did not attempt to fix his choice on any order in particular, and discreetly abstained from revealing his purpose to any one, albeit the Barnabite fathers much more than suspected it, and cherished the hope of possessing him one day themselves. But from this hour, no longer doubting but that he was called to that perfect life of self-immolation, which the religious by his profession adopts, he felt himself urged to practise the same abnegation in the world and in the court, so far at least as it was possible. Hitherto he had accepted without reflection the use of certain accommodations, luxuries belonging to his rank, which, indeed, the delicacy of his constitution now seemed to render almost essential to his health. Winter in Northern Italy is often very severe, and, as a matter of course, a fire was lighted in the young prince's room at that season, which was all the more needed as he spent there so large a portion of his time. But religious have no fire in their cells, and so Lewis would renounce this comfort also as an unnecessary indulgence. Nay more, when in company, he would avoid all approach to the blazing hearth; or, if courtesy obliged him sometimes to draw near, he would dextrously place himself so as to enjoy its warmth as little as might be. Yet he was extremely sensitive to cold, and suffered much from its severity. His faithful *cameriere*,* Clemente Ghisoni, who survived his young master and furnished Cepari with many traits of the saint's youth, compassionating the state of his hands, swollen, inflamed, and even bleeding as they were from the effects of cold, prepared an ointment which he begged him to apply to them. Lewis expressed his thanks with his usual graciousness, and the ointment speedily disappeared, but it was certainly not by use: it was probably locked up safe out of sight where no one could mark its unbroken surface, for the saintly boy had no desire for the removal of his pains, but rejoiced to have something to suffer for his Lord.

His books of recreation were, we need hardly say, not profane tales or romances, which he never so much as opened, nor, indeed, any work of which the reading could bring no profit to his soul, but the lives of Saints, in which he greatly delighted. For his classi-

* In princely houses like that of Gonzaga, the term *cameriere* implied something higher in grade than the appellation of valet conveys to our modern ear; and Clemente himself (according to Cepari) seems to have been a person of some trust and importance.

cal studies he selected those pagan authors who treated of morals, such as Seneca, Plutarch, and Valerius Maximus, and he used to avail himself of apt quotations from their pages when exhorting others to lead a Christian life. The discourse which flowed from his lips on these occasions not only astonished the hearers by its touching eloquence, but suggested the irresistible persuasion that much of the science of divine things which he possessed was infused knowledge, so far beyond the natural capacity of his age did it appear.

The marchese's term of office being expired, he and his family returned to Castiglione, where, to his exceeding annoyance, he observed that, so far from moderating his austerities, Lewis continued to increase them. Much, of course, remained unknown to his parent, for the boy shunned observation, from the double motive of humility and discretion, but much also there was which could not escape the knowledge of all. The food which he took seemed insufficient to preserve life without a miracle. Donna Camilla Ferrari,* a lady belonging to the marchesa's household who had had the charge of Lewis in his infancy, weighed one of his ordinary repasts, and found that it barely reached an ounce. When at table, he would choose whatever seemed the worst, just taste it, and eat no more. But he now added three regular weekly fasts, besides such as were either occasional or prompted by his devotion. On Friday, in memory of our Lord's Passion, he took nothing but a very small amount of

* Formerly Maynardi, whom we noticed as presiding over the nursery. She had lately married.

bread dipped in water. On Saturday he fasted in the same manner, in honour of the Blessed Virgin. Wednesday he kept as an ordinary fast-day of the Church. What his quondam nurse did from affectionate curiosity, he himself in after years habitually practised from a desire to avoid all superfluity and to adhere strictly to what he found absolutely necessary for the support of life. But these were not his only mortifications. His desire for suffering made him ingenious. He possessed no instrument of penance, and no facility for procuring any; accordingly he searched amongst the old lumber of the castle, where he found some castaway leashes of dogs and fragments of old iron chain, which he carried off as a treasure. With these he disciplined himself as he knelt, in which act he was often surprised by his attendants, who also, in making his bed, discovered pieces of rope stained with blood, carefully concealed under the mattress. They showed them to the marchesa, but her son was a saint in her eyes, and she dared not interfere with the holy excesses of his fervour. Not so the marchese; when this distressing information reached his ears he exclaimed: "That child will kill himself," and sent for Lewis, to whom he bitterly complained of his imprudence, at the same time representing the affliction which it was causing to himself; nevertheless, he seemed marvellously restrained from issuing any prohibition to his son.

Lewis was resolved to be a saint. Saints have not slept on down, and so, unable to change the bed provided for him, he placed pieces of wood and other hard substances underneath him; and in order not to want for suffering during the day, being unable to procure a hair-shirt, he devised a novel instrument of penance in a cincture of his own manufacture, made out of the rowels of some old spurs, which he wore next his delicate skin, and which pricked and tormented him at every movement. To these mortifications must be added the bodily fatigues he underwent during his incessant devotions. His first morning act was an hour's mental prayer, measured, however, rather by devotion than by a timepiece; this was followed by his vocal prayers. He then heard one or more masses, which he also frequently served; besides which he attended the different offices in the neighbouring religious houses. The remainder of his time he devoted, in the secrecy of his own apartment, to meditation, contemplation, and spiritual reading. In the evening, before lying down to rest, he made one or two hours' unbroken prayer, so that the valets, who were waiting without to undress and see him into bed, as was usual with persons of his rank, thought he would never have done; but, instead of being wearied, as we suspect would be the case with most servants in our modern days, they were much edified at their young lord's piety, and beguiled the time with peering at him through the aforementioned treacherous chinks. Nor can we refrain from noticing by the way the respectful appreciation, not to say hearty admiration, for that high perfection and sublime devotion which is attained by few; and is, indeed, unattainable to the great mass of men, which meets us at every turn in these times, beginning with the great marquis, whose ambition, pride, and treasured hopes were thwarted by his son's vocation, and ending with the domestics, a class who are seldom behindhand in valuing the pomp and worldly advantages of the great houses in which they serve. Deep must have been, in the midst of the many corruptions of the 16th century, the hold which the Catholic faith in all its fulness had nevertheless upon the hearts of the multitude, for it to have influenced so powerfully their standard of judgment. Vice, laxity, and even neglect of religious duties might abound, but piety was certainly not despised.

To return to the poor marchese, for whom we think it is scarcely possible, despite his blamable opposition to God's designs respecting his child, not to feel a certain degree of natural compassion—he was constantly lamenting that he could not get his son out of his room, and he himself related to P. Prospero Malavolta how he had often, upon entering it, found the spot where his Aluigi had prayed all bedewed with his tears. Even when the boy was compelled to leave his retirement, he carried that retirement along with him in spirit; and the subject of his meditation, whether a mystery of the Passion, or any other, was so deeply impressed upon his mind that whatever he was doing, or whatever of necessity superficially occupied his attention, it was still in its hidden depths intent on this heavenly theme. But, not content with praying well-nigh the whole day long, he rose in the silence of night, in the cold night of a Lombard winter, and there on his knees, in the centre of his room, with no other covering but his night-dress and with no support to his feeble body, he would pray, all shaking and trembling from head to foot; and when his attention was thereby somewhat distracted, imputing it to imperfection and determined to conquer, he would still pray on and meditate, until his soul became so rapt from his senses that he no longer felt the cold. Often however, he became so benumbed and exhausted that, resolved neither to sit nor to support himself, he would at last fall prostrate on the floor, and thus continue his meditation. As we contemplate this picture, our minds revert to the great St. Dominic, of whose youthful sanctity Dante sings in his Paradiso:—

"Many a time his nurse, at entering, found
That he had risen in silence, and was prostrate,
As who should say, 'My errand was for this.'"*
(Cary's Translation.)

It is little, if at all, short of miraculous that Lewis did not contract some mortal complaint in consequence of these holy indiscretions. One life-long malady, indeed, was the result of this intense application of mind, if it were not rather the consequence of the nervous depression caused by defective nourishment and sleep, a painful headache, from which he habitually suffered, and which he cherished in memory of our Lord's crown of thorns. It reminded him of the Passion of Jesus, and, like the sufferings of other saints, and unlike those of common men, it did not seem either to oppress his powers or in general to interfere with his occupations. Sometimes, however, he had such violent attacks, that he was obliged to take some bodily rest; and having retired one night on this account betimes, and remembering that he had not said the seven Penitential Psalms, he would not close his eyes till he had acquitted himself of this his customary exercise; so calling the servant, he bade

* "Spesse fiate fu taçito e desto
Trovato in terra dalla sua nutrice,
Cum dicesse: Io son venuto a questo."—*Canto* XII.

him place a candle by his bed, and then dismissed him. Scarcely had he finished the Psalms when, overcome with the stupefying pain and with bodily exhaustion, the eyes of the young saint closed, and he slept. The angels of God watched over him, or he had closed to open them no more. The candle in burning down set fire to the bedclothes. They did not, however blaze, but smouldered on, the fire twisting and writhing about like a coiling serpent. The curtains of the bed, three mattresses, and a paillasse were thus consumed, and yet, strange to say, with an absence of all flame. Lewis awoke, and, finding himself intensely hot, attributed it to fever; but when, upon stretching his hands and feet to other parts of the bed, he found them equally warm, he marvelled a little, yet endeavoured to go to sleep again. But the stifling heat increasing almost to suffocation, he got up and called to the servants. No sooner had he left his couch and opened the door, admitting a current of air, than the smothered flames burst forth, enveloped the whole bed, and would have set fire to the room, but for the prompt exertions of the soldiers of the fortress, who threw everything which had ignited through the window into the castle-ditch. The circumstances appearing quite inexplicable by natural causes, what wonder if, taken in connection with the holiness of their young lord, the people of Castiglione should have deemed them miraculous? Possibly they were right: it is hard to draw the line between extraordinary Providences and supernatural interventions. Lewis himself appears to have regarded his preservation as a *grazia* if not a positive miracle.

It was, indeed, by no means his first experience of

the special protection of Providence, and nothing could surpass the confidence which he placed in the Divine care and help. These sentiments had their source in his constant practice of referring everything to God for counsel and help. No little child ever looked more continually to its parent's hand and eye to prefer its requests and seek for guidance, than Lewis turned to his Heavenly Father in every need, in every doubt. We have, moreover, his own recorded testimony that he never recommended anything to God, whether great or small, without obtaining his desire, and this in cases even of much difficulty, and where others quite despaired of success. Hence in this boy, so humble and so lowly, there dwelt a certain loftiness of spirit. Like Abraham, the "friend of God," with whom he negociated his every affair, and talked face to face, and who, fresh from the majesty of this presence, despised the Paradisaical fruitfulness of the Jordan plain and the princely guerdon proffered by the king of Sodom, our Aloysius contemned in his heart all that the world could show of wealth, glory, and magnificence; so that, in sweet scorn, the youth was fain to laugh within him, and could scarce, indeed, suppress his merriment, when witnessing the style and splendour of court, so imposing in worldly eyes—the gold, the silver, the rich furniture and attire, the pompous etiquette, the obsequious bearing of the courtiers, and such like vain circumstances and concomitants of earthly rank and station. He who all the day long dwelt in the court of the King of kings, could see nothing in all these things but what was utterly and (one may even say) ludicrously unworthy of the least esteem. Amongst all the gifts with which

God had munificently endowed him, there was none, indeed, upon which Lewis set a higher value than upon this elevation of soul above every earthly interest and desire. We may think of him as continually singing in his heart, *Regnum mundi et omnem ornatum seculi contempsi, propter amorem Domini nostri Jesu Christi,* a kind of perpetual pæan of his exodus from Egypt.* Often, in confidential conversation with his mother, he would express his wonder that everybody did not embrace the religious state, considering its advantages, not for the future life alone, but for the present also; whence the marchesa inferred that her son had certainly himself set his heart upon it; but she said nothing. His delight in the company of religious was another indication of his secret purpose. He who so sedulously shunned all society, not only visited frequently the monasteries in Castiglione, but if any monks from other convents chanced to make a passing stay, he never lost the opportunity of seeing and discoursing with them. He used, in particular, to rejoice when any of the Benedictines of Monte Cassino came that way, and these fathers were afterwards to add their testimony to the holiness of Lewis. He loved also much the Dominicans, who, in the heats of summer, used to spend their recreation time at Castiglione or in its neighbourhood; and we cannot better close this account of our young saint's mode of life at this period than by quoting from the deposition of the Dominican father Claudio Fini, a doctor in theology and celebrated preacher of Lombardy, which he con-

* "The kingdom of the world and all the adornment of the world I have despised, for the love of our Lord Jesus Christ." —*Pontificale Romanum: De Benedictione et Consecratione Virginum.*

firmed on oath, before the tribunal of the bishop of Modena:—

"I knew personally and had frequent familiar conversations with the most illustrious Signor Don Aluigi Gonzaga, heir of the marquisate of Castiglione, when I used to be at Castiglione for recreation, or in other places feudatory to his house. An extraordinary love of humility displayed itself in all his familiar words and sayings; frequently did he extol detachment from greatness and worldly dignities. Upon one occasion, amongst others, he said to me at Castiglione, 'High birth ought not to inflate us, because, any way, a prince's body when it turns to corruption is indistinguishable from that of a poor man, except that the prince's may very likely stink the most.' At this tender age no childishness ever appeared in him; he had a singular modesty, and at times a retiring taciturnity, thoughtful, grave, devout. Often had he these words on his lips; 'Would to God that I could love Him with the fervour which His Infinite Majesty deserves! My heart weeps because Christians show such ingratitude towards Him.' So exquisite were his modesty, delicacy, and purity, that it is impossible to conceive anything surpassing them; so sensitive was he in this respect, that if any one, albeit but in jest and frolic, ever so little declined from the rules of the strictest decorum, he blushed and sorrowed with an expression of exceeding shame, showing the compassion he felt for another's fault. If any one spoke to him of spiritual things, or of some one who had entered religion, he manifested great joy; his whole countenance lighted up in a manner that quite changed his appearance; and he would say with interrupting sighs,

'Oh how great must be the blessedness of Heaven in actual enjoyment, since even when talking of it here below one experiences such delight! Sometimes I accompanied him to the church, and, young as he was, he surpassed the oldest religious in acts of most humble devotion, in which he was as one perpetually weeping. Sometimes he would fix his eyes on the image of some saint with such attention that he seemed to have passed out of himself; for if, on these occasions, any one called or spoke to him he did not hear or answer immediately. He told me more than once that he had a special devotion to the Blessed Virgin, and felt himself melted to tenderness if he only heard her named. I never knew him after he entered religion, but I clearly perceived from his whole behaviour that he inwardly purposed to leave the world."

We have here the simple statement of one who knew Lewis well in his early youth. Solemnly attested, it comes to set its seal on what has been stated upon the best and surest testimony. Such was the tenour of Lewis's life in the midst of the world and of a court, supported only by his mother's secret sympathy, yet so marvellously shielded by the hand of God that, to use Cepari's remarkable expressions, "no one dared to ask, Why doest thou this thing or wherefore that?' Such was the species of awe which this boy of thirteen impressed on all who surrounded him.

CHAPTER IV.

LEWIS AT THE COURT OF SPAIN.

PHILIP II., king of Spain, had taken as his fourth wife his niece, Anne of Austria, daughter of Maximilian II., emperor of Germany, and of the Infanta Maria of Spain. In the year 1581, to which our story has brought us, the empress-dowager was to pay a visit to the court of her brother, and Philip, desiring to do her honour, signified his wish that some of his great feudatory nobles of northern Italy, through whose territory she was to pass, should accompany her; Don Ferrante di Gonzaga, for whom, as well as for his wife, Donna Marta, the king retained a high regard, being specially invited. Kings' invitations are commands, at least they were so considered in those days, and the marchese, perhaps nothing loth, prepared to obey the summons. To his lady-wife the removal from their home and the long voyage were far from agreeable. She had to leave behind her three youngest children: Francesco, but five years of age; Fernando, only three; and Cristiano, a babe just weaned. But she had the consolation of taking her "angel" with her, as well as his brother Ridolfo and the little Isabella, who was never again to set her foot on Italian ground.* Don Francesco del Turco accompanied them.

* Isabella of Gonzaga was left at the court of Philip to be brought up with the Infanta Isabella Clara Eugenia, and became her lady of honour. She died a few years later.

The marchese and his family sailed in the ship which bore the empress. Cepari collected, from the marchesa's own lips, a few characteristic traits of her son during the voyage. The Mediterranean was at that time infested with pirates; and Lewis, hearing some apprehensions expressed of being attacked by these infidel corsairs, exclaimed, in an excess of fervour, "Would to God that we might have the opportunity of becoming martyrs!" The galley touched at some ports on the way. On one of these occasions the boy landed, and, walking along the beach, with his eyes, no doubt, cast down as usual, observed and picked up a stone. What was it that had attracted the notice of one who seemed devoid of all mere natural curiosity? The stone bore upon it marks of a blood-red hue, which to Lewis's eye seemed to represent the Five Wounds of our Lord. He took and showed it to his mother. To him, who looked upon no incident in its purely natural relations, but as a link in a chain of circumstances connected with the hidden supernatural life of grace, it appeared that God had placed this stone on his path as a token that he was to be conformed to the Passion of his Lord. "See, Signora," he said, "what God has made me find;" adding triumphantly, with a naive conviction that he was urging an invincible argument, "and after *that*,"—after what? would many say to whom the things of faith are shadowy abstractions rather than living realities—"after *that*, could my father hinder my becoming a religious?" From this anecdote we gather that Lewis had by this time confided his intention to his mother, although we know well that as yet the marchese remained in ignorance.

Doubtless Donna Marta had told her son that she feared that his father's consent would never be obtained, and it was to this that he made allusion. The boy long preserved the stone as a devotional treasure.

The marchese on his arrival resumed his office of chamberlain at the court of the Catholic king, and Lewis and Ridolfo were made pages of honour to the Infante Don Diego, Philip's eldest son. Lewis had finished his humanities before leaving Italy; he now applied himself closely to logic, in which he received lessons from a distinguished ecclesiastic, while by Dimas, the king's mathematician, he was instructed in the use of the globes. He had a daily lesson also, after dinner, in philosophy and natural theology, in which he made such great proficiency, that, when visiting Alcalà some two years later, while a student was defending in the school some theological thesis, P. Gabriel Vasquez, afterwards his own master in theology at the Roman College, invited Lewis, young as he was to take up the argument. The subject was the knowledge which may be had of the mystery of the Blessed Trinity by the light of the natural reason. He acquitted himself with so much skill and grace that the audience were filled with admiration. Study, it will be seen, occupied now a considerable portion of Lewis's time, and then there was the needful courtly attendance on the little prince, to intrench upon what remained. The marchese had, no doubt, reckoned much upon the effect which this new mode of life would have upon the whole current of his son's thoughts and feelings. Change in itself acts as a distraction; its beneficial as well as its evil results are grounded on this well-known fact. Ordinary good Christians find that they have to make an effort, not always altogether successful, to resist the disturbing effect of new scenes and of a revolution in their usual plan and routine of life. And here was not change only, but change to circumstances far more unpropitious to devotion. Yet we need scarcely observe that Aloysius was not an ordinary good Christian, nor even an extraordinary good Christian. He was a saint. A saint is one who breathes in the atmosphere of prayer. The breath and food of sanctity is prayer. It is indeed by throwing us out of our regular habits of prayer, chiefly if not wholly, that change of place and scene works its common evil results. We relax our hold on God's hand, we forget to eat our daily bread, to replenish our lamp, and the lamp flickers for want of oil; but he who at every moment of the day, alone or in company, was leaning on the arm of Almighty strength and drinking at the Infinite fountain of grace, receiving continually, drop by drop, into his soul the Divine unction, as the bowl on the golden candlestick was fed by the sons of oil which the prophet saw in mystic vision*—he who was thus invigorated by that almighty Spirit before whom the mountains become plains—was proof against the influence of external circumstances; or if in any way they interfered with his devotional exercises and sensible fervour, God, who knew that the fault was not in his servant's will, was sure to provide a stay or an antidote. And, in fact, his biographer Cepari, alluding to the interruptions to which Lewis was

* Zach. iv.

subject at this period, when the curtailment of his available time rendered even his participation of the sacraments less frequent, says, not, indeed, that his general fervour had cooled, but that he felt less pressed by the consuming desire which he had lately experienced to leave the world immediately and enter the religious life. Perhaps also the difficulties in his path presented themselves more strongly to his mind, when less able to fortify himself to meet them by long solitary communings with God. The world seemed to hedge him in and block up his path of escape. But never for one moment did the holy youth relax in his fixed resolution of living in the world, if there perforce he must remain, the mortified life of at religious. Yet his delicate sense of the spiritual affections of his soul, to which those who live in close union with God within them are as keenly alive as the bodies of the sensitively organized are to changes in temperature, caused Lewis to take alarm, and in his necessity he sought the advice of some good director.

The Jesuits had several houses in Madrid. It was in one of these that Lewis found the guide of his soul. He chose for his confessor Padre Fernando Paternò, a Sicilian, and, under his direction, communicated frequently, and made fresh progress in evangelical perfection. What his life was, even in the midst of the daily distractions and disadvantages which his presence at the court entailed upon him, may be gathered from the testimony of this very father, given after the saint's death, to his purity of conscience. Not only, he averred, had Lewis never committed a mortal sin, having ever abhored the very thought of it, but many and many a time the padre could not in his confessions discover sufficient matter for absolution. In innocency a child, he describes him at that time as already a man in intellect and judgment; a great enemy to idleness, always occupied in some good exercise, and specially in the study of Scripture, in which he took great delight, and manifesting singular modesty in word, look, and deed. When walking through the streets, Lewis never raised his eyes, so that, had he not been accompanied, he would have mistaken his way, whether in Madrid, where he spent more than two years, or in other places, as he himself upon occasion stated in after years. And if palaces and buildings courted his gaze in vain, so also was it with all the pageantry of that court, the most sumptuous and gorgeous in Europe. Queens, princesses, and their glittering attendants passed before him as in a dream, in which nothing of detail is marked or remembered, or as unseen objects of which the shadow alone crosses our field of vision; nay, Lewis confessed to the same Jesuit father that even the empress, in whose galley he had sailed and in whose presence he almost daily found himself with Don Diego, he had never really seen; never had he looked in her face so as to be able to recognize her; and had he met her elsewhere, he would not have known her.

It was during his residence at this splended court that Lewis began to exhibit in a marked manner, not only a love for simple attire, but a predilection for old and mended garments. This propensity for shabby clothing was extremely distasteful, as may be supposed, to the marquis, who reproached his son with dishonouring his family; and the subject became one of frequent discussion between them, if discussion that could be called which was chiefly on one side, for Lewis always replied with filial respect and with perfect meekness. Yet undoubtedly, he opposed a passive resistance, dictated by that Spirit which pressed him to this despoilment and renunciation of all the outward trappings of his station. Indeed, had it not been for his perseverance in this course, the marchese might never (humanly speaking) have been brought to recognize his son's vocation to the religious life. It would not appear, however, that Lewis presented himself before royalty, or paid his court to the Infante, in dress derogatory to his father's rank; and with the usual apparel of his attendants he never interfered. But he ever pertinaciously refused for himself all that savoured of pomp; he rejected the golden chain worn by grandees in those days, and no brilliant was allowed to glitter on his person. When he could indulge his own taste, and had but his personal honour to support, he returned to his old clothes; going about with patches below the knee (as Cepari tells us) such as men of the obscurest fortune would have been ashamed to exhibit in public. In vain the marchese had new suits of clothes made for his heir; Lewis wore them once or twice and then slipped back into his faded garments. All this, it must be allowed, was sufficiently trying to the father. We, who view these humiliations in connection with the glory of the beatified saint, see in them so many jewels which were making up his crown; but to the marchese, albeit cognisant of his son's great holiness, they did not wear that aspect: it was all simple shabbiness, the result of exaggerated views, and he was heartily ashamed of it. We must therefore consider it as no little credit to a man of Don Ferrante's spirit and temper that he gave up the battle, not simply from its uselessness, but, in a great measure, from sheer respect for the constancy of that inexplicable son of his, and even could not withhold the tribute of his admiration from what on other grounds he entirely disapproved. We cannot, however, attribute altogether to the influence of Lewis's sanctity, a forbearance which must be considered remarkable in a man of the marchese's proud and imperious disposition; for a large part must be ascribed to the commanding power of a very superior mind, and of a calmness against which passion spends its force in vain. The marchese clearly perceived the strength of intellect, the maturity of judgment, and the consummate discretion of his son; he honoured these great qualities, he was proud of him, and thought with complacency, amidst his own increasing infirmities, of possessing in his heir such an efficient coadjutor during his lifetime, and such an excellent successor in the government of his estates and people.

Meanwhile, as may be imagined, Lewis's extraordinary piety did not pass unnoticed by those who were in habits of social intercourse with him. So grave and religious was his conversation with the great courtiers, that when they saw him coming, their free talk would cease, and they would compose their whole bearing and demeanour; and this not only out of respect for the angelic modesty which guarded every word and look of the youth, but because they knew that, gentle as he was, he would not tolerate, whether in jest or earnest, the slightest departure from decorum. It was as if some being from a purer realm had suddenly stepped into the circle. The saying, indeed, went about among the barons of the court: "The marchesino of Castiglione is not made of flesh and blood." Never did Lewis let pass any opportunity when he could say aught for the glory of God or the good of souls. One day when the little prince Diego was standing at an open window, through which a strong wind was blowing, which annoyed the child, the heir of all the Spains—destined, however, never to reach the eminence to which he was born—turned round with babyish indignation, and said, "Wind, I command you not to trouble me;" upon which Lewis, who was near him, smiled, and gently observed, "Your Highness can, indeed, command men, and they will obey you; but you cannot command the elements, because they belong to God only, whom your Highness is also bound to obey." As everything which concerned the Infante was sure to be retailed to the king, this little incident reached Philip's ears, who expressed himself much pleased with so judicious and well-timed an observation.

Although Lewis deferred to his father in everything where conscience did not forbid compliance, he had by no means the same consideration for the wishes of friends and acquaintance. Most persons allow such wishes, expressed or implied, to have very great weight with them, and often burden themselves thereby with an intolerable load of imaginary obligations. The fear of displeasing and the desire of winning or keeping affection easily take the shape of an amiable regard for the demands of kindness; but with numbers it comes so much as a matter of course that they must do what they are expected to do, that it would be difficult to analyze the complex feelings which go to form their actuating motive for making themselves the slaves of friends or of society, and of the received opinions and customs of the circle in which they move. Persons who value their own time will thus often allow it to be pillaged and devoured piecemeal by those whose sole object is to squander and get rid of their own. Lewis had small regard or concern for such chimerical duties, and had no mind to be a martyr in so thankless a cause. During the early part of his residence at the court, many of the youthful nobility would often come to visit him. Lewis, to avoid their importunity, used to retire to a hiding-place he had found for himself—an uninhabited apartment with a closet, where firewood was kept. Here, while the house was scoured for him, he calmly pursued his devotions, and although diligent search was made, yet as no one thought of looking for the marchesino in a dusty closet, he was never discovered. In vain the marchese complained, in vain even his mother gently remonstrated at what she feared might pass for unsociable rudeness: Lewis preferred the heavenly communications he enjoyed in this dingy hole to the company of all the nobles of the court of Spain. That neglected apartment, with its mean receptacle, was to be participant of the glory of the saint who so often prayed there, and to be raised to a far higher honour than belongs to the saloons of any earthly potentate; for after the saint's beatification it was converted into a chapel, in which the Adorable Sacrifice was offered. The friends and acquaintance perceiving at last that their company was undesired, ceased to molest him, and disposed of their idle hours elsewhere.

The holy youth at this time had found a more congenial companion in Lewis of Granada's treatise on mental prayer, which gave him a fresh stimulus in the ways of contemplation. What he read in this precious volume, concerning the necessity and manner of fixing the attention, put him upon a marvellous undertaking,—to pray without any, even casual, distraction; and, what is still more marvellous, he accomplished his object. Lewis, we may note—for it is another of those points in which he stands forth as a special pattern to the young—never (to use a homely phrase) allowed himself to be beat. His perseverance when he had a point to gain was something perfectly astonishing. Youth is generally not wanting in fervour or in zeal for undertaking great things, which have commonly an attraction for ardent and aspiring spirits; but the very ignorance of its powers, which leads it to aim high, is apt also to induce discouragement at the first unlooked-for difficulty. And this is the more unfortunate, because if there is a time for forming habits the acquisition of which demands strenuous labour, it is that period of life when the flexibility and spring of the mind is the counterpart of the pliancy and activity of the physical frame. But our saint's undertakings were not the dictates of simple natural fervour. We may think of him as one who has passed through that night of the senses, external and internal, of which St. John of the Cross treats in his Ascent of Mount Carmel. In the mystical canticle of that saint, the soul thus describes itself as issuing from its house, at the call of divine love:—

"In that happy night,
In secret seen of none,
Seeing nought myself,
Without other light or guide,
Save that which in my heart was burning."*

Thus it was with our saint. He had so gone out of himself, that the divine life had passed, as it were, into him, with its motives, its inspirations, its science, replacing the natural or mixed promptings of the heart and the short-sighted knowledge derived from the workings of the human intellect. What Lewis willed and undertook we may well believe was at the dictation of this inner guide, and by the light of this solitary lamp which shone within his soul; and so the triumph was secured. His first determination was to make daily, at least, one consecutive hour of mental prayer, absolutely free from even a momentary wandering of the attention. Placing himself on his knees without support, as was his habit, he commenced his meditation; and if, after half an hour, or even three quarters, he had the smallest distraction of thought ("*una minima distrazioncella*"), the first half or three quarters of an hour reckoned for nothing, and he began again. For some time he experienced a difficulty, and had occasionally to make so much as five hours' prayer, or more, before succeeding; but he *did* succeed at last. To this heroic victory over himself, may be attributed the wonderful gift which he possessed of commanding his attention and of fixing it on

* "En la noche dichosa,
En secreto, que nadie me veia,
Ni yo mirava cosa.
Sin otra luz in guia,
Sino la que en el corazon ardia."

such objects alone as he desired to consider. The hand does not more freely follow the movement of the will, than those usually rebellious subjects, the imagination and the memory, obeyed Lewis's volition. He had, as he himself afterwards confessed, the power of thinking or not thinking of just what he pleased.

The close of the year 1582 brought a heavy affliction to the Spanish monarch. A malignant fever carried off his eldest son, Don Diego. The death of the boy-prince freed Lewis from his court attendance. We meet with him, however, in March, 1583, figuring on a very public occasion, much doubtless, against his own inclination; being selected to deliver a Latin address of felicitation to the monarch at his solemn entry into Madrid on his return from Portugal, the diadem of which kingdom he had just placed upon his brow. Lewis's selection at so early an age for this office marks, not only the high consideration in which the marchese was held, but the opinion entertained of his son's capacity. The calamity which had fallen on the royal family was to Lewis personally a providential release. For when he had resided a year and a half in Madrid, and had consequently nearly completed his fifteenth year, he felt himself inwardly moved to execute the resolution he had formed in Italy, and, under the light of Divine guidance, make choice of the religious order into which he should enter. For this end he prayed much and reflected much, and confided his reflections to his pious mother. As he had so strong an attraction for mortifications, his first inclination was to join the Discalced Franciscans (the Capuchins of Spain); but whether he judged that, his constitution being so much enfeebled, there might be some danger, if found unable to persevere in so austere a rule, of his being removed and brought back to the world, or whether the representations of the marchesa, who strongly dissuaded him from this election, had weight with him, or from both reasons combined, he gave up this first thought, and debated for a time upon the advantages of entering some order relaxed from its primitive strictness, with the view of labouring for the glory of God, by bringing about its reform. But his low opinion of his own merit and capacity made him abandon the idea of an undertaking not, as he believed, within the compass of his powers, and in attempting which he might even entail injury to his own soul. To orders entirely devoted to the active life, and to corporal works of mercy, he did not feel himself called, not judging them comformable to his disposition; but his inclinations strongly leaned towards a life of pure contemplation. Those orders which, either in the deep solitudes of nature or strictly cloistered in the heart of cities, gave themselves to silence, prayer, psalmody, meditation, and sacred studies, were in his eyes havens of holy peace and joy; but as his great desire was to seek, not merely his own repose and the glory of God, but, above all, the greater glory of God, he weighed the matter well in his mind; and here he began to reflect that, according to the opinion of many, and of St. Thomas in particular, those religious orders hold the sublimest rank which do not give themselves exclusively to contemplation, but also strive to lead others to the knowledge of the great objects of their contemplation, and teach, preach, and labour for the salvation of souls; because they thus more perfectly imitate the life of the Son of God, who was not always in the desert and on the mountain-top, holding solitary communion with His Heavenly Father, but descended to instruct the ignorant, to evangelize the poor, and to work miracles of mercy in the cities of Galilee and amidst the multitudes which gathered around Him on the shores of its lake, and even followed Him into the wilderness, and who, if He withdrew at night to the Mount of Olives, was again in the daytime found teaching in the Temple. And so for the love of God, Lewis would wean himself from this exclusive love of solitude, and would choose some order in which the mixed life was practised.

After comparing minutely all the different orders, he fixed at last upon the latest which had sprung up in the Church, the Company of Jesus. The chief reasons which recommended that great Society to his preference seem to have been the following:—First, that religious observance was now flourishing there in all its first vigour; secondly, that in the Company a particular vow is taken, not to accept any ecclesiastical dignity save by the Pope's special command: this was a matter of great importance in Lewis's eyes, who dreaded being one day dragged again into the world, through the ambition of his family, to be promoted to some prelacy. Thirdly, the Company does so much for the instruction and religious training of youth; and Lewis esteemed this to be one of the works most pleasing to God. Fourthly, the Company sets before it as one of its special objects, the reclaiming of heretics and the conversion of the heathen in foreign lands; and he hoped that possibly some day he himself might have the good fortune to be sent to China, Japan, or the New World, to win souls to the faith. In order that he might be the more assured that his choice was according to the designs of God, Lewis recommended the matter to the intercession of Mary, communicating with that intention on the feast of her Assumption, 1583, being then fifteen years and five months old. For this communion he prepared himself most diligently; and while engaged in fervently beseeching our Blessed Lady to obtain for him the knowledge of God's will, he received the desired answer in the form of an anterior word, pronounced so plainly in the depths of his soul, and bringing with it so strongly that indescribable conviction which God imparts in such purely intellectual communications, that he could no longer doubt but that he was divinely called to enter the Company of Jesus. All joyous he returned home, and that very afternoon disclosed to his confessor the intimation with which he had been favoured, for so the Divine voice had enjoined him to do, and begged him to intercede with his superiors for his admission.

Padre Paternó, when he had heard and examined the whole matter, judged the vocation to be a good one, but assured Lewis at the same time that the Company would certainly never receive him without his father's consent, and that it behoved him therefore to endeavour by all the means in his power to obtain the paternal sanction. Lewis sought no delay. The length of time he had taken for deliberation was owing to his desire to ascertain with certainty God's will. The desire to execute that will, as soon as it was known, now prompted him to instant action. Before the day was closed he told all to his mother. She rejoiced exceedingly, and gave fervent thanks to God, to whom, like another Anna, she offered her son anew, as she had already offered him before his birth, to be entirely dedicated to the service of his divine Majesty. Desirous to spare her child the first outbreak of his father's wrath, she undertook herself to make the disclosure to him. It was a task requiring no small amount of courage; that courage which gentle and quiet souls often possess in so eminent a degree. Terrible was the marchese's anger when he learned his son's purpose; a purpose in his eyes so wild and preposterous that, whatever at times he might have vaguely apprehended, this, at any rate, had never for a moment crossed his imagination. And Donna Marta herself actually favoured the mad design! Not only did she strive to deprecate his indignation and stand as a shield between him and his infatuated boy—that were but natural perhaps in a fond mother—but she pleaded his cause, she justified his desire. And then one of those suspicious fancies which will enter the brain of angry persons, who, along with self-command, seem to have lost for the time even the power of sane judgment, got possession of the marchese's mind. His wife preferred her second son, and had worked upon the religious temperament of Lewis to urge him on to a sacrifice which should promote Ridolfo to the honours of the eldest-born. This, however, was too absurd a notion to last long. A few days elapsed, and then Lewis himself sought an interview with his father; and while, with all humility and respect, he disclosed to him the state of his soul, he at the same time manifested the firmness of the determination he had formed to serve God for the remainder of his life in holy religion. The marchese could not contain his fury; it flamed in his countenance and burst forth in ungovernable language: with hard and menacing words he drove the meek boy from his presence, threatening to have him stripped naked and caned by his varlets. Lewis humbly bowed his head: "Would to God," he said, "that He would grant me the grace to suffer such treatment for the love of Him!" and with these words on his lips he withdrew.

The marchese remained utterly prostrated with sorrow and amazement. He could not be angry long with his sweet son; nay, his very anger was a form of love; selfish love, it is true, as mere natural love is so prone to be, but still love; love in a bitter mood, but ready to soften into tenderness, and casting about for an object on which to discharge its gall, that it may spare, if possible, the too dear offender. Don Ferrante now remembers that his son goes to confession to the Jesuits. Ah! the confessor—he is the culprit: it is he who has had the audacity to insinuate this fancy into the mind of Lewis, and attempt to deprive a noble house of its prop and its hope. Never did the marchese for a moment admit the notion that a boy of fifteen, and *his* boy in particular, and the heir of Castiglione and of Solferino and of Castel Goffredo, could have a vocation. Some one, of course, had put it into the youth's head. Who so likely as Padre Paternò? And so he sends for the father, and, at once taking for granted the correctness of his surmise, loudly complains of the attempt made to rob him of his firstborn. The Company, both collectively and individually, were, as we have seen, quite innocent of the imputed larceny. Padre Paternò was able to state that Lewis had never spoken to him on the subject until the festival of the Assumption, when, after dinner, he came and imparted to him the answer he had received that morning in prayer and his already formed resolution. Nevertheless the padre freely acknowledged that although Lewis had never communicated with him on the subject of his vocation, he was by no means surprised when made acquainted with his determination. Lewis was now sent for, in compliance with the Jesuit father's request, to attest the truth of his assertions. The marchese could not but give full credit to what he heard; he had by this time become a little calmer, and, perceiving the boy's unshaken resolution, he lowered his tone, and said, "My son, I should at least have wished that you had made choice of any other religious order, which would not have interfered with your exaltation to some high ecclesiastical dignity, whereby the honour of our house would have been maintained, but this can never be if you join the Company, which refuses all such promotion for its members." To which Lewis replied, "But, my lord and father, this is one of the very reasons for which I have preferred the Company to other orders: that it closes the door against ambition. If I coveted dignities, I should remain in the world, and enjoy my marquisate, which God has given to me as my birthright and heritage, nor should I quit the certain for the uncertain."

The next idea which seized upon the unhappy marchese's fevered imagination was that the whole affair was a menace, a bravado, a pious stratagem on the part of his son to turn him from the habit of gaming, to which he was unhappily addicted. Nor, indeed, did the marchese stand alone in entertaining this suspicion: it was very largely shared by the court; and many loudly commended the prudence of the youth in thus endeavouring to deter his father from high play by the fear of a more serious loss. What gave colour to this notion was the pain and chagrin which Lewis had not seldom evinced when seeing his parent thus engaged, often retiring to his own room in tears; and his attendants had frequently heard him say that it was much more the offence committed against God which he deplored than the pecuniary loss which it entailed. The marchese, as it happened, had just lost at play several thousand scudi; and the very day he heard of his son's resolve he sat down in the reckless mood which disappointment will often create, and gambled away another six thousand. But as time went on and the marchese perceived no faltering in his son's purpose, who continued perseveringly to beseech his father's permission to follow the Divine inspiration, he was fain to acknowledge to himself that Lewis was, at any rate, thoroughly sincere in what he professed; nay, when he reflected upon the angelic life that son of his had led from his very infancy, he could not but perceive that it was much more than credible that he might indeed be called by God to His special service. It must be remembered that Ferrante was a sincere Catholic, and neither abstractedly denied the existence of religious vocations, nor had the boldness to pretend openly to contend with God, or to dispute His supreme right to dispose, as He chooses, of the souls He has created. Doubtless he said to himself that, if thoroughly convinced, he would give in; unfortunately, persons strongly attached to their own will and wedded to worldly interests, are very hard to be persuaded of anything which, on their own confession, must legitimately involve a renunciation of these cherished idols. And so the marchese *was* extremely difficult to convince; so difficult, that the task seemed hopeless. The poor man was, in short, afflicted with the proverbial and well-nigh incurable blindness of those who will not see.

Nevertheless he could not rest, and took steps which seemed to argue a desire to be enlightened. The Father General of the Franciscans was a noble of the house of Gonzaga, and a cousin of Don Ferrante, to whom he was also closely united in friendship. He was at this time visiting the convents of his order in Spain, and, being at Madrid at the close of the year 1583, the afflicted father applied to him, and begged him to examine his son's vocation. After two hours' strict investigation, the Father General told his relative that there could be no possible doubt but that Lewis's call was from God. Reasonably, the marchese could now offer no objection; neither did he attempt to contravene what one so well qualified to judge, and selected by himself for this office, had so solemnly decided; but he could not bring himself to let the desired permission pass his lips; he temporized, and put the matter off with indecisive or ambiguous words; and so days passed on, and then he said no more. Was he going to let the matter drop? Such was not at any rate Lewis's intention. His father had now ample light upon the subject. If he continued to oppose his vocation, it must be knowingly. What more could his son hope from entreaties and representations? He thought the time was come for some decisive step; so one day, as he was walking with Ridolfo, he took the direction of the Jesuit's house, and when they had reached it, addressing his brother and the attendants, he told them they might return to the palace; for, as for himself, he was going to remain. After reasoning some time with him, and finding that he was not to be dissuaded, the party left him, and went home to report the strange occurrence. The marchese was in bed with the gout; unable therefore to rise, he called hastily for Don Salustio Petroceni, the auditor of his affairs, and sent him to the Company's house to bring back his son. Lewis, however, calmly told that gentleman on his arrival that what must be done to-morrow might as well be done to-day; that he desired to remain where he was, and begged that he might not be deprived of his happiness. When the marchese received this reply, he became much alarmed, and said it would be too grievous a dishonour to him that the affair should terminate in such a manner, for that it would be the talk of the whole court. Accordingly he again despatched Salustio to his son, with peremptory orders for his return. Lewis then obeyed.

The marchese had gained his point for a time; but for how long? Passion plays a losing game against calm and conscientious perseverance; and we may add that parents also contend with their children generally at a certain ultimate disadvantage, unless they are prepared to exercise compulsion. Humanly speaking the marchese would in all probability be beaten at last, if Lewis only persevered; but he was not beaten yet. Far from it. Against him, however, stood an opponent stronger than the might of his son's constancy—One whose Will sooner or later will cause every created will to bend or break. But Lewis had yet much to endure; God so ordered it for the increase of his merit, and, doubtless, also for the worldly father's own good; the virtues which his long opposition to his child's vocation called into exercise under his eyes, were in due time to overcome the resistance of rebellious nature, and bend his proud soul to tardy but fervent penitence. The marchese now had again recourse to his cousin the general of the Franciscans, and besought him by all the ties of kindred and friendship to dissuade Lewis from his design. He set before him what an irreparable loss his son must be to him; a son of such great promise, of such mature sense and judgment, one who would govern his people religiously, and confer untold blessings on his dependants. If his revered relative would but represent to Lewis that he might thus serve God most devoutly while remaining in the world, it would be possible perhaps to bring him to reason. To this appeal, the Father General replied that the marchese must excuse him from undertaking such an office; for not only would it be inconsistent with his profession, but it would be repugnant to his conscience. The marchese then entreated him at any rate to prevail upon Lewis not to take the habit in Spain, but to return home with his family; their departure was imminent, and he promised that, when in Italy, his son should have leave to follow his own inclination. But the father knew what slender reliance was to be placed upon such promises, made in order to gain time, and really implying some conscious or unconscious reservation of paternal rights, which to the possessors are apt to appear so sacred as to override on occasion all contravening stipulations. He, too, had gone through a trying ordeal on his entry into the Franciscan order, and he remembered how, under similar circumstances, and at this same court, his parents had tried to coax him back into Italy in the hopes of there succeeding in turning him from his purpose; but, aware of their object, he had refused, and had taken the habit in Spain. Could he persuade Lewis to risk his dearest hopes and interests in a manner which he had judged to be perilous in his own case? He therefore candidly exposed to the marchese the scruple he felt in taking any such responsibility upon his shoulders. At last a compromise was agreed upon; he was to speak to Lewis, simply stating to him the offer and promise made by his father, but adding no arguments of his own to enforce compliance

Accordingly the Father General communicated to his young relative what had passed, including his own reluctance in any way to second the marchese's request, notwithstanding his pledged word of future consent. But the good youth either entertained no mistrust as to his father's faithful adherence to his promise, or at any rate considered it his duty at once to accept the terms he proposed. He therefore told P. Gonzaga that he was most willing to give his parent this satisfaction, and that he had no difficulty in making this concession; that he had forseen all possible contingencies, and felt within himself an immovable resolution, which, by God's grace, would stand him in as good stead in Italy as on foreign ground. The answer was reported, and the treaty thus concluded. Each had gained all he could at present hope to secure: Lewis, a promise which he could hereafter plead; his father, a delay by which he might find the means to profit.

CHAPTER V.

Return to Italy and Disappointed Hopes.

The Father General did not immediately lose sight of his young cousin, for whom he felt the warmest sympathy. It was settled that the marchese and his family should return to Italy with the galleys of Giovanni Andrea Doria, who had been recently appointed admiral of the navy of the Catholic king, and P. Gonzaga seems to have arranged with Don Ferrante that they should sail in company; not sorry, as may be inferred, to watch over Lewis's interests as long as he could, and enjoy the pleasure of his society. It was while journeying to Barcelona, the place of embarkation, and passing through Alcalà that Lewis, as already noticed, sustained with applause a thesis in the theological school. At Saragossa the noble family received hospitality in the palace of Don Diego de Espez y Mendoza. The whole house was at that moment in the deepest anxiety, from the extreme peril in which the young wife of that grandee was placed coupled with the fear that her infant would not live to receive baptism. It was a parallel case with that of our saint himself, who touched with the tears of the afflicted husband, began to pray most feverently, exhorting all to join him in imploring the mercy of God on mother and child. The sudden deliverance of both from the very jaws of death was regarded by all as a marvel which the almighty power of God could alone have brought about.*

The voyage was much more agreeable to Lewis than that which he had made three years before in company with the empress and her brilliant suite. He had now the congenial society of P. Gonzaga to whom he looked up as a perfect pattern of the true religious; and he himself afterwards told P. Cepari how diligently he observed and studied every word and action of his venerable companion, that he might store up the lessons they afforded for his own profit. The Father General was, indeed, a man of high spiritual attainments and distinguished piety, as was afterwards apparent to the world when he was raised to the dignity of the Episcopate, and occupied first the see of Cefalu in Sicily, and afterwards that of Mantua; treading in the footsteps of the most saintly of his predecessors, and becoming himself a model to those who should follow him. The time glided pleasantly on as the galley sped its way over the Mediterranean waters; Lewis discoursing one while with his revered friend on some passage of Holy Writ or other like topic, at another proposing to him doubts on questions arising in his own spiritual life; and so in the month of July, the voyage was brought to a happy conclu-

* The oratory in which Lewis offered his petitions on this occasion continued to be held in high veneration, although the mansion passed into other hands; the saint being there held in special honour on account of the miraculous recovery granted to his prayers.

sion, and the Gonzaga family once more set foot on Italian ground after a three years' absence.

It was Lewis's reasonable expectation that he would at once receive from his father the promised license. As, however, not a word was said upon the subject, he earnestly renewed his suit. The marchese made no direct opposition; he could hardly, for very shame, have recalled his so recently pledged word. Accordingly, he gave an evasive answer, intimating that he must send Lewis and his brother to the courts of several Italian princes, to compliment them in his name on the occasion of his return. This plan he devised not only in order to put off the evil day of parting with his son, but in the hopes, never really abandoned, of seducing him from his purpose or of wearing out his constancy by delay. Lewis should see the pomp of these little states; the glory of the world should be unrolled before him; its blandishments should woo him in varied succession; he should be the object of all that flattering and respectful homage by which, as the heir of a great house and the representative of his father, he was sure to be surrounded. Lewis was now in his seventeenth year; he was emerging from childhood, and there is something peculiarly agreeable to the self-love of the boy-youth when he finds himself for the first time treated as a man. The world itself seems to wear a different aspect to him, as he takes his first independent step into its charmed circle. Thus, doubtless, argued the marchese; parental fondness, and ambition so blinded him, that he did not see that he was playing the seducer's part. Woe to him, had he succeeded! But the fatal triumph was out of his reach. Equally was it out of his power to vex the spirit of him whom he thus persecuted, with so much as a passing temptation. Whatever trials and sufferings Lewis had to endure in accomplishing his vocation, they were all so to say, external to him. The sunlight of grace beamed always bright upon his path; no obscuration ever came over even the inferior regions of the soul, dimming for a season his sense of divine things, or his clear view of that upward track which was marked out to him by God. Such, was, perhaps, the special reward of his unflinching perseverance, and of that unremitting faithful correspondence with the slightest movements of grace for which he stands forth so singularly conspicuous even amongst the most exalted of God's servants; reminding us of that one spotless, glorious creature who shines far above in a sphere of her own, and who, with a perfection immeasurably above that of holiest saint or highest archangel, "heard the word of God and kept it."

However much disappointed by the delay, and whatever weariness of soul he may have experienced at the prospect of a mission so repugnant to his habits and inclinations, Lewis thought it his duty to accept the office laid upon him. His father's infirmities had increased, and Ridolfo was too young to figure by himself on such an occasion. If, therefore, the delivery of this round of compliments was a social necessity, or, at least, judged to be so by his parent, he would not refuse him this last service, albeit it involved a painful sacrifice on his part. And so the obedient youth prepared for his journey, or rather, held himself in readiness, while the marchese made great preparations in form of splendid court dresses for his children, who were to be accompanied by a numerous and well-appointed retinue. Ridolfo, as may be imagined, strutted about in his gorgeous attire with much satisfaction, but upon Lewis this sumptuous wardrobe was wasted; he persevered in wearing his simple dress of black serge. Obedience compelled him to undertake this worldly commission, but no consideration should make him don the livery of the world, or forego the continual assertion of his purpose to forsake it, which the simplicity of his garb silently but forcibly expressed. Upon this point he was immovable, and not so much as once would he gratify his father by putting on the splendid habiliments whose gold trimming scarcely allowed the rich material of which they were composed to be visible; in which garb the ostentatious marchese designed him to pay his court to her serene highness the duchess of Savoy.

While the party was on the road, Lewis now prayed, now meditated, and omitted none of his usual fasts or religious observances. On arriving at an inn, he searched about for some retired apartment, and if it contained no image or picture of the Crucified, he would with coal or ink trace a cross on a piece of paper, and kneeling before it make his long evening devotions. When he reached any city in which the Jesuits had a house or college, as soon as he had paid his visit of ceremony to the princes, in obedience to his father's commands, he at once sought the society which alone he relished; he went to see the fathers, but first, he would always go straight to the chapel, to honour the Divine Majesty in the Blessed Sacrament; a practice which he invariably observed under whatever roof, secular or religious, his dear Lord made His abode. Two characteristic anecdotes are related of our saint during this expedition. At Turin, declining the pressing invitations of the duke and duchess, he lodged at the archiepiscopal palace, with the Cardinal della Rovere, his mother's cousin. One day when he was sitting in company with many young nobles, there happened to be present in the juvenile circle an old gentleman of seventy, who began to talk in a free, immodest manner; upon which the habitually mild Lewis turned indignantly towards the hoary sinner, and boldly said to him, "How is it that an aged man of your lordship's quality is not ashamed to talk in this wise before all these young gentlemen? this is to give scandal and a bad example: for St. Paul says, *Corrumpunt bonos mores colloquia prava.*" As he said these words he rose, took a book, and, with a countenance of exceeding displeasure retired to another room, leaving the septuagenarian much abashed and the rest of the company greatly edified.

Signor Ercole Tani, Lewis's maternal uncle, having heard that he was at Turin, came to press him to pay a visit to Chieri for the gratification of his relatives, who were very desirous to see both him and his brother Ridolfo. To this request Lewis acceded; meanwhile Signor Ercole prepared a banquet in honour of his nephews, to which all his connections and noble friends were invited; the entertainment to be followed by a ball! To have to sit at a luxurious festal board, the centre of this worldly circle, was sufficiently distasteful to our mortified saint, and had he been aware of his uncle's intention, his well-meaning kinsman would probably never have succeeded in getting him into the trap; but—the ball! this was too much. Lewis would absolutely not be present at the ball. Then the good uncle urged all those reasons which are so hard to combat: those nobles and their wives, and, in particular, those gentlemen and ladies who claimed kinsmanship with Lewis, had been asked for the express purpose of meeting him; they were coming with that very expectation. Was it reasonable, was it gracious, was it kind to disappoint them, and throw a gloom over a whole social party by retiring, with such seeming rudeness, from their company? Besides, such conduct would place him, as the host, in a false position. Of course Lewis need not dance, since he did not like it; but he must not refuse to enter the ball-room. The nephew accordingly was fain, under these conditions, to accept the false position for himself, in order to relieve his kind uncle from a dilemma. But he was not going to be let off so easily. One concession to the world—as Lewis well knew—entails application for another; and so the stand must be made at last. Our saint would gladly have made it on the threshold, a course which he approved as the most consistent and the least embarrassing, but he had scarcely had a choice. No sooner, then, had he sat down than a young lady, to whom cousinship gave a title to familiarity, came and playfully begged him to be her partner in the dance. And who could blame her? there is small difference between looking on and joining in a diversion. Lewis's reluctance could hardly be of a nature, therefore, which forbade a friendly assault. Enough; our saint, without answering a word, rose, and leaving the astonished siren to her own reflections, escaped from the gay saloon. Signor Ercole soon missed him, and went in search of the recreant, but without success; at last, having occasion for some reason to pass through one of his servants' rooms, he caught a glimpse of the black serge of his nephew. He was kneeling in a corner between the bed and the wall, absorbed in prayer. His uncle did not venture to disturb him, but after gazing a moment with admiration, left the room and rejoined his company.

Lewis and his brother returned to Castiglione at the end of September; and, no doubt, the marchese asked and received a detailed account of all the visits they had paid to the different courts. All this, of course, must come first; and afterwards, as was but just, it would be question of what Lewis had most nearly at heart, the permission which his father had solemnly pledged his word to grant; but again were the youth's hopes doomed to bitter disappointment. The marchese had now shifted his ground, and when compelled to allude to the subject, he treated it no longer as a settled affair, but either as a matter never arranged, or as one which there were reasons for reconsidering; these reasons being, in fact, the old objections revived: Lewis's youth, and the consequent chances that his wish proceeded from a mere effervescence of juvenile fervour, and was not the fruit of a mature and solid vocation. Don Ferrante had been busy preparing a battery to try the firmness of his son, or rather, to speak more accurately, to vanquish and destroy it. The first shot came from no less a personage than the great head of the house of Gonzaga, who had always entertained a singular affection for Lewis. A bishop* made his appearance at the

* P. Cepari does not mention the prelate's name.

marchese's castle one day, charged with a message from Duke Guglielmo to the young heir of Castiglione. It was to this purpose: that if the life of a layman was distasteful to him, let him embrace the ecclesiastical state; wherein he would be able to do more for the glory of God and the good of his neighbour than as a religious; examples were not wanting in proof thereof: witness the many eminent saints and holy men both of ancient and of modern times, of which last, not to speak of others, the illustrious Charles Borromeo was a shining instance; for in the high dignity to which he was raised he had done more service to the Church than many religious could have accomplished. The prelate, who had been specially selected for his persuasive tongue, was very eloquent upon the subject, and concluded with what was the gist of the matter, in the marchese's estimation at least, that his serene highness would exert all his interest to open a similar career to Lewis, and secure his promotion to an exalted rank in the Church. Lewis heard him with respect, but, without hesitation, replied in detail to all the alleged reasons; in conclusion, he begged the duke's ambassador to convey his warmest thanks to his serene highness for the love which he had ever shown him, and which had prompted these offers; but, as he had already renounced all that his family could do for his advancement, so also must he decline the favours which the duke so liberally proffered; indeed, it had been his special inducement to make choice of the Company of Jesus because it refused all dignities, and he had decided to take God for his sole portion in life.

The bishop now disappears from the scene, but another actor is waiting to come forward. There is something almost ludicrous in the way in which these combatants of Lewis's vocation appear in rapid succession. The marchese, as a good general, had determined that the assault should be hotly maintained, and had his fresh troops in reserve to replace their foiled precursors. The second attack was from the illustrious Signor Alfonso Gonzaga, Lewis's uncle. He had a peculiar personal interest in the matter. His nephew would inherit his own fief of Castel Goffredo. Aluigi, the father of Ferrante Gonzaga, in bequeathing it to his son Alfonso, had stipulated the return of this property to the house of Castiglione in default of male heirs; and as this nobleman had no son, it had been arranged between the brothers that Caterina, his only child, should be married to the heir of Castiglione, and by this means retain the enjoyment of her father's estate. Lewis would have been all that the uncle could desire; he could not therefore see a son-in-law in every way so admirable as well as suitable escape him with indifference. What might Ridolfo, yet a boy, turn out? As may be imagined, where the bishop failed, the uncle was not more successful. He was followed by another personage * of much weight in the family. After urging many reasons to dissuade Lewis from his intention, he began to speak against the Company, exhorting him, at any rate, to make choice of some other order, such as the Capuchins or Carthusians: in so doing he would also more completely attain his end—separation from the

* Cepari does not name him; probably because the life was published at a time when a great number of the persons alluded to were still living. It might possibly be the Cardinal Vincenzo Gonzaga, whose father was prince of Guastalla and duke of Molfetta.

world. It is hard to assign the motive for this piece of advice. Possibly the object was simply to divert Lewis from his present plan, by the hope of meeting less opposition if he made a different election, and then to take occasion of this change to plead his inconstancy and variation of purpose as an argument against the soundness of his vocation; or again, the orders suggested being extremely austere, it might have been more easy hereafter to hinder him from embracing one of them on account of his delicacy of constitution, or to raise difficulties in his way upon this ground; or, finally—and this is far from improbable—in order to reserve the power of one day promoting him to some ecclesiastical dignity. The humble discalced Franciscan might find his espousal of poverty no protection, if influential persons so willed it, against his being made the unwilling occupant of an episcopal throne; the rigid Carthusian might be dragged from his rugged solitude, and forced to lay down his spade to carry a crosier; but the Jesuit was separated from the world by a barrier which nothing but the command of the Vicar of Christ could remove. Lewis briefly replied that he did not see that it was possible to withdraw more completely from the world than by entering the Company, for by their complete renunciation of all property, its members practised poverty with perfection; and as for honours and worldly dignities, they precluded themselves by vow from accepting them, save by the express command of the Pope, albeit offered by prince or king.

Lewis had to run the gauntlet with several other honourable assailants. Amongst these, Monsignore Pastorio, the arch-priest of Castiglione (whom he highly esteemed), endeavoured to persuade him to be contented with governing his marquisate, but in this case his adversary was not simply foiled but converted; and so fully was he won over, that he became the son's advocate with his father, and everywhere declared that he held Lewis to be a saint. The marchese now enlisted Padre Francesco Panicarola, a good Dominican and famous preacher, in his service. This father undertook the office reluctantly, and only because he did not know how to refuse; nevertheless, having promised to use all his eloquence in the attempt, he kept his word; but his representations produced as little effect as the arguments of his predecessors. "I was set to do the devil's work with that youth," he said afterwards to an eminent cardinal (probably Cardinal Vincenzo Gonzaga.) "I did it well and with all the skill and ability I was master of, yet I prevailed nothing; for he was so firm and immovable that it was impossible to shake him." Still the marchese hoped that some impression must have been made by these repeated assaults: accordingly, one day as he lay chained to his bed by the gout, outwardly racked with pain, and inwardly torn by anxiety, and in the very worst possible humour, he could bear his suspense no longer, and, sending for his son, asked him how he was now minded. Lewis, reverently but distinctly, stated that he was in the same mind as heretofore, to serve God in that religious order of which he had made choice. At this reply, the marchese, bitterly disappointed, flew into a violent passion, and, turning upon his son a countenance of fury, he bade him begone from his presence, and get out of his sight. Lewis took these expressions as a literal command, and at once retired to the convent of Santa Maria, belonging to the Frati Zoccolanti (Recollects). The marchese had himself established these monks on his estate, in a charming valley about a mile from his own castle. The convent stood on the border of an artificial lake, formed by the damming up of the streams that trickled in numerous rills down the adjoining hill. After his marriage, Don Ferrante had caused a kind of artificial cave, existing at the foot of the hill, to be enlarged and beautified, dividing it into several apartments. Antique mosaics adorned the flooring and walls, and the waters, conducted thither by some ancient channels, lent the refreshment of a cool and sparkling fountain, which was suffered to expand into a lucid basin. To this subterranean retreat, thus singularly adapted for the combined purposes of recreation, repose, and devotion, the different members of the family were in the habit of resorting, each having his own special room. Hither then Lewis retired, causing his bed, books, and furniture to be removed to the spot, and in this quiet refuge he gave himself unremittingly to prayer and the exercises of penance. No one dared to name him to the marchese, who, still in bed, was probably too proud, and for some time too angry, to make any inquiries. At last the question passed his lips· Where was Lewis? Upon being informed that he

made his appearance, sharply reproved him for his disobedience and insolence in leaving the house, for the sole purpose of causing him greater displeasure. Lewis meekly and humbly replied that he had thought to act in obedience to his father's commands in removing from his sight. The marchese added many threats and harsh words, and ended by bidding his son retire to his own apartments. Lewis bent his head: "I go," he said, "from obedience." Once in his room, he closed the door and, falling on his knees before the crucifix, shed many tears, begging of God constancy and fortitude in his trials. Then, baring his shoulders, he inflicted on himself a long and merciless discipline.

Meanwhile a great combat was going on in the marchese's mind. He was passionate and irritable, but he had a tender heart. We must do this poor man full justice: little has reached us descriptive of his character, save in connection with his reprehensible interference with his son's vocation; he comes before us as the persecutor of our Aloysius, and as one who did his best to rob us of a glorious saint and patron; but this must not make us judge him with harshness. He had, as we have said, a tender heart,—not merely a heart of paternal tenderness; many a hard and selfish man retains a soft corner within his bosom for his children, but not a few little circumstances prove that the great marquis was of a kind and compassionate nature. He was evidently not only a good master, but a merciful ruler of his feudal subjects; and we cannot suppose that it was altogether a pretext when he so often pathetically deplored that they should lose so good and pious a lord as his Lewis would have proved. Nay, we have strong proof also of his estimable and lovable qualities in the tender affection which his son, who suffered so much at his hands, ever bore him. For Lewis himself averred, when he entered religion, that his father was what was dearest to him on earth; making no exception, as it would seem, even of his mother, who had special claims upon his love. A re-action, then, had taken place in the father's mind. His conscience was not quite easy; he did not wish to offend God; and his feelings began to relent towards his child. He saw his meek countenance of gentle sadness as he left his presence: perhaps his rough reproof might have been too much for the youth's feeble frame; and so he summoned to his presence the intendant of his property, who was in the antechamber, and bade him go and discover what his son was about. The intendant found a valet at the door of Lewis's apartment, who told him that the prince had locked himself in, and did not wish to be disturbed; but the governor, intimating that he came by the marchese's orders, approached the door of the room, and with the sharp point of a dagger gently enlarged a crack in the panel so as to be able to see through. Lewis, it would seem, had now a new suite of apartments, which were on the same floor with those of his father, and the doors of which appear to have been in comparatively good repair. The spectacle which met his eye, touched the intendant's heart. His young master, whom they all quite worshipped, was on his knees before his crucifix, weeping and disciplining himself to blood. It was too much for the good man. He returned sobbing to his lord, and could scarcely tell his story for excitement. "If your Excellency," he exclaimed, "had only seen what your son, the Signor Aluigi, is doing, you certainly would not try and prevent his becoming a religious." "But what have you seen?" asked the impatient marchese, "My lord, what I have seen in your son would move any one who beheld it to tears" When the scene had been described, Don Ferrante could hardly credit the account, and desired to have ocular proof. He bade the intendant be on the watch the following day, who, as soon as the audible report of the discipline gave token of what had begun, hurried off to his gouty master, who, despite his indisposition, insisted on being placed in an arm-chair and conveyed to the spot. The marchesa accompanied him. With his eye at the hole which the intendant had made, Ferrante saw all; Lewis on his knees, his bare shoulders already torn by the discipline, and receiving fresh unsparing strokes every instant, the tears all the while streaming from his eyes and bathing the floor. It was a sight which stirred to its depths the father's heart. The tears which dimmed his own eyes soon obscured the vision before him, and he sank back in his chair as one who had received a stunning blow, and for a brief space remained speechless from emotion. Recovering himself, he bade his attendants make a slight noise as of persons arriving, and then knock at the door. Lewis heard at last, and opened. The chair was pushed in, and the whole party were in presence of each other. That might have been a scene well worthy of a painter's pencil: Lewis standing, with abashed and gentle, yet calm and collected, mien; the mother silently contemplating her son with a face of mingled love and veneration; and the father—how shall we describe the father's countenance? We can see him in imagination, with his face buried in his hands, through which the big tears are forcing their way, while his bosom is heaving with irrepressible sobs; tears and sobs which said more plainly than words could tell, "My son, you have conquered." Yes, Lewis had conquered at last. When now he knelt at his father's feet and renewed his entreaties, we can well conceive he was no longer repelled with angry words or bitter taunts. The spectacle of the blood and tears of his son had expelled all anger and bitterness from the parent's bosom. Lewis had conquered,

Not long after a letter was penned by the marchese to the illustrious Signor Scipione Gonzaga,* patriarch of Jerusalem, and afterwards cardinal, commissioning him to offer on his part to the Rev. Father General of the Company, at that time P. Claudio Acquaviva, his eldest son, the dearest thing he had on earth, and on whom his best hopes had centered; begging at the same time that his Paternity would name some place for the performance of the noviciate. In writing these lines, the marchese felt, we may imagine, like another Abraham raising the knife to slay his son, though altogether lacking that sublime love which made the

* He was brother to P. Francesco, the General of the Franciscans, and a distant cousin of P. Claudio Acquaviva. The house of Gonzaga was at that time divided into five principal branches:—1. The elder branch, the dukes of Mantua. 2. The princes of Guastalla. 3. The counts of Novellara. 4. The princes of Bozzolo. 5. The marquises of Castiglione. They were all descended from Lewis, or Aluigi, Gonzaga, who first reigned at Mantua. The inhabitants of that city having revolted against and slain their governor, Passerino Boncossi, the captain of Mantua, in 1328, Aluigi, the son of Guido Gonzaga, marched against, defeated them, and took possession of the town. He was recognized as vicar of the empire, with the title of prince-viscount of Mantua for himself and his descendants. In 1433 the Emperor Sigismund raised Mantua into a marquisate, in reward for the services of Francesco II. In 1530 Charles V. erected it into a duchy. Several intermarriages had more nearly connected some of the collateral branches.

patriarch's sacrifice a fervent act of the will. The poor marquis made his sacrifice from dire necessity, and no voice from Heaven was to come and stay his hand. That he still hoped for a reprieve, however faint that hope may have been, there can be no doubt. He clung indeed to a slender thread of hope, almost to the end, as his subsequent behaviour abundantly testified. But at present all went smoothly for Lewis's prospects. It seems that the marchese, while referring himself to the Father General's pleasure for the selection of the place where Lewis was to make his noviciate, insinuated to P. Scipione that he should make choice of Novellara; his secret motive being the neighbourhood of certain members of the Gonzaga family. But this was a reason for Lewis to dislike the plan; accordingly, he himself wrote also to P. Scipione acquainting him with his father's strong opposition to his vocation, and his own personal desire to make his noviciate at Rome, which would remove him further from all interference of his relations, and especially from all fresh assaults on the part of his father. P. Acquaviva took the hint. After writing such a letter as was suitable on the occasion to the marchese, and raising no objection to Novellara, he shortly after communicated to him his selection of Rome as the most suitable place for Lewis's noviciate; signifying this resolution, as would appear, through P. Scipione. The marchese acquainted his son with the result, without any demonstration of displeasure. Lewis, full of joy and gratitude, immediately wrote as follows to the General of the order:—

"I thank your Reverence for this great benefit, but words fail me to express as I should wish the extent of my gratitude. I offer and give myself up entirely to your Reverence, while awaiting the time when I shall be permitted to go and throw myself at your feet. If I do not fly instantly to Rome, it is because my father requires me to make a formal renunciation of all my hereditary rights to the marquisate of Castiglione, in favour of my next brother. Although the consent of the emperor is needed for this transfer, since the fief is independent, I hope soon to have terminated this affair."

With this affectionate letter the general was much pleased, and replied in terms expressive of the cordial pleasure with which he was prepared to receive him. Lewis had no other wish in this matter of the renunciation but that it should be speedily accomplished; but so anxious was the marchese that the instrument should be drawn up with the strictest attention to legal forms, that he not only caused it to be examined by several doctors of the law, but even laid it before the senate of Milan. Lewis therein made a full resignation of his hereditary claims upon the marquisate, as well as his title to all other successions. He was to have the sum of four thousand scudi to employ in any way he pleased, and a life annuity of four hundred scudi. The document was then forwarded to the Imperial court. The marchese, of course, was in no hurry, and was more than willing to let the courts of law and the courts of princes intervene with all their customary tardiness between him and the dreaded separation. Not so Lewis, who applied to his kind friend, the duchess of Mantua, Eleanora of Austria, to use her influence in his behalf. She readily complied with his request by writing at once to her nephew the

Emperor Rodolph; and the strong interest she expressed on the subject was of considerable service in expediting the business.

CHAPTER VI.

Renewed Trials and Final Success.

Some affairs of importance demanding the marchese's personal presence at Milan occurred at this time, and, as he was still disabled from active exertion by the gout, he commissioned Lewis to transact the business for him. He had already, in several instances, employed his son in negociations with several princes, and Lewis had always conducted everything to his father's satisfaction. On the present occasion he displayed, as usual, the consummate prudence and skill for which he was so remarkable, and succeeded in accomplishing all that the marchese desired. The time during which he was detained in the capital of Lombardy was not, however, lost to Lewis as respected his own mental progress, for he took advantage of the opportunity to study physics in the Jesuits' College of Brera, and made notable proficiency. Nor can it be considered less than marvellous that a youth of seventeen should at one and the same time acquit himself of a negociation requiring all the qualities of mature age and in a manner which excited the admiration of his seniors; pursue his studies with the ardour of a collegian who has as yet no occupation to distract his mind from the acquisition of knowledge, and—which is the crowning wonder—be leading all the while a life of prayer, penance, and contemplation; nay, every day making giant strides in the ways of perfection. Each morning he assisted at the early lectures at the college, and when his father's affairs prevented his personal attendance, he sent one of his gentlemen to take down the lecture in writing, that he might study it at home. He also took his turn among the other disputants in the schools; but while manifesting on these occasions, as he could not fail to do, the acuteness of his intellect, never did a sharp or vehement expression escape his lips, but his whole demeanour was a pattern of the most engaging modesty; so that if any one had been asked to single out the humblest, gentlest, and most retiring scholar on the benches, he must have pointed to Aluigi Gonzaga, the heir of one of the most illustrious families of Italy, a prince of the empire, and allied in blood to more than one crowned head. But Lewis, who despised all worldly honours and titles, would admit of no distinction in his favour, striving ever to seem the least of all, yet always winning, unsought, universal love and admiration. Besides his other studies, he attended a daily lecture on mathematics, and, as this was simply read, not dictated, immediately on going home he repeated it *verbatim* to one of his attendants, who committed it to paper. This man afterwards told Father Cepari that Lewis made this dictation with the utmost facility and clearness. The papers had been treasured up as relics at Castiglione, and the father to whom the amanuensis showed them was astonished at the perspicuity and accuracy which they displayed.

It was a lesson in modesty, not inferior to the sermon which St. Francis of Assisi preached by walking with his disciples through the town, which every day might have been learned by those who beheld this young noble go forth, not in bravery of attire, but in a plain dress of black serge, with no sword at his side, and, declining the horse caparisoned and drawn up at the door—doubtless according to the prescribed paternal etiquette,—take his way on foot mixed with the common crowd, though not unmarked, for his obligatory suite trod on his steps to do honour to the son of so great a house, while he, with his eyes cast down, walked on in silence, and never turned to say an idle word till he reached the college of Brera. It must have been a great alleviation of the trials of suspense, this continued intercourse with those who dwelt in the home of his affections: for every son of St. Ignatius was a brother of his love, or, rather, a father to whom he paid a loving and, so to say, passionate reverence. He spent all his spare time at the Jesuits' house, discoursing with one or other of its inmates; and his master in philosophy recorded the extraordinary respect which he used in conversing not only with them, but even with seculars vested with authority, scarcely ever raising his eyes to look his interlocutors in the face. He cultivated an intimacy with the lay brothers also, and particularly with the porter, whom he would persuade to entrust him awhile with the keys, and thus innocently amuse himself with the imagination of being a member of the Company, perhaps even hoping to be mistaken for such by some casual visitor. Nay, he almost passed the fond illusion upon himself, and nothing, by his own confession, could exceed the delight of those moments. Then he would wander out into the country through the Porta Comasina, always selecting Thursday for this stroll, and after bidding his attendants remain hehind, he might have been seen loitering on the way, now reading, now picking violets, as though to while away the time, like one who is watching and waiting for some expected meeting. Bye and bye, in the distance might be descried the black figures of the Fathers approaching. They were returning from Chisolfa, a villa which they possessed about a mile and a half from the town, and where every week they spent some hours of recreation on that day. Lewis would now stand close to their path; he had watched for the joy of that moment, to salute them courteously and reverentially as they passed; he would then follow softly on their steps, leaving such discreet interval as should remove him from their company, but keeping his eyes intently fixed on their retreating forms, as if he beheld so many blessed angels defiling from the gates of Paradise: and blessed, indeed, did he esteem them, able as they were to serve God without hindrance. Pausing as he neared the city, he continued watching them till, entering its streets, they vanished from his sight; then he would turn and hasten back to intercept another detachment, and nenew the pleasing process. Such actions forcibly remind us of the extravagances of the lover, extravagances in the eyes of the indifferent spectator, who shares not his ardent feelings: but love makes children of us all; nay, it is said to make fools of us, of the staid grown man as of the impetuous youth; and such-like little pastimes, in which a lively affection finds its satisfaction and delight, are perhaps stronger proofs of its force and tenderness than greater acts might be. And so divine love has its follies too, more reasonable than all the wisdom of the world.

Such, certainly, were the only follies in which Lewis ever indulged. When the mad fooleries of Carnival time began he took refuge in the college, to avoid the very sight of them, and to refresh his soul with talking of God; he used to say, indeed, that his spectacles and diversions were the Fathers of the Company, whose society was his greatest earthly pleasure. Yet on one occasion he did appear at a great worldly show, a tournament, which brought the whole city of Milan together. There might be seen all the young cavaliers of Lombardy splendidly arrayed, and mounted on spirited chargers richly caparisoned. On such a day, we may well suppose, there were few, if any, in the assembled crowd who had not done their utmost to appear to the best advantage in the brilliant scene. One, however, there was who had horses feeding in his stall inferior to none in Milan, and after whom was daily led, though not by his desire, a steed with velvet housings: to-day indeed he is mounted, but the animal that bears him boasts neither cloth of gold nor velvet in its trappings; it is a beast that spends its days in ignorance of such adornments, a sorry little mule, fit for some decrepit old man who can scarce raise his foot to the stirrup. Thus it is that the heir of the proud house of Gonzaga passes through the streets of this great city, whose balconies are crowded with merry dames, and amidst the jostling throng of nobles, with their garrulous attendants, who fill the thoroughfare. Two servants follow him: possibly *they* felt shame—history has not recorded their sentiments—but of Lewis we know that he passed on inwardly laughing at the world, as the world around, no doubt, audibly laughed at him. Many religious, however, to whom he was well known, noted the act of mortification and were greatly edified. To the Jesuit Fathers Lewis was, in truth, as great an object of admiration as they could be to him. Every Sunday and festival day, when he communicated at their church of San Fedele, the sight of his deep humility and devotion was a fresh stimulus to their own piety: in their eyes, indeed, he shone like the very impersonation of those graces, which seemed to breathe, so to say, in every look, gesture, and act. P. Carlo Reggio, who preached the Lent in that church this year, affirmed that whenever he desired to excite in himself sentiments of fervour and devotion, he cast a glance at Lewis, who was always stationed in front of the pulpit; the very sight of him causing a sensation of interior sweetness and emotion such as is experienced when contemplating some sacred object. Of Lewis's ordinary devotions we need say little, for it would be but to repeat what we have already described. His feet, as may be supposed, often trod the ways that led to the venerated churches and shrines in Milan and its neighbourhood; in particular, he frequented the Madonna di San Celso, much resorted to at that time in consequence of the many miracles wrought in this favoured sanctuary of our Lady.

The Imperial confirmation of the deed of renunciation had now been granted. Lewis was aware that it had been received at Castiglione, and was in daily expectation of a summons, which, however, did not arrive; neither was any explanation of this delay communicated to him. Suddenly, one day, the marchese made his appearance. A fresh storm was evidently impending, but this time it was to be in the scarcely less, if we might not rather say the more, afflictive form of supplication. It is very hard to be entreated by a parent, by one, too, accustomed to command and little prone to descend to petition. How must that proud heart be rent with grief and humbled by sorrow to become the suppliant of his own child! The marchese first inquired what were Lewis's present intentions, and when he found from his reply that they were as fixed as ever, his first movement was one of anger and resentment; but, suppressing the rising ebullition of displeasure, he assumed a different tone. He began to reason kindly with his son: he was not so bad a Christian as to wish to act in opposition to God's will, but his judgment told him that this desire of Lewis's was rather an ardent natural preference than the fruit of a divine vocation, because both filial piety, so strongly enjoined by God, and many other reasons grounded on the peculiar circumstances of his case, stood in direct contradiction to this passionate love of his for the religious state. He then went on to urge every motive which affection could suggest, to deter him from the execution of a design which, he affirmed, would prove the utter ruin of his house. He could not plead in its favour the danger which would accrue to his soul by remaining in the world; for God had endowed him with so much strength of purpose and made him so rich in virtue that he had no cause for alarm on this head. He could have perfect freedom to live as strict a life as he pleased, and be able at the same time, by his conduct and example, to lead the subjects over whom Providence had placed him, to walk in the fear and love of God. He reminded him of the devoted love which his vassals bore to their future lord: had they not all at this very moment their hands joined in prayer, that they might one day have the happiness to be ruled by their prince Aluigi? Was not this a hopeful prospect? was it lightly to be abandoned? God, too, had given him favour in the sight of the princes of Italy; what untold good might he not effect by the credit he possessed with them! Then the marchese turned to speak of Ridolfo, on whom the burden of rule must fall if Lewis withdrew from its support. He had good dispositions, excellent abilities, and gave fair promise for the future, but as yet this was a distant future; at present he was altogether inapt for the charge of governing others; he had not learned to govern himself; he was full of the fire of youth, impetuous, impulsive; needing a curb himself, he was not fit to hold the reins. And how soon might they not fall from his old father's hands! Here was the pathetic climax. "See me," he concluded, "a sick, infirm man, tortured and crippled with perpetual attacks of gout; it is with difficulty, as you know, that I can even move; so that my relief from the cares of government is become an urgent necessity. From this intolerable burden you are able at once to release me; but if you forsake me and go into religion, affairs will arise to which I shall be quite unequal; and thus, worn with anxiety, fatigue, and suffering, I shall sink under their united pleasure, and you, Lewis, will be the cause of my death." Touched with the picture he had drawn of his own lamentable condition, the poor marchese here burst into a genuine fit of sobbing, which was only interrupted to give utterance to some tender and affecting appeals to his son's compassion. Never had Lewis been so painfully tried, After listening respectfully to his father's argument, he first humbly thanked him for all his love and paternal solicitude, and then, instead of endeavouring to combat any of the objections that had been urged, he, on the contrary, readily admitted their weight and importance, specially as regarded his duty of filial obedience, which came next to his duty to God: indeed, he had himself pondered all or the greater part of the reasons alleged for his remaining in the world, and he felt that were it not for God's call, he should be doing wrong in overlooking considerations of so serious a character; yet seeing that he entered religion from no caprice, but in obedience to that call, he had reason to trust that He who sees and knows all would provide that no injury should ensue to his family or to their subjects; the Divine Bounty would order all things for the best.

It seemed to the marchese that he had gained a point in this admission of his son that, did he not firmly believe in a heavenly call, he would not insist upon leaving the world: if this persuasion could only be removed or shaken, something might still be effected. And so the whole process had to be gone through again, and the investigation resumed, as if Lewis's vocation had not been abundantly proved already. The good marquis seemed to argue thus: "It is so next to impossible that God should ask for *my* son, that much more proof is required than in ordinary cases:" it was question, indeed, if *any* proof could ever establish so unnatural a fact. Various persons, secular and religious, were now called upon to examine Lewis in succession; but the same result attended every trial. Still the marchese choose to remain in doubt: he must have some evidence so satisfactory as utterly to exclude every possibility of error. One day accordingly he has himself carried in his gouty chair to San Fedele, and, asking to see P. Achille Gagliardi, who enjoyed a very high repute in Milan, he told him he had determined, in so important an affair as the parting with the hope of his house, to abide by his judgment; but first he must require the father to come and set before his son every motive which his ingenuity and experience could suggest against the design he entertained. P. Gagliardi accepted the conditions, and, Lewis having been summoned, he examined him in his father's presence for the space of a full hour, not only as respected his vocation in general, but, in particular, as to his choice of the Company; and on this latter point he insisted so strongly, and raised such a host of difficulties, that Lewis was actually led to suspect that his interrogator was not simply proving him, but expressing his own genuine convictions. To so searching an ordeal he had never before been subjected, and the high esteem which he entertained for P. Gagliardi rendered it peculiarly trying. He replied, however, to all his questions so pertinently and frankly, fortifying his positions by the Sacred Scriptures and the Doctors of the Church with such theological ability, that the father at last exclaimed, "Signor Aluigi, you are right; it is indubitably as you say; you have completely satisfied and much edified me." We may imagine Lewis's relief at these words; if not as gratifying to the marchese, he at least could not dispute their justice, or complain that the father had not well played his part; indeed, he professed himself also as completely satisfied, and, perhaps, he was so at the moment; for he proceeded to give P. Achille an account of the devout life which his son had led from his very infancy, and finally expressed his willingness to allow him to join the Company of Jesus according to his desire. A few days later the marchese returned to Castiglione, whither Lewis, after despatching some further business, was to follow him, in order to complete the renunciation of his worldly inheritance.

Lewis could now feel little confidence in the stability of his father's promises; although the sky was clear at present, he had reason to apprehend some future storm. In order to be provided against such a contingency, he wrote a letter to the Father General Acquaviva, in which, after relating his recent troubles, he earnestly solicited leave, in case of his father's raising any fresh hindrance or delay to his entry into religion, to take refuge in some house of the Company. He did not obtain his desire. The Father General, while compassionating the youth's difficulties and trials, did not judge it to be prudent to accord permission to do that which in other instances has been even recommended. He told Lewis that he must by all means obtain his father's free consent. It would be for the greater glory of God, and his own greater good, as well as that of the Company. Nothing, then, remained for Lewis but to continue his course of patience and perseverance, of which he was to offer so perfect an example. He left Milan in the early days of July, in the year 1585, and before returning to

Castiglione visited Mantua. The whole city was in a turmoil at that moment from the daily expectation of the arrival of the ambassadors from Japan. The Christian princes of that island, the theatre of St. Francis Xavier's recent marvellous Apostolic labours, had sent their representatives to lay their homage at the feet of the Supreme Pastor of the Church, and these magnates, before their return home, had been visiting the Holy House of Loreto, and many of the cities of Lombardy. The duke Guglielmo and his son Vincenzo were preparing to receive them with regal magnificence, and a large concourse of people had been attracted to the capital, not only to witness the festivities and shows, but to gaze also on these wonderful Orientals, in their splendid and novel costume, these first-fruits to the Church of lands invested in those days with a mysterious interest. There was another stirring circumstance of the time, the approaching espousals of Prince Vincenzo with Eleanora de' Medici, whom the reader will recognize as the little girl who, with her sister, now queen of France, endeavoured to entice Lewis to join in their sports. Upon the occasion of this marriage the duke Guglielmo, in compliance with the will of his uncle, Ercole di Gonzaga, had just founded a college of the Company; thus bestowing upon his subjects an advantage they had long solicited and desired for the education of their children and the spiritual benefit of the whole duchy.

To this house our saint took his way. As it may well be supposed, the festivities of the city had neither attraction nor interest for him; he sought perfect retirement, and there, in a narrow cell of the college, during the great heats of the season, he imprisoned himself, giving night and day to prayer and meditation, and practising an abstinence so rigid that it made Fra Michele Angelo Pasqualini, who had the charge of carrying him his slender repast, declare that he believed that this young prince existed by miracle. Here he followed the Spiritual Exercises of St. Ignatius; and, if the lay-brother was edified by the youth's mortification, the fathers Antonio Valentino and Lelio Passionei, who gave him the Exercises, were not less charmed by the purity of his conscience, the fervour of his piety, and his high spiritual gifts. The Constitutions and Rules of the Company were now shown to Lewis, and, after diligent perusal, he declared that they presented no difficulty to his mind.

Fortified against coming trials by the invigorating spiritual course through which he had passed, he left Mantua, and returned to Castiglione. If he had followed his natural bent, he would immediately have requested that the great affair he had at heart might be concluded; but, desiring to conform to the Father General's advice, and not run the risk of causing irritation, he kept silence for some days, waiting for his father to take the initiative. To mark, however, his entire separation from the world, as well as to follow the movements of grace which were ever urging him forward, he lived a life in which his seclusion of spirit must have been more than ever palpable to all. If he left the rock fortress and descended into the town of Castiglione, his whole bearing was as reserved as we have seen it amidst the perils of a court and the throng of cities. His eyes were ever bent to the earth, and it was only when any of his vassals made obeisance to him as he passed, that he would raise them slightly to return the salutation; which he always did most courteously, uncovering his head to the least as to the greatest. But every eye lovingly and reverentially followed him, and sorrow mingled with the love and veneration at the thought that the happiness of possessing such a ruler was too precious a boon to be accorded to them. When he and his brother heard mass in the churches, fald-stools with velvet cushions were placed for them side by side, but his own remained vacant, as if he had already deserted in the body the rank which he had long resigned in heart. He knelt on the floor, and there, immovable, with eyes cast down, he remained at his devotions after mass was over. On festival days and Sundays especially, when he always communicated, his thanksgiving was so long, that Ridolfo was accustomed to leave him and go and take his morning exercise; but when he returned to seek his brother he would still find him praying. In the castle he kept still more strictly than ever to his own apartment, and many days would often pass during which he scarcely spoke a word. How deep was the silence he kept may be gathered from what he himself afterwards said to the Fathers: that he talked more in one day as a religious than he had done in many months as a secular; and that if he had ever occasion to visit his native country he would have to change his ways, and set a watch over his tongue, that he might not give scandal to those who had known him previously, and who would conclude that his conduct had become more relaxed than it had been in the world; and yet he was reckoned by his brethren in religion as a most exact observer of the rule of silence. The reason of the difference is sufficiently obvious. In religion he could freely talk of God; whereas such opportunities were naturally rarer in his father's house, and except from necessity, he never opened his lips save to converse of divine things. To all else he was as one dead; and his outward appearance was in accordance therewith. The attenuation of his frame, and the transparent whiteness of his complexion, made him look more like a shadow than a form of flesh and blood, while the heavenly expression of his delicately-chiselled features spoke of the home in which his spirit dwelt. The light of God's countenance, in which he was ever sunning his pure soul, was signed upon him: *Signasti super nos lumen vultus tui.* He undoubtedly, at this time, greatly increased the strictness of his fasts; and, indeed, it was one of the arguments used by the marchesa to induce her husband to grant their son the permission he so earnestly requested, that they were sure to lose him anyhow if they kept him in the world, since it was impossible he could live long if he persevered in his present system; but if they gave him to religion his fervour would be restrained. It turned out exactly as she said; for Lewis afterwards confessed that religion had benefitted his body as well as his soul, through the charity of superiors, who "checked his indiscretions." At the period of which we are now speaking, he interested himself much about his younger brothers, endeavouring to lead their minds to devotion. He taught the little ones how to pray, and used to caress them and give them sweetmeats to encourage them. He must have found a somewhat unpromising pupil in the elder, Ridolfo, now sixteen, yet in him, no doubt, he fostered many seeds of good, which were not wanting in him. Francesco was always his favourite amongst the younger ones, and it would appear that he had some secret prescience regarding the boy; for the marchesa related how one day, when Francesco was quite a child and playing with the pages, she heard a scream, and fearing they were too rough with him, she hastened to the room-door and said to Lewis, "I am afraid of their hurting that child;" but Lewis replied, "Signora, never fear but that Francesco will know how to defend himself; and mark what I say: it will be Francesco who will sustain the honour of our house;" a prediction which events, then distant and unforeseen, fully justified. But, as his governor Del Turco assured Cepari, this was not the only prophecy uttered by his saintly pupil, who foretold to many of his vassals things which afterwards took place precisely as he had said.

Days passed, and the marchese said nothing about Lewis's affair; at length he himself ventured gently to introduce the subject, and to remind his father that the time seemed to be come for the promised completion of the business. To which the marchese, now driven to answer plainly yes or no, a situation he would gladly have avoided, replied that he was not aware that he ever had given the promise and permission which Lewis assumed that he had received; and, what was more, he had no thoughts of giving it, until his son's vocation was more matured, and until he had gained sufficient bodily strength to enable him to follow it, as he might by the time he was about twenty-five years of age. But, of course, if he chose to take his own way, he might go if he pleased, but not with his father's good will; and in such case he would no longer regard him as his son. This announcement fell on Lewis like a thunder-stroke. Excuses for delay he had feared; nay more, he had anticipated them; but that the promise which secured to him the eventual attainment of his hopes would be denied and set aside, this he had never imagined to be possible. As one who, hearing a cruel and unexpected sentence of death pronounced upon him, entreats for his life, so he besought his father, with lamentations and tears, for the love of God not to do him this wrong; but the marchese had steeled himself beforehand to resist, and was proof against all supplications. Lewis left him, and retired inconsolable to his room, to weep and take counsel within himself as to his future course. The plan which approved itself to him, on reflection, was to do nothing definite until he should receive a reply from the Father General, and in the mean time, he would recommend the matter earnestly to God; but the marchese, who was resolved on carrying his point, so hurried and pressed him to decide between the two alternatives which he had set before him that, unable to wait for the opinion of the General, he chose as the lesser evil to propose a compromise. He told his father that although nothing in this life could be more painful or more disturbing to his peace of mind, he was willing to delay his entrance into religion for two or three years, in order to content his Excellency, to whom, after God, he most desired to give satisfaction; moreover, the Father General had enjoined him to seek by every means which his duty to God would permit, to obtain his father's acquiescence; but only on two conditions could he assent to this arrangement, and if either of these should be infringed, then he should be freed from his own promise; and since he could not in conscience prefer the will of his father to the Divine will, he would, rather than make any further concession, fly far away from his paternal house and country, if the Jesuits should refuse to receive him into their Company. The two conditions were, first, that, while awaiting the appointed time, he should live at Rome, where he could better preserve his vocation and attend to his studies; secondly, that, to obviate all further difficulty, the marchese should give his consent at once in writing, and send it to the Father General.

Don Ferrante was extremely angry at having these terms offered to him by his son, not only because they altogether thwarted his plans, but also from a dislike to commit himself on paper, and this to a third party. The oral engagements of parents to their children are commonly regarded by them as mere expressions of their present mind and intention, liable to be changed, of course, with altered humour and circumstances. In this light, no doubt, the marchese, who was a man of honour and strict adherence to his word on other occasions, had regarded the promises which, when in a softened mood or from motives of temporizing prudence, he had made at different times to Lewis; but to bind himself by contract and take the Father General to witness was quite another affair. He stood firm in his refusal for two days; but, at last, whether from a sense of justice, or because he feared that a prolonged denial might drive his son to the adoption of some desperate resolution—for he well knew that neither courage nor determination was wanting to him—he gave a reluctant consent. Lewis wrote at once to acquaint P. Acquaviva with the concession which with deep regret he had been forced to make. His victory indeed was far from satisfactory. His heart was inconsolable at the delay, and with many tears he deplored that he was born the heir of a noble house; regarding with a holy envy such as, belonging to an inferior station, have fewer impediments to the accomplishment of their vocations. But God had compassion on His afflicted child, and an unexpected deliverance from all his troubles was near at hand.

In making it a condition that he should spend his period of probation at Rome, Lewis had certainly reckoned on being placed at the seminary of the Jesuits. But the marchese did not so interpret the agreement, or, at least, had no intention of so understanding it. He wished to locate his son in the splendid palace of the Cardinal Vincenzo Gonzaga, and to place him under the tutelage of that dignitary. He accordingly begged the duke of Mantua to write to their illustrious relative, and make this proposition. Guglielmo, who had a special affection for Lewis, willingly acceded. Why any subsequent discussion should have arisen, it is hard to say, except that God, who rules men's minds disposes them to adopt measures which lead to the accomplishment of His own purposes. Lewis, indeed, always regarded it as a special Providence in his favour that, the duke and his father differing amicably for some reason or other as to which should write first to the cardinal, the project was abandoned, and he was thus delivered from a position most repugnant to his inclinations and from a species of bondage he so much dreaded; that which springs from intimate association with relatives, and from the consequence of which it would (as he said) have taken years completely to free himself.

The marchese's next idea was that his son should have his own private apartments at the seminary, with such attendance as was suitable to his rank, where he could at the same time prosecute his studies under the superintendence of the Company; but as this arrangement was quite unprecedented, and opposed to the rules of the order, he sent a special messenger with a letter to the Signor Scipione Gonzaga to beg him by all means to obtain this favour from the General. His cousin warmly interested himself in the matter, but, convinced by the reasons alleged for refusal, he wrote in this sense to the marchese, who, with the pertinacity which distinguished him, and which Lewis seems to have inherited in a purer form,—the natural quality being, moreover, in him sublimated by Divine grace,—now pressed his son to apply to Madama Eleonora of Austria, the duchess of Mantua, to whom the Company were under great obligations, in order to prevail upon her to ask this favour of the General; but for many reasons Lewis refused to comply. Not only did he deem the proposed plan to be adverse to his own spiritual interests and disparaging to his credit, if supposed to be desired by himself, but he considered that any application of the sort to Madama Eleonara on his part would be a glaring inconsistency and even impropriety, after his previous application to her in the case of the renunciation. Some other scheme had therefore to be devised.

Meanwhile Lewis took heart, and with renewed fervour gave himself to supplications, fastings, and penitential exercises, always communicating with the same intention, that God would be pleased to remove the impediments from his path. One day, after spending between four and five hours in prayer, he felt a sudden inward movement, accompanied with a marvellous spiritual strength, prompting him to seek his father, who at the time was confined to his bed with gout, and make a new effort to obtain his consent. Believing this impulse to come from the Spirit of God, he rose from prayer, went straight to the marchese's room, and without preamble spoke thus:—"My lord and father, I place myself entirely in your hands; do with me what you will; but I protest to you that I am called by God to the Company of Jesus, and that in resisting this call you resist the will of God." Then, without waiting for an answer, he turned and left the room. These few words seemed to carry with them a marvellous force and keenness to reach and pierce the heart. The marchese remained for a time like one transfixed and speechless; and then his long persistent opposition to his son's vocation rose up before his mind in colours such as it had never before assumed, and his soul was assailed by the fear of having herein offended God; while he seemed to realize more deeply and sensibly than ever the goodness, the sweetness, the angelic virtues of his son. To lose such a son, or to offend God! Unable to support the intense violence of the conflict which was going on within him, he turned his face to the wall and, to use the expressive language of Scripture, he "lifted up his voice and wept." It was the loud, uncontrollable burst of grief of one who is wont to refrain himself: when the spirit gives way, sorrow breaks forth like a flood. As the Egyptians and all Pharaoh's house heard, with amazement, through the closed doors, the sobs of Joseph weeping, so the marchese's servants in the anteroom listened to the mighty clamour of distress which came from their lord's chamber, and wondered what had happened. What could have excited this paroxysm of grief! The marchesino had been there, it is true, but he had tarried but a moment, and heaven's peace abode always on his fair, unruffled brow. Bye and bye the marchese summoned one of the attendants and sent for his son. Lewis came. "My son," he said, "you have wounded me to the heart, because I love you, and have always loved you, as you indeed deserve to be loved. In you I had treasured up all my hopes, and the hopes of our house; but since God calls you, as you say, I will not hinder you: go, my son, whither you list, and I give you my blessing." These words, uttered with the deepest tenderness and feeling, were followed by a fresh outbreak of sobs. Lewis, after briefly thanking his father with much affection and gentleness, left him to recover his calmness of mind, for the very presence of his son at that moment only increased his anguish. Hastening to his own room, he cast himself on his knees, and, with his eyes raised to heaven and his arms extended, poured forth his soul in tears of gratitude for the inspiration he had received; and while offering himself anew as a perpetual sacrifice to the Divine Majesty, so great were the joy and sweetness with which his soul was flooded, that it seemed to him as if he could remain for ever in the attitude of adoration, never satiated with blessing and praising God for this His crowning mercy.

CHAPTER VII.

Lewis joins the Company of Jesus,

The news that Don Ferrante had given his consent to part with his son spread with electric rapidity through the castle and through the town. It was a day of great lamentation among the vassals of the house of Gonzaga; for the few days that Lewis remained amongst them, he could not stir out without every one, men, women, and children, rushing to doors and windows to catch a sight of their dear young lord and to show him reverence. The countenances of those who could not make free to do more than express their feelings in looks, told of their heartfelt regret; and he himself, who had become so dead to all mere earthly affections, could not but be touched by the genuine love exhibited by these simple people. Some who were able to approach him nearer ventured tenderly to remonstrate with him. "Signor Aluigi," they said, "why do you leave us? you have such a fine estate, and such loving vassals, who, over and above the ordinary love of subjects for their natural prince, have also a particular devotion to your person; we have all of us set our affections on you, and laid up our hopes in you, and now, while we were looking to have you for our ruler, you forsake us!" To which Lewis replied, "It is because I wish to go and gain a crown in Heaven; it is very difficult for the lord of an earthly state to save his soul; no one can serve two masters, the world and God; I wish to make sure of my salvation, and I exhort you to do likewise."

It may well be imagined that Lewis was solicitous to exchange the house of his earthly for that of his heavenly Father; but it was necessary to wait some weeks, both for the return of the marchesa his mother from Turin, whither she had gone to visit the duchess of Savoy, and also to arrange a meeting of several princes of the house of Gonzaga, whose presence at the signing of the renunciation had been expressly stipulated by the Emperor; the object being to avoid any future litigation in the event of a failure of the marchese's direct heirs. For their accommodation Mantua, where these nobles chiefly resided, was selected, and hither the marchese, still in a very infirm condition, would have himself conveyed. It was a sorrowful procession which left Castiglione in the October of 1585. With the exception of a single glad heart, all were sad and mournful, and tears were on every face. One, indeed, there was, who, if he sorrowed that day a little, could not have sorrowed very deeply, and whose tears, if he shed any, which, from the contagion of grief and the impressibility of a young heart, he probably did, were at any rate not bitter tears. This was Ridolfo, upon whom the deed, the first act of which was being performed, bestowed a splendid inheritance, to the value of which he was far from being insensible. One universal wail arose on every side as the ponderous carriages rolled on at their usual slow pace, a wail which was taken up and echoed throughout the length and breadth of the little state. All Castiglione and its neighbourhood had turned out to take a last look of him who was going from them never to return; and on that day, and for several days after, there was no talk but of the young Aluigi's rare virtues, all lauding him as a saint, not only for the holiness he had manifested in his high estate, but for having waged as long and arduous a battle to rid himself of earthly honours as others have fought to win them.

In Mantua some further delay occurred to the signing of the deed. Don Ferrante, as will be remembered, had made a special reserve of an annuity of 400 scudi for his son's personal use, but on ascertaining from the Rector of the Company in that city that no religious was allowed to retain the private use of property (a practice which would directly contravene the vow of poverty) and that, consequently, the proposed allowance must remain at the disposition of the superior, the marchese withdrew this condition from the deed. Whether he was nettled at being defeated in this last attempt to preserve a little worldly distinction for his son, or that he felt to owe the Company a grudge for robbing him of his most valued treasure, and was therefore unwilling to enrich it by the contribution of even so paltry a sum, does not appear. The measure in itself presented no difficulty either as respected the Company, which asked for nothing and coveted nothing, or as regarded Lewis, who cared not in what form the renunciation was made so as it were speedily made; but certain legal authorities suggested that if any clause of the deed were expunged, it would no longer be the same document which had received the Imperial sanction, and hence a risk might arise of invalidating the whole proceeding. Many doctors were now consulted, and several days were passed in debating the point, to the renewal of Lewis's painful anxiety. But seeing that the question was of a purely technical character, and that Lewis and the princes of his house were willing to affix their names to the deed, after the withdrawal of this unimportant clause, it would be easy to obtain the Imperial confirmation for what had been thus done with the assent of all. Anyhow Lewis pleaded his cause so well that the objection was waived, and the renunciation was signed, with all the required securities and formalities, upon the 2nd of November.

The marchese's palace of San Sebastiano was the scene of this concluding act, which set its seal on the accomplishment of Lewis's long-cherished hopes. Hither the Princes Vincenzo and Prospero Gonzaga, the nearest of kin, with other lords of the house of Gonzaga, repaired on the morning of that day, accompanied by all the necessary witnesses and other connections and friends of the family. While the notary was reading the deed, which seems to have rivalled our modern legal documents in lengthiness, the poor marchese wept without ceasing, like the chief mourner at a funeral. It was, indeed, the interment of his fondest earthly hopes at which he was assisting. The chief actor and self-immolator on this occasion was serenely joyous, although he had that morning been subjected to some vexatious assaults upon his resolution from certain of the Gonzaga princes, who took the liberty of relationship to make themselves extremely disagreeable. While Prince Vincenzo was endeavouring to pacify the marquis, for whose grief a species of solicitous concern was exhibited which conveyed an implied reproach to its cause, these lords jested at Lewis for his design of becoming a religious, trying to make the youth, who stood alone in an imposing circle which represented the united authority of his family, feel as if he were playing a fool's part in the affair. Minds less strong than that of Lewis, or less strengthened by grace, know that an ordeal of this kind is painful even where it is not trying. Seeing that their teasing pleasantries made not the smallest impression, Lewis's relatives began to offer serious remonstrances, for it was yet time to draw back so long as the fatal signature did not stain the parchment. But Lewis heard their grave dissuasions with the same imperturbability as he had listened to their banterings. Both failed even to ruffle the surface of his mind, and Prince Prospero afterwards affirmed that he had never before seen his cousin in such spirits. No sooner had our saint set his name to the deed, and his presence was not legally required, than he retired to his own apartment, where, on his knees, for above an hour, he gave thanks for his deliverance from all earthly possessions; and it would, indeed, seem as if it had been to content his great love of holy poverty, that God so ordained that he should enter the Company empty-handed, through a strange perversity on the part of the marchese, who acted upon this occasion in opposition to his natural disposition, which was liberal even to prodigality. His behaviour was, in fact, at that very moment matter of comment amongst the noble cousins, who were unable to understand how the magnificent Don Ferrante could have betrayed such a niggardly spirit; in the case, too, of a son so beloved, and when he himself had been the originator of the proposed settlement.

Meanwhile Lewis, on rising from his long thanksgiving, called Don Ludovico Cataneo, a venerable ecclesiastic who had accompanied him from Castiglione, and begged him to bless an ecclesiastical habit which he had secretly caused to be made after the fashion of that worn by Jesuits, and then, stripping himself of all his secular attire even to his very shirt and the silken leggings worn by gentlemen in those days, he put on the clerical dress and went down to the dining-hall, where the whole noble family were already seated at table. We are told by Father Cepari that all were moved to tears at the sight—for of jests and reproaches we now hear not another word—and more than all—need it be said?—was the marchese affected, who, in spite of the strong effort he made to control himself, wept incessantly all dinner-time. Lewis, taking his place, began with a modest cheerfulness to speak of the great risk so often incurred in the world of offending God, of the vanity of transitory goods, of the special difficulties which beset princes and nobles in the way of salvation, and how every one ought seriously to attend to this one great affair. With such grace and authority did the youth express himself that the lordly guests listened with respectful attention; nor was the impression he made a transitory feeling, for when Cepari wrote the life of the saint, the survivors used still to retail with admiration the discourses he held with them at that parting banquet.

On the next day, the 3rd of November, Lewis took leave of the ducal family, and in the evening, before retiring to rest, he knelt at his parents' feet and humbly asked their blessing. The marchesa, as may be imagined, was as deeply affected as her husband when the last farewell had to be pronounced, but spiritual consolation mingled with the pious Marta's tears. For this hour she had prayed, and for this result she had toiled, and the natural sorrow of the mother's heart could not swallow up that joy which sprang from a higher source. But the poor marchese had to devour his grief as best he might; though doubtless, he found a secret support from the inward consciousness that he had at last yielded what God had been so long demanding of him.

The next morning Lewis set off for Rome., with the suite appointed by his father. The party consisted of Don Ludovico Cataneo, his governor Signor Pier Francesco del Turco, and the Doctor Giovanni Battista Bono, with the addition of the cameriere Clemente Ghisoni, and many other attendants. The newly made heir, Ridolfo, accompanied his brother in the carriage as far as Quistello, a few leagues distant, where he was to embark on the Po for Ferrara. Lewis's natural affections had been so completely absorbed and lost in divine charity, that he exhibited none of those sensibilities the absence of which on such occasions in ordinary persons might justly incur the reproach of want of feeling. Such, in fact, is the judgment commonly passed by the world external to the Church, and, we may add, the world within it also;

for whoever is not ruled by the mind of the Spirit thinks and judges according to this merely human and natural spirit, albeit he may avoid mortal offences and be a living member of the Church. If such an one had seen our saint leaving the home and friends of his youth (as Clemente Ghisoni afterwards attested) without shedding a tear, and scarcely addressing three words to his brother during the last brief hours which, possibly, they were ever to spend together, the sight would, at the least have been accounted strange and unintelligible. But Lewis was not leaving the home of his affections; long had the home he sighed for been elsewhere, and he had dwelt as a stranger amongst his brethren. All personal sorrow, the selfish though amiable source of so many of our sociable and kindly tears, was absent in him; and although in the order of charity his parents and brethren occupied, without doubt, the place which was their due, yet, on the other hand, the family tie, potent for much good in cases where the vocation does not raise a soul above the domestic sphere, to him had been a chain, an impediment, and a snare. Who could wonder that he rejoiced that at length the snare was broken and that he was delivered; or, that, in the spirit of the Apostle, who said he no longer knew any man after the flesh—no, not even Him in loving whom there could be no exceeding—Lewis also had none of those gentle infirmities and soft relentings which belong to natural love, and which, while they make it so attractive in our eyes, stamp its imperfection and attest its earthly origin? When one of the gentlemen in the boat observed, "I think Signor Don Ridolfo must feel not a little joy at succeeding to your estate," Lewis simply replied, "His joy at succeeding to it cannot equal mine in renounceing it."

Alfonso d'Este, duke of Ferrara, had married Margherita di Gonzaga, the daughter of the duke of Mantua; and it had been considered fitting that Lewis should make his adieux to his noble cousin and her consort before leaving the world. This ceremony being dispatched, our saint took his road to Florence through Bologna, purposing to pay the same devoirs to the grand-duke Francesco. This last visit was to be followed by one far more congenial to his inclinations, to which, moreover, a pious sense of duty urged him. A pilgrimage to the Holy House of Loretto, it will be remembered, had been vowed by his mother for herself, and her infant in their peril. The vow had been commuted, it is true, but Lewis, who owed to the Mother of God's intercession his natural life, not to speak of unnumbered graces since received through her hands, felt nevertheless a strong desire to fulfil his earthly parent's original intention, while satisfying his own particular devotion. When he reached Pietra Mala, on the confines of the ducal states, he was not allowed to pass on, the frontier being strictly guarded on account of suspicion of plague existing in the neighbouring provinces. Retracing his steps to Bologna, Lewis now wrote a letter to the grand-duke, expressing his regret at being hindered from taking personal leave of that prince, as he had designed, and pleading his haste in excuse for not awaiting the permission to proceed to Florence, which, no doubt, would have been forwarded. Pressed and hastened, indeed, he was by the love of God, which would brook no loitering or delay. But to Loreto he must needs go. Here he spent two days, that is, two nights and one whole day; and what ineffable consolations he there received from Ged and our Lady, while kneeling in the Santa Casa well-nigh the whole time of his stay, words could not tell. He himself used to melt into tears at the very recollection. He even declined the offer made by the Fathers of the Company that he should lodge at their house, preferring the inn on account of its proximity to the sanctuary. The first morning he heard four or five consecutive masses in the holy chapel, and then communicated. Cold must be the heart which could without deep devotion receive its Lord on the spot where He became Incarnate; vainly then may we attempt to conceive what were the interior sentiments of this great lover of Jesus and Mary. Meanwhile it got about who he was, and what was the purpose of his journey to Rome. Immediately he became an object of intense interest, and no sooner did he issue from the church or from the inn than he was pointed out and watched with curiosity and admiration. Youth, rank, and wealth, all combined to give splendour to the sacrifice he was making, while the consummate sanctity he had already attained adorned the victim with a garland of beauty as he travelled to the altar of God, there to be offered and consumed as a holocaust of divine love. But this vision, the very sight of which edified, had soon vanished, and Lewis, after hearing mass and again communicating the next day, resumed his journey.

Every morning, after a short mental prayer, he recited prime, sext, and tierce with Don Ludovico, who instructed him in the method of saying office; this was followed by the Itinerary, and he then mounted his horse. Knowing that solitude and silence were so dear to him, the party would drop a little behind, while Lewis went on for many miles meditating and praying with as much recollection as if in the privacy of his chamber; occasionally he would stop and call Don Ludovico to his side, when they would proceed awhile in company, discoursing of holy things. When they stopped to refresh and rest the horses, they had a slight collation; Lewis then said vespers and compline with the priest, and forthwith they were again in the saddle. His conversation naturally turned on what was before him, and he particularly adverted to the subject of penitential exercises, for which he had so much attraction, and which he hoped in the Company to have every facility to practise. Don Ludovico probably thought that his superiors were more likely to curtail his austerities than allow of their increase, but he knew that this would be a very different thing from the interference of relatives, who, while lacking spiritual authority, are commonly actuated by purely human views. If Lewis should be restrained in his practice of penance, this very restraint would give larger scope to the virtue of obedience. For that virtue he had as much love as for penance, and he cheerfully obeyed Cataneo, his temporary superior, by foregoing his weekly fasts of bread and water during this fatiguing journey in severe weather. Another favourite topic was the conversion of the heathen and the missions to the Indies, upon which he hoped some day to be sent; in short, just as a young man starting in life has his head full of his future career, and willingly talks of the worldly prospects which are unrolling themselves before him, so Lewis's imagination was rife with the anticipations of the new existence on which he was entering; only that life was all spiritual, as also were the affections and aspirations with which he yearned after it. On arrival at their night's halting-place, a good fire in the guest-room of the hostelry was a welcome sight to the cold and weary travellers, but Lewis would not go near it, not even for a brief space to thaw his benumned limbs; his fire was within, and he was off immediately with his crucifix to his room, where for two hours he would give himself to prayer, his sighs and sobs ever and anon reaching the ears of the company he had left, who would gaze at one another silently with mingled sentiments of wonder and compunction. He finished with a long and severe discipline, after which he called Don Ludovico, and with him said matins and lauds; this concluded, he joined the party at table, and partook of a sober repast. He refused all assistance when retiring to rest, and one evening, when the priest, accidentally perceiving him engaged in laborious efforts to get off his stockings, made of a different material and fashion from that to which he was used, hastened to his aid, he found his feet not only painfully swollen by the effects of long riding, but almost frozen with the cold; yet the patient sufferer had not uttered a complaint, and could not even then be persuaded to warm them. Lewis nursed his sufferings as others cherish their comforts.

We have reason to think (though Cepari does not name the day) that it was on the 21st of November that Lewis reached Rome and dismounted at the house of Scipione Gonzaga, whence, after a short rest, he hastened to the Gesù that he might present himself to the General of the Company; and it is a pleasing thought that it should have been on the festival of the Presentation of our Lady, that Lewis offered his pure and child-like soul to the perpetual service of her Divine Son. The Padre Acquaviva descended into the garden to meet him, and Lewis, prostrating himself at the feet of his new father with more than filial submission, seemed all unable to rise, but the General, affectionately assisting him, kissed him on the forehead, and received him as his son. Aloysius then gave him a letter from the marchese, which ran as follows:—

"Most illustrious, most reverend, and most honoured Sir,—As I have hitherto judged it proper to defer granting leave to Don Aluigi, my son, to enter into your holy order, fearing some inconstancy of purpose on account of his youth, so now, believing that I have reason to be assured that he is called by our Lord, not only have I not dared to trouble him by farther interference or a prolonged delay in according the permission which he has continually and urgently sought, but, on the contrary, for his satisfaction, and to tranquillize and console his mind, I have sent him to you, most reverend Sir, as to one who will prove a more profitable father to him than myself. I do not ask for any special personal attention to him, only I can certify you, most reverend Sir, that you become the possessor of my dearest earthly treasure, and of the chief hope to which I looked for the maintenance of my house; which will henceforth place great confidence in the prayers of this son, and of you, most reverend Sir, to whose favour I recommend myself, praying our Lord to grant you all the blessings you desire.

"From Mantua, Nov. 3, 1585.

"I am, most illustrious and most reverend Sir,

"Your most affectionate servant,

"The Prince Marquis of Castiglione."

Before taking up his quarters in his new home, Lewis had some visits of ceremony to pay; for several members of the Sacred College were allied to him by blood, and others were connected in some way with his family. When these obligatory courtesies had been performed, Lewis visited devoutly the Seven Churches and the other principal places of devotion in Rome.

The Pope's benediction was to conclude all, and send him to his new home freighted with spiritual blessings. It was on a Saturday, the 23rd of November, that he was admitted to the presence of Sixtus the V. The report of the youth's sanctity had reached the ears of the Roman court, and while waiting for his turn in the ante-chamber he was surrounded by a circle of observers, who gazed on him as on a living miracle. After kissing the foot of the Vicar of Christ, he presented to him the letters he had brought from the marchese. The holy Father asked him many questions regarding his vocation, and in particular whether he had well considered the arduous life which he was embracing. The youth's attenuated form and pallid countenance doubtless contributed to suggest this enquiry to the Pope. Lewis replied that he had pondered all for a long time past, upon which his Holiness approved his resolution and fervour, and, after conferring his benediction, dismissed him with many demonstrations of affection. Don Cataneo's prohibition had, it seems, only extended to the journey, for Lewis, we find, had resumed his Friday's rigorous fast of bread and water; and having deferred his repast on Saturday to a late hour, in order to have audience of the Pope, his strength gave way, and on regaining Scipione Gonzaga's house, he was taken so ill that he feared some fresh delay might be the result. However, this indisposition passed off, and the next morning we find him communicating at the Gesù, in the chapel of SS. Abondio and Abondanzio under the high altar, then ascending into the choir to hear the sermon, and, with the Patriarch Gonzaga, remaining to dine with the fathers in the refectory. The admiration with which that prelate regarded his cousin knew no bounds; and, in particular, he expressed his wonder at the discretion of his tongue. "It is marvellous," he said, "how this youth never utters one word amiss, but all that falls from his lips is duly weighed, measured, and adapted to the occasion" The edification he had given in the patriarch's house was, indeed, general, and specially were the household touched at the sight of the tears he shed at the elevation every morning at mass in the chapel, tears which he vainly strove to conceal, but which were betrayed by their very abundance.

This 24th of November was his last day in the world. On the morning of the 25th, Lewis joyously ascended Monte Cavallo, to enter the noviciate house of Sant' Andrea. He was followed by all who had accompanied him from Mantua, and Scipione Gonzaga himself said mass and communicated him with his own hands. As they entered the house, Lewis turned to his people and reminded them to give heed to the affair of their salvation. He thanked the doctor Bono for his company on the way, and commissioned his governor, Don Francesco del Turco, now appointed major-domo to prince Giovanni de' Medici, to deliver his letters and compliments to the grand-duke of Tuscany at Leghorn. To the cameriere Clemênte Ghisoni he gave the charge of saluting his lady mother in his name, while to Don Ludovico he entrusted the delivery of this short verbal message to the marchese his father: "*Obliviscere populum tuum et domum patris tui*—(forget thy people and thy father's house);" desiring, doubtless, to convey the assurance that he should never regret the step he had taken. When asked if he had anything to say to his brother Ridolfo, he replied, "Say to him, '*Qui timet Deum, faciet bona*—(He that feareth God, shall do good things).'" With these words he left them, and they went their way weeping for their loss of so good a lord. Such are the parting adieux of saints, calm, grave, free from perturbation, for the rending of earthly ties has been, in fact, made long before, and all those chords which vibrate so painfully at the word farewell have been already snapped and severed. Finally, he took leave of Scipione Gonzaga, who had remained to dine with the Father General, affectionately thanking him for all the kind interest he had taken in the matter of his vocation, and promising to remember him in his prayers. The patriarch could not restrain his tears, and acknowledged that he felt a holy envy for one who had known how to choose the better path, telling the fathers that they had that day received into their house an angel of paradise.

The world now dismissed, Lewis was led by the master of novices, to a chamber where he was to remain in strict privacy and silence for some days, in order to undergo his probation, according to the custom of the Company. As he entered, it seemed to him as if he passed the portal of heaven: "*Hæc requies mea in sæculum sæculi*," he said; "*hic habitabo, quoniam elegi eam.*—(This is my rest for ever and ever; here will I dwell, for I have chosen it." Ps. cxxxi. 14). Left to himself, he knelt down and, with tears of loving gratitude and sweetness, thanked God who had brought him out of Egypt's bondage to the land of promise, flowing with the milk and honey of heavenly consolations; once and again he renewed the solemn dedication he had so often made of himself to the Divine Majesty, praying for grace to dwell worthily in the house of his Lord, and to live and die in His holy service. Lewis ever celebrated with much devotion the anniversary of his entrance into religion, and chose St. Catharine, whose festival is kept on that day, for his special patroness and advocate with God.

PART II.

THE SAINT IN RELIGION.

CHAPTER I

Lewis's Entry into the Noviciate.

We have seen our saint in the world, yet from his very cradle not of the world; for years sighing and struggling to leave it for that higher state in which the counsels become by vow obligatory on those who embrace it, as the precepts are binding on all Christians by the baptismal covenant. We have now to contemplate him in this more exalted sphere. All—at least all Catholics—confess the superiority of the religious to the secular calling, but to one who viewed the matter only externally, it might seem that Lewis Ganzaga's life in the world, when his sanctity was displayed in shining contradiction to all its maxims and customs, in a generous contempt of its allurements, and in an heroic conflict with all the efforts of flesh and blood, of kindred and friends, to detain him, offered a more splendid and striking spectacle than the years he passed in religion. For his light, brilliant as it was, was there, to use Cepari's expression, hidden under the bushel of domestic discipline; he was no longer the object of daily observation to a large worldly circle, neither had the time come for him to be brought before the eyes of men in a new and sublimer character, for he died before he had entirely completed his theological studies, or had attained the age at which he could be raised to the priesthood. As a Jesuit, Aloysius Gonzaga had never any public life; received into the bosom of the spiritual family which was to nurture and train him for a fresh career, he expired in the arms of his adopted mother ere his religious adolescence had passed away. Add to this that during the brief years he lived the care of superiors restrained his fervour, and that he had to forego many of those austerities which he had been wont to practise in the world, and restrict himself within more moderate bounds. Moreover, what he now did was no longer by the movement of his own free election, but was performed simply in virtue of obedience; and unreflecting observers might therefore judge that his actions had lost something of their grandeur, and something also of their merit, by submission to direction, and that Brother Aloysius was not so marvellous a prodigy of grace in the Company as was the Prince Aluigi in the paternal castle. But a slight consideration will suggest the immense increase of perfection and merit which this very submission of obedience conferred, for we all know, however apt me may be practically to forget it, that it is not the matter of a work which gives it its value in the eyes of God, nor even the energy with which it is performed: its worth wholly comes from its being done for God and in God; so that not only is the end supernatural, but the motives from which it springs and the spirit in which it is carried out remain equally so. But it is much harder to exclude self from intermeddling when the act is one of our own choosing; the humility inseparable from true obedience embalms our good deeds, and excludes the secret corrupting influence of self-love; not to speak of the fresh merit imparted by the exercise of an additional virtue, and one of such intrinsic excellence that of Christ it is emphatically said that He was "*obedient;*" summing up in that one word the transcendent merit of His sacrifice. Certainly in the humble and docile Lewis we at no time find a trace of self-love, yet his strong desire to be placed under obedience shows the estimation in which he held it, and the profit which he hoped to derive from it.

Amongst the many heroic virtues which he was enabled to practise with more consummate perfection in religion may be noticed his humility and his exactness. We have seen him in the world rejecting and even abhorring all the distinctions of his rank, and, as much as was possible in his condition, choosing the lowest place, the meanest dress, the plainest fare. It might seem little, then, that he should with facility conform himself to the common life of a religious order, and not only perform with readiness the humblest domestic offices, as if he had always been a servant,instead of having always been served, but even desire and delight in them. Yet the fact is worth notice, because there is some difference between rejecting honours, luxuries, and comforts—while all around us are proffering to us in their hearts, nay, even pressing upon our acceptance, the reverence, the privileges, and the rights which we forego—and the finding ourselves simply despoiled of them. In religion all are equal, and it comes as a matter of course that we should do what we are bid, accept what is allotted to us, and take the lowest place, if so required, without exciting either notice or admiration. A parallel difference exists between the humility exercised in the lowly condescension and self-abasement of one in a confessedly honoured rank, and that which is called into play by the rough and contemptuous treatment which the same person might receive should some reverse of fortune sink him into poverty and obscurity. If in the first case there be more splendour, in the last there is more perfection, and more security. Lewis, then, proved the genuineness of his humility by adapting himself with ease and pleasure to his new circumstances, and in them, doubtless, it received its finishing and finest touches.

The virtue of exactness was also singularly exhibited by our Aloysius. His conception of the true religious was one who conformed in every particular to the rules of the holy institute to which he belonged, making no distinction in his own mind between the great and small, the important and the non-important, in what came to him stamped with the same revered authority. We shall have occasion to notice some examples of this marvellous fidelity and punctuality. It has caused him to be regarded as a special pattern to all who embrace the religious state. But we may add that it makes him no less a model to persons in the world; seeing that we each have our state of life with its corresponding duties, which bind us as strictly as the rules of a religious order bind its members. To us these duties come with a like sacred obligation, and to us they trace the pattern to which we are to conform ourselves. Aloysius, then, is a model also to seculars, not always in what he did, but in the punctuality and exactness with which he observed the rules and duties of his state.

So much having already been said with respect to his eminent virtues, as they were incidentally called into action in the world, we shall, in following our saint through this second portion of his life, strive to avoid repetition by selecting for notice chiefly such applications of them as his new state peculiarly elicited. Aloysius's time of probation was shortened by his superiors on account of an indisposition which attacked him at this juncture, and which rendered it desirable to curtail his period of seclusion; a matter of the less importance because his vocation had been sufficiently proved before he came, and he had recently gone through the Spiritual Exercises at Mantua, where he had also studied the Rules and Constitutions of the Order. He was immediately committed to the doctor's care, until he should be sufficiently recovered to enter on the common life of the noviciate. We shall find superiors placing a certain check upon that severe castigation of the body to which Aloysius had so powerful an attraction: on the other hand, they subjected him to mortifications of a different kind, less injurious to health. Our saint, while regretting to be deprived of those austerities of which his soul was so greedy, could derive sweet nourishment from their milder substitutes and, above all, from compliance with the will of God as signified to him by superiors, whether their voice bade him to bear or forbear.

The master of novices, P. Giovanni Battista Pescatore, was a holy man. No sooner had his new charge been entrusted to him than his watchful eye discerned what looked like a singularity, and furnished him at once with matter for the pruning-knife. We have more than once alluded to Lewis Gonzaga's practice of walking not only with eyes bent down but with a decided inclination of the head, which was scarcely ever raised even in conversation. This habit Aloysius carried with him into religion. Forthwith P. Pescatore has a stiff pasteboard collar made for the youth, which compels him to keep his head in an erect position, and which, he tells him, will cure him of the trick he has contracted. Aloysius submitted not only with a good grace but even with pleasure, and he to whom laughter had been a strange thing made it matter of gentle merriment when he appeared among his companions with his head set in this singular frame. He wore it for a considerable time, but we strongly suspect that whatever profit he may have derived from this discipline, it did not entirely cure our saint of the downward glance which we associate with his meek image. Yet it may possibly have led to some discoveries which he made at this time. His beretta, he perceived, was of a different fashion from that of his brethren, his own being square and clerical; he begs to have it changed. The cloth of their habit is of a coarser texture than that which he had procured for himself at mantua; he requests his superiors to let him have the same material as the rest. Notwithstanding his love for simplicity, Lewis in the world, surrounded by luxury and grandeur, had not so much as noticed the costliness or embellishment of some of the things of which he habitually made use; but when he saw the breviaries of the other novices, with their plain bindings, and compared them with his own in its gilded cover, he was shocked, and taking it at once to his master, begged for a common one; and so by this summary process, he had soon got rid of all which, as he playfully expressed himself, smelt of Egypt.

Many who have followed our saint's progressive steps in holiness up to this period may have felt some surprise at hearing nothing of those internal trials and temptations, those seasons of dryness, desolation, and temporary shrouding of God's countenance, so usual in the spiritual life. Trials he had undergone, but they had all been brought upon him by extrinsic causes; his inward life had kept on its ever serene and unclouded course. The first consolations and sweetnesses of conversion, with him contemporaneous with the dawn of reason, appear never to have been withdrawn, and his soul, which had generously abandoned all earth's satisfactions, seems to have sat at a perennial banquet of delights. But it was not the Divine will that he should be deprived of the special value of these trials, which, coming immediately from God, have so mighty an effect in purifying, refining, and exalting His work of grace in the soul. Lewis's trial—his period of obscuration, when he was thrown upon the pure life and support of faith, stripped of all sensible consolation—was not long, but it was sharp. Surrounded in religion by all that was calculated to refresh and sustain his spirit, he fell into a state of interior desolation, utterly unknown to him while in the world. It produced in him, however, no perturbation of mind, nor caused him the slightest uneasiness; he was grieved at his loss, but it was a placid and submissive grief, and God consoled him by lightening the burden laid upon him when directly engaged in prayer. It was not long before the sun burst forth again with renewed radiance and warmth. One other inward trial only was the novice called to undergo. It came in the form of a question:—What possible use can the Company make of you? What have you come here to do? But as he clearly saw that pusillanimity, and not humility, would be the result of entertaining this question, he at once recognized the quarter whence it came, and, putting it aside as a temptation, was never more troubled with its recurrence. Henceforward he preserved a peace and tranquillity which may be described as imperturbable,

How little any outward calamity or affliction had power to move him was shown in his behaviour on the occasion of his father's death, which occurred just two months and a half after he had joined the Company. As our readers, doubtless, feel a compassionate interest in the poor marchese, whom we so recently left to the dubious consolations of a half-hearted sacrifice, they will, we believe, willingly return with us to the world without for a brief space, to attend the death-bed of the lord of Castiglione. He had made, as we have said, what certainly looked like a most reluctant sacrifice to God; but God is very good: He is no hard task-master; He waits and watches, so to say, for an excuse to be satisfied. Men reject scornfully a gift offered ungraciously; they call it an unwilling offering, and as such, regard it as unworthy their acceptance. But God, who can read the secrets of the heart, dives, so to say, to seek the one grain of sincerity which perchance lies beneath,—that hidden sincerity of which none but He is judge, and which atones, in His eyes of infinite pity, for the churlish manner and the rebellious disinclination which may outwardly clothe and disfigure the act. And so may we believe it was with Ferrante Gonzaga. His sacrifice had that one sterling grain, and God accepted the tardy renunciation of will, and repaid it in streams of grace and pardoning mercy. From the very moment that Lewis had entered religion an entire change came over the marchese. He altogether gave up his inveterate habit of play, and entirely applied his mind to devotion. Every evening he had a crucifix which his Aluigi had left, brought to the foot of his bed, to which the gout confined him, and recited the Penitential Psalms and Litanies, accompanied by his son's late cameriere, Clemente Ghisoni, whom he had taken now for his own personal attendant, and by the marchesa and his children. The gift of tears seemed to be a boon which the saintly Lewis had won for his parent by his own groans and prayers, and had bequeathed to him as his parting legacy, for they poured in floods from the old man's eyes, bespeaking the deep contrition which moved him; and so he himself believed it to be, for when, taking the crucifix in his hands and striking his breast, he would exclaim, "*Miserere Domine; Domine peccavi, miserere mei,*—(Have mercy, Lord; Lord, I have sinned, have mercy on me)," he marvelled at his own facility to weep, and said, "I know well whence these tears proceed; I owe all to Lewis; Lewis has obtained for me this contrition from the ever blessed God." He sent for Don Ludovico Cataneo on his return from Rome, and, accompanying him to the church of the Madonna of Mantua (doubtless because it was there his son had loved to pray), he made with much devotion a general confession of his whole past life. From this moment his fervour never abated, but his bodily sufferings daily increased. Accordingly, he had himself conveyed to Milan, with the view of seeking fresh medical advice, but he went there only to die. Late one evening the Padre Francesco Gonzaga repaired to the marchese's room: it was to announce to his old friend and relative his approaching dissolution. The sick man, seeing him at that unwonted hour, at once divined the object of his visit, and begged the father to choose and send him a confessor. No time was lost; he made his confession that very night, and his testament the following day; after which he consoled his family, telling them they ought to rejoice at seeing him die in such good dispositions. On the 13th of February, 1586, he departed, and his body, by his desire, was carried to Mantua, and buried in the church of San Francesco.

One there was who did, indeed, purely rejoice, and that was his own beloved Aluigi. Long had he silenced in his bosom all mere natural sensibilities, and divine charity had sublimated all his affections, so that, dearly as he loved his father, it was in God only, as all else besides. To a heart thus exclusively filled with supernatural love, the tidings of his father's truly Christian death was a message of life, full of joy and consolation. Strange to our heavy ears are the words and ways of saints. He began his letter to his mother with thanking God that henceforth he could with more entire freedom say, "*Pater noster, qui es in cœlis.*" The saints, even while sorrowing, can rejoice in spirit when the fetters of earthly love are broken by death, and to the world such joy may seem to argue insensibility; but Donna Marta knew her son and understood him well. The calmness of the novice Aloysius surprised even those who had been long schooled by religion to mastery over their feelings, and, in particular, such as were aware how greatly he had loved his father. He himself confessed that had he regarded the loss of his parent simply in itself, no doubt it would have been a severe grief to him; but that he was unable to feel sorrow for any dispensation of God, or for any event which he knew to be agreeable to the Divine will. Such was the happy incapacity at which he had arrived, fortified as it was by that singular privilege he possessed, his power over his own mind. On one occasion, indeed, being questioned by one of the fathers whether the remembrance of his relatives ever intruded itself painfully upon his mind, he replied in the negative; because, as he said, he never recollected them save when he recommended them to God; adding, in conformity with what has been stated, that by God's grace he was so entirely master over his thoughts, that he never reflected upon anything but what he desired.

If it was a singular mercy of God which prolonged the marchese's days to an hour of grace, when he was able to make a good death, that delay had proved also a providential blessing to his son. Had his father died but three months sooner, before the deed of renunciation had been signed, Lewis's reception into religion would probably have been indefinitely deferred. Not only would his relatives have, with every show of reason on their side, deprecated his leaving the government of the estates in the hands of his young and inexperienced brother; not only would the vassals, who could then claim him as their lord, have clamoured to retain him, and used an affectionate violence, hard to resist when justified by so fair a plea, but the Father General himself might have refnsed to receive him under the trying circumstances in which his family were placed; while Lewis himself might have felt bound to postpone the fulfillment of his heart's desire. But God, in His love to his youthful servant, had removed the son from the bonds of the world, before He took the father to Himself. The act was irrevocably accomplished, and Lewis was safe.

CHAPTER II.

The Perfect Novice.

The Jesuit noviciate, as our readers are probably aware, lasts two years. It is, so to say, a prolonged retreat, during which a deep foundation of humility and of all the solid virtues is to be laid. Such was the intention of the great founder, St. Ignatius, for which reason the period of noviciate was to be devoted wholly to the science of divine things. "Prayer, prolonged meditations, the practical study of perfection, and, above all, the most entire self-abnegation, the courageous reformation of all the natural inclinations, the daily and faithful struggle against the love of false honour and false enjoyments, the continual use of the Spiritual Exercises and commune with God, the acquaintance with a whole hidden world in the depths of the soul and with a life altogether interior —these," says P. Ravignan, "are the things which fill up the hours of the noviciate. Aloysius's life, indeed, may be said to have been one long noviciate, for these words give an exact description of the aims and occupations of his existence for the last ten years, —in fact, ever since he had attained the age of reason; but he was now going to enter upon the work afresh, with far other advantages and under very different circumstances.

We may imagine the joy and alacrity with which the holy youth addressed himself to the task before him. He was in the habit of saying that his father had impressed upon him the necessity and obligation which lie upon everybody of using his best endeavours to acquit himself as perfectly as possible of whatever he has undertaken to perform. If Don Ferrante had himself strictly adhered to this rule in his secular affairs, much more did his son feel it incumbent upon him to apply it in the affairs of God. To shut out all that had no reference to this one all-important matter, he judged to be the indispensable condition of its due performance. Accordingly, the guard which he kept over all his senses, those avenues between the outer and inner world, was as unrelaxing as it was severe. We need hardly speak of his rigid mortification of the taste; scarcely could it be more complete in religion than it had been in the world. He appeared, indeed, to have lost all perception of the flavour of food, and it might have been supposed that he did not know whether what was set before him was good or bad, but for his habitual selection of the worst. At table his mind, when there was no spiritual reading, was occupied with meditation on some pious subject. At the morning meal, it was the Saviour's gall and vinegar; at the evening repast, the mysteries of our Lord's Last Supper with His disciples. No one remembered ever seeing him so much as regaling himself with the sweetness of a flower; rather he sedulously sought to mortify all natural repugnances. When he went to the hospitals to serve the sick (a favour he often requested), he bestowed the chief share of his attention on the most offensive objects, never showing the slightest sign of disgust at what was often well-nigh insufferable. His ears were utterly closed against all that was idle and unprofitable; if the news of the day or such like topics were alluded to in his presence, he changed the subject as speedily as he could; and if the speaker was one whose position commanded respect, his silence and reserved deportment betrayed the disinclination which he did not feel it fitting to express.

His frequent ejaculatory prayer was, "*Pone, Domine, custodiam ori meo, et ostium circumstantiæ labiis meis*, —(Set a watch, O Lord, before my mouth, and a door round about my lips." Ps. cxl. 3); and he was often heard to say, "*Qui non offendit in verbo, hic perfectus est vir; et si quis putat se religosum esse, non refrænans linguam suam, hujus vana est religio*,— (If any man offend not in word, the same is a perfect man; and if any man think himself to be religious, not bridling his tongue, this man's religion is vain." Jas. iii. 2; i. 26). By him therefore the rules of silence were not felt as a restraint; indeed, he infinitely prefered holding his peace to speaking, for the double reason of the risk of offending God by the tongue, and the desire not to lose the internal spiritual sweetness which conversation interrupted. When compelled to speak, it was always with much consideration and parsimony of words; and he would occasionally stop short in what he had begun to say, as judging it better for some reason to refrain. He invariably interpreted the rule to the advantage of silence; one day, for example, when he was sent out in company with a priest, having heard that permission to leave the house did not always imply licence to talk, he took a little spiritual book, and alternately read and meditated the whole time without saying one word to his companion, who, far from feeling offended, was much edified, and betook himself to the like pious exercise.

We have seen how he guarded his eyes while in the world; in religion he kept still stricter watch over them. As he thought only what it pleased him to think of, so he seemed to see only what he desired to see, and that was little enough. Had it not been for some slight occurrences which happened to attract attention, the extent to which he had blinded himself could hardly have been suspected. The novices used occasionally to be sent for recreation to a *vigna** in the neighbourhood; Aloysius of course went with the rest, but when, for some reason or other, the party had visited a different country place from that which they had previously frequented, and our saint was asked on his return which of the two he preferred, he inquired with some surprise if he had seen more than one; and this, although the road had led in quite another direction, and the disposition of the house and grounds was by no means similar. Then, reflecting for a moment, he recollected having observed a chapel in the place last visited, which he had not seen before; and this,

* A sort of farm-house with vineyard and garden attached. The *vigna* differs from the *villa* in its object, being cultivated solely for profit.

it would appear, was all of which his eyes had received licence to take cognisance. Again, after dining three months in the refectory, he was not familiar with the order in which the tables stood, for one day, the father minister having sent him for a book which he had left in the rector's place, our novice had to ask some one to show him where the rector sat. He carried the repression of all curiosity to a point which persons who have but ordinary notions of Christian holiness might set down to scrupulosity. We will give an instance or two of his exactness in this and other points. He mentioned to the master of novices, a few months after his arrival, as a thing which troubled him, that he had incidentally and without design —evidently it would seem almost mechanically—upon two or three occasions turned to look at what a person sitting next to him was doing, and he feared that this movement had been prompted by curiosity; he added, however, that it was the first time since joining the Company that he had reason to suspect in himself any defect of that sort. Again, it is the custom for all who leave the house to inform the porter where they are going; the novices were often sent to the professed house, to serve masses or to hear sermons or lectures on feast-days; and Brother Aloysius applied to his superior to know whether it were uttering an idle word to say, "I am going to the professed house," or whether it were not sufficient to say, "I am going to the house." Such a question would of course provoke a smile of contempt in men of the world, but even to many amongst ourselves it may be difficult to realize such extreme nicety of conscience, albeit our reverence for so great a saint will restrain us from criticising what we cannot understand. Certainly if such a question were put to his instructor by any ordinary youth it would, perhaps not unjustly, be regarded as a puerility or a foolish scruple. But the difficulty we may feel in understanding these minute actions of the saint is solved when we remember that adequately to estimate perfection we must ourselves have made large advances therein. Every one is capable of valuing and appreciating something considerably higher and more exact than that which he makes the object of his personal aims; but this capability has its limits—limits indefinitely increased with his own progress in virtue

The man who is living in habitual mortal sin can still admire the state of one who keeps God's commandments; the precepts he can understand; the counsels are generally repugnant to him. Another in the state of grace and desirous to save his soul by avoiding grievous offences, will be sensible of the beauty of the counsels, though he feels no attraction to follow them; but his views of their application are very narrow, and he is apt to judge them by his human reason. And so it is in its measure even with those who have entered on a higher path, much still remains unintelligible to them; they are often content to accord an unreasoning admiration, which they believe, rather than feel, that they owe. It is a common expression that much in the saints is to be admired rather than imitated, perhaps it would be more correct to say *copied*. Thus, much that St. Aloysius did lies, it is true, beyond the horizon of our spiritual ken; we could not ourselves without affectation act as he acted; we may even wonder how this were possible to any one; but the spirit which prompted the act is palpable and plain, and this is, and can always be, the object of our imitation. With such a rule ever kept in sight, there is no saint's life which is not both imitable and profitable. It seemed well to make this passing observation, seeing that St. Aloysius is pre-eminently set forth as a pattern to youth in general, including necessarily a large proportion of beginners in the ways of spirituality, of whom, moreover, a considerable number may never perhaps be called by God to the practice of any high degree of perfection.

Aloysius was certainly not subject to scrupulosity; true it is, his purity of conscience was exquisite, and though his spiritual discernment as well as his natural judgment was acute and penetrating, he was in the habit of referring the minutest points of conduct to his superiours. But that he judged himself with that calm and dispassionate temper to which the scrupulous mind is a stranger appears from the following instance. He continued in religion to preserve his love for old clothes, and so much did he dislike a new habit, that when one was ordered for him by his superior, even the tailor observed a certain mortification in his manner. Upon his mentioning this little trouble to the master of novices, he was advised to examine himself as to whether some subtle form of self-love might not lie concealed under a seeming humility. For many days Aloysius watched his thoughts and inward movements to detect the origin of the feeling he had experienced, and the result was that he could not discover anything reprehensible in the motives which actuated him; nay, so perfectly impartial was the sentence which he passed upon himself that, while allowing that in the early days of his noviciate some thoughts of self-complacency had arisen in his mind, yet, by God's grace, he said, he had offered so firm a resistance that he did not believe he had so much as once yielded consent; and the better to secure his victory, he had for some months directed his meditations on the Passion to the extirpation of every root of self-love and to the acquisition of a holy contempt and hatred of himself. His confessor in after years, the great Bellarmine, has recorded his testimony to the extraordinary discrimination which our saint possessed in discovering the secret springs and motives of his actions. It almost seemed as if he beheld with his corporal eyes the precise point at which a thought or desire had arrived in its progress towards consent, so illuminated by grace was his mental vision. When by close scrutiny he had satisfied his mind, so as to enable him to make a true confession, he gave himself no further anxiety; for, like St. Teresa, he confessed that his garden naturally produced only briars and thorns. "Forgive me, Lord," he would say, "and grant me grace not to do so again;" after which he was perfectly tranquil, and made his confession briefly, clearly, unembarrassed by a shade of scrupulosity.

He sought with special eagerness all such mortifications as serve to repress the desire of obtaining credit and reputation in the eyes of others; he was in the habit of saying, that to persons of good judgment these were more useful and more essential than bodily austerities; and yet we know how high a value he set on corporal penances. He would often beg permissian to go about Rome in a tattered habit, with a bag on his shoulder, to solicit alms; and when asked whether he felt any shame or repugnance in this occupation, his reply would be that he set before him the imitation of Christ and the eternal reward, and that this was quite enough to make him do it with joy; adding with that good sense which distinguished him, that, after all, he could not see any real cause for mortification: "People who see me either know me or they do not. If they do not know me, I ought not to care what they think; and if they do know me, I really lose none of their esteem; on the contrary, they may probably be edified; so that, in fact, there might be more danger of vain-glory than of shame, for even the worldly often admire those who make themselves poor for the love of God." It was with the same gladness of spirit that on festival days he would go and teach Christian doctrine to the poor and catechize the children in the streets and piazzas of the city. Beholders were charmed with the modesty, zeal, and lowly deportment of the novice, and great prelates would sometimes stop their coaches to listen to the youthful teacher. So successful was he in his humble apostleship, that he more than once brought to the Gesu for confession persons who had lived for many years without the sacraments.

He continued to exercise himself with fasts, hairshirts, and disciplines as much as his superiors would permit, but, as we have already observed, they restrained him considerably in this matter on account of the delicacy of his health. Nothing caused him more sorrow than this restriction, and he told Father Decio Striverio in confidence, that he was not allowed to practise half the austerities which he had allowed himself in the world; but that he took consolation in the thought that in religion men are like seamen in a vessel, who make equal way whether they are bid to handle the oar or to remain idle. His superiors, however, knew how to find him matter for mortification of another sort. Having requested and received permission to fast on bread and water on some vigil, he was observed by the master to eat scarcely anything; he therefore bade him return the next time the table was served, and eat as much as should be given him. Aloysius punctually obeyed. When the meal was over, P. Striverio laughingly said, "Our dear brother has found out a fine way of fasting, to eat a little once, and then come back and eat double." Aloysius modestly replied, "What would you have me do? '*Ut jumentum factus sum apud te*' ('I am become as a beast before you')," implying that he acted from obedience. Our saint never indulged in self-justification; and so rigidly did he adhere to this rule that on one occasion he even incurred a reproof for not having spoken in his own defence. At the professed house, to which he was afterwards sent, as we shall notice by-and-by, P. Girolamo Piatti, desirous for his health's sake to distract him a little from his mental application to prayer, bade him remain a longer time at recreation; although he had eaten at the first meal, he was to stay on with those who had sat down to the second. The father minister, who was ignorant of this order, gave him a public penance in the refectory for transgression of the rule. Aloysius performed the penance, without explanation, and the next day by a repetition of the same conduct, provoked a second penance from the somewhat astonished minister. Father Piatti then sent for the youth, and told him he had given scandal by this apparently repeated breach of rule. Aloysius replied that the fear of scandal had occurred also to himself, but that, dreading some secret plea of self-love, he had resolved to accept this second penance and to mention the order he had received, should the father minister speak again to him on the subject. The patience and cheerfulness with which he received and performed penances was truly edifying, but the occasions, as may be supposed, were not very frequent; and of these the greater part were founded on error, the delinquencies of others being at times imputed to him. Yet he invariably submitted as if the fault had been his own, and had it not been for the compunction of the true offenders, who could not endure to see him suffering their punishment, the truth would never have been known.

The master of novices, observing how circumspect he was not to offend in any point, bethought himself of trying him in some employment with which he was not familiar, and which would therefore afford occasion for fault-finding. Accordingly, for a few days, he made him help the lay brother in charge of the common refectory, who was to occupy him in cleaning, sweeping, and arranging that apartment, and who received private directions to make himself particularly exacting and vexatious, and complain of all that his associate did. But although the brother carried out these instructions to the letter he never could get Aloysius to excuse or so much as explain anything, so that he expressed his amazement at a humility of which he had never beheld the like.

There was but one thing in which the novice, by his own confession, felt any sensible mortification; it was when he was publicly reprimanded for his faults; and this, not because he felt any annoyance at the diminution of credit in the eyes of others (for of this he made small account), but simply from the pain which he experienced at the thought of his defects, thus forcibly set before him; and for this reason there was nothing for which he so earnestly and frequently begged as to be reprehended before all. This pain, moreover, was entirely voluntary on his part; owing to the complete mastery which he possessed over his imagination, he might, with the utmost facility, have distracted his mind from what was going on, so that, hearing, he would have been as one that did not hear; but this he would have considered as defrauding holy obedience of its claims and himself of its merits; he compelled himself therefore to taste as well as drink the cup presented to him, and rejoice at suffering something which might the more assimilate him to Christ our Lord. He persevered in this desire even after he had made his vows, and with this view used to give in a list of his faults to his superiors; but they, unable to detect anything reprehensible, would send him away with praises, and so he ultimately gave up the practice, saying that he lost more than he gained by it.

We have said that it was only when publicly reproved that our saint was able to experience any sensible mortification, but we ought to add that he felt far greater pain—a pain, moreover, which he did not seem able to discard at will—when any praise was bestowed upon him. Especially did he abhor any reference to his advantages of birth, and one day, when the doctor who was attending him began to descant on the glories of the house of Gonzaga, and to compliment his patient on the noble blood which flowed in his veins and his near relationship to the ducal sovereign of Mantua, Aloysius showed evident displeasure, and gravely said, "We are religious, and we are no longer what we were." Nothing, indeed, could be more distressing to the humble youth than to manifest any esteem for him on the ground of his high parentage; and after he had utterly crushed and subdued every other passion, he appeared unable to master a certain resentment at the slightest commendation or token of respect awarded him on that account. Praise in every form, indeed, was altogether distasteful to one who entertained of himself the lowest possible opinion, and he carefully avoided doing or saying anything which might redown to his own credit, concealing as much as was possible his intellectual powers, his knowledge, and his talents. The very apprehension of praise was enough to call the blood to his cheek, and if any one desired to witness the delicate blush which would mantle on that ingenuous countenance of more than maiden modesty, he had only to try the infallible receipt of a little laudation. We shall have occasion to notice his humility so frequently as we proceed that we need not here further dwell upon it. What the fathers thought of him may be gathered from the reply of the Rector to the Patriarch Scipione Gonzaga, when he visited the noviciate one day and drew him aside to inquire after his cousin "Signor, all I can say to your illustrious lordship about him is, that we have much to learn from his example." In fact, even in these early days of his noviciate, he presented a compendium of all those virtues which adorn the perfect religious. The novices, his companions, regarded him as a saint, and would even kiss with devotion things which he had touched or of which he had made use; while others, and they not novices, but his elders in religion, eagerly sought to obtain objects hallowed by having belonged to him, as though they had been the relics of one already in glory. The novices, after undergoing preliminary training at S. Andrea, were sent to the professed house for a few weeks, where, occupying a separate apartment under the superintendence of a prefect of their own, they were employed in serving masses, reading at table, and other suitable offices. Here they were entrusted to the care of P Girolamo Piatti a very holy religious, who, in a letter addressed to P. Muzio Vitelleschi at Naples, testifies at much length to the eminent holiness of Aloysius; thus proving the high estimation in which he was generally held. P. Piatti had not at that time the intimate personal knowledge of the saint which he afterwards possessed. When he came to know him as his confessor and director, we need only say that he told P. Antonio Francesco Guelfucci, who was then at Siena, that when he contemplated the heroic virtues of this youth, it was a matter of amazement to him that he did not perform a great many miracles; and Cardinal Bellarmine also marvelled that evident miracles, such as should become publicly known, were not worked by his hands. From these remarks we do not think it can be inferred that St. Aloysius (as some have asserted) had never during his lifetime a single miracle attributed to him, but rather the reverse. It was the absence of splendour and publicity, and of those indubitable proofs which can alone entitle to publicity, to which they would seem to advert.

It was a subject of much rejoicing to Aloysius when, after three months passed at the noviciate house, he was sent to the Gesu, partly because he would thus have the advantage of observing more closely and copying more accurately his fathers in religion, and partly on account of his great devotion to the Blessed Sacrament, which had made him, while in the world, embrace every opportunity of serving mass. This absorbing devotion was well known to all, and it was the source of the abundant tears which gushed from his eyes at the elevation. His whole life, indeed, may be said to have been one act of adoration of Jesus in the Blessed Sacrament, for he was in the habit of making each communion the preparation for the next. Thus Monday, Tuesday, and Wednesday he devoted to adoring the Three Persons of the Blessed Trinity, thanking Each in particular for the graces received in his Sunday communion; while Thursday, Friday, and Saturday were allotted to begging from Each grace to receive with due disposition on the coming Sunday. To these devotions he added many other practices directed to the same object, and on Saturday his whole conversation turned upon the Adorable Mystery of the Altar. With such depth and unction did he discourse on this subject that even some of the fathers used to seek his company at recreation on those days, that they might rekindle their own fervour by hearing the burning words which flowed from the novice's lips, and never, as they testified, did they celebrate mass with more devotion than on the following mornings.

Subsequently his days of communion became much more frequent; and afterwards at the Roman College he is described by one who shared his room with him, as communicating not only on Sundays but on all the days of devotion that were appointed by the Church, as well as on many other days besides: to these he added the Fridays in March; and, indeed, he communicated as often as he received permission.

His sojourn at the Gesu was, by the arrangement of his superiors, prolonged to the unusual term of two months. Every day, after his hour's mental prayer, he went to the sacristy, and remained serving five or six successive masses with undiminished fervour; yet, though himself never yielding to bodily weariness, he had such a tender compassion for others that, when he observed any of his companions to be delicate or weak, he would give a private hint to his superior, in order to prevent their strength being overtaxed. Between the masses he either meditated or said our Lady's office in some corner; and if he had to ask the sacristan any question, he would uncover his head and join his hands across his breast, addressing him with such exceeding respect and obeying his directions with such submission that the good man, unaccustomed to this reverential treatment, was quite confounded. Indeed he was not the only person who had to complain of the unusual grievance of meeting with too much consideration. The prefect, himself a novice, and therefore not exalted above his companions, save as regarded the very limited authority committed to him in virtue of his temporary office, could not have been treated with more respect by Brother Aloysius had he been the General of the Order. Never did he casually pass but

Aloysius was at once on his feet, and his beretta lifted from his head with the profoundest veneration, till, unable to endure it any longer, the prefect spoke to the superior, who bade our novice moderate his demonstrations of respect. We need scarcely observe, that there was not a shadow either of exaggeration or of affectation in this behaviour. Alloysius really felt what his demeanour expressed; regarding our Lord Himself in every one, and especially in such as were the depositaries of authority, he listened to their voice and obeyed their behests as if God had spoken directly to him; and in acting with promptitude and submission it was not so much, he declared, that he sought the additional merit of ready obedience as that he followed the impulse of the delight he experienced in serving his Lord. He added that he obeyed subalterns and inferior officials with even greater joy than superiors of a higher grade, not so much from humility as from a species of pride. For the service of God, he said, was always supremely glorious, whereas the service of man is humiliating. The less therefore he who is set over us has to recommend him on his own account, the more does all that is human disappear, and the better do we realize that it is the Lord Himself whom we obey.

During the course of the day Aloysius was commouly employed in visiting the prisons and the hospitals, in company with one of the fathers, who heard the confessions of the inmates, while the novice catechized the others, and disposed and prepared them for confession. On his return to the Gesu his avocations consisted in sweeping and other humble domestic offices. These last were not the least valued or appreciated of his occupations; and it is related how one day, while engaged in folding some linen, he remembered that he had not yet read a portion of St. Bernard's writings, as was his daily habit. He had a mind to leave his employment to fulfil this act of devotion, for he was free to do so, as were all the novices, when a certain time had been devoted to the allotted work; but on second thoughts he forbore, saying to himself, "If you were to read St. Bernard, what else would he teach you but obedience? Reckon, then, that you have read him, and are attending to the lesson you have learned." No consideration of human respect, not one of those causes usually considered as implicitly dispensing from rigid attention to rule, could ever make him swerve from it in the minutest degree; for instance, it is recorded that his Eminence Cardinal della Rovere, a near relative of his own, having gone into the sacristy one day to speak to him, he excused himself on the ground that he had not permission to break silence, and went to ask the Father General's leave, much to the cardinal's admiration.

Aloysius returned to the noviciate house charmed with the holy examples he had seen at the Gesù, himself, to edify no less the inmates of S. Andrea by his own faultless demeanour. It was impossible for any one to perceive the minutest defect in him; nay more, he could not himself detect any, notwithstanding the continual severe dissection to which he subjected, not his acts alone, but his thoughts. Troubled at being unable to discover in himself, after the strictest examination, anything which amounted to even a venial offence, he communicated his anxiety to the master of novices. What if he had fallen into a state of spiritual deadness and blindness? The complete dominion he had acquired over his passions was, doubtless, mainly owing to his having begun to combat and mortify them in his very infancy, and before they had acquired strength by indulgence. Hence the species of impassibility to which he had attained, for he does not appear to have felt so much as their first movements. Earthly objects had lost all power even to stir him; his passions appeared to be utterly expunged; his loves and his hates were all in God and for God. Yet by nature he was neither phlegmatic nor dull, but quick, ardent, and sensitive, with perceptions and feelings at all times beyond his years. The victory was therefore all the triumph of God's grace, operating in conjunction with an indomitable will and an untiring perseverance. Having set before himself the importance of never acting by the impulse of affection —a habit which, he said, was very dangerous and the cause of many errors—he had always taken care to test and rectify his motives, and to resist the smallest temptation to eagerness, an infallible sign that the human spirit, even if it has not supplanted the supernatural, mingles largely with its operations. For this reason he was never heard to contend about anything, or try to get the better in argument; he said simply what he thought; if others contradicted him, or disputed his assertion, he let the matter drop, unless the cause of truth seemed to demand a reply, which he then made calmly and gently; but if his opponent maintained his ground he insisted no further, just as if the matter in no way regarded him. This same indifference he sedulously cultivated at all times by driving away every desire, even were its object some good and holy work, if he perceived that it made the slightest inroad upon his tranquillity of mind. The result of this long discipline was a profound peace, which had become so habitual as to seem to form part of his nature. A state of such mental quietude could only have been brought about and maintained by an abiding sense of the presence of God, and this again was fed by prayer. Here was the secret of all. His life-long study had been to pray much, to pray well; to pray always; and so convinced was he that prayer is the great lever in spiritual things, that he used to say that it was well-nigh impossible for any but a man of prayer and recollection to acquire full dominion over himself or attain a high degree of sanctity, a truth which experience fully confirms, All those unmortified tempers, all that perturbation of mind, disquiet, and discontent, which are occasionally observable even in religious, our Aloysius referred to one single cause, deficiency in the exercises of meditation and prayer, which are the short road, as he said, to perfection. Much, indeed, did he wonder that any who have tasted the sweetness of communing with God should ever abandon the occupation, and deeply did he sorrow as well as marvel that there should be found preachers who, having been hindered on occasions by urgent press of occupation from making their daily meditation, allow this omission to pass into a habit when the excuse no longer exists.

Although much has been said already about our saint's wonderful gift of prayer, a few remarks may here be added. By long experience he had acquired so much knowledge of its secrets, that when Cardinal

Bellarmine was giving the Spiritual Exercises to students of the Company at the Roman College, after making some valuable suggestion in reference to meditation, he would add, "This I learned from our Aloysius." The saint although he lived in an atmosphere of prayer, was in the habit of preparing himself carefully for his morning meditation, according to the method with which all are, at least theoretically, familiar, including a previous short consideration of the subject, before retiring to rest, with a renewed recollection in the morning before entering upon it. He took care therefore to be in readiness some time before the signal was given, his occupation being the perfect tranquillizing of his mind by the exclusion of every other thought and feeling. Solicitude and desire—these are the great foes of all prayer, but much more of contemplation. It may be possible to repeat vocal prayers with a certain degree of attention where they are not entirely banished, but with prayer of a higher order they are simply incompatible; and this because in the latter case the mind is in a passive state, or, at least, its activity is of a delicate and subtle kind, so as at times even to escape consciousness. Now by one active thought and consideration we may, it is true, make some head against another, but the very conditions of contemplation, in which the discursive reason is silent, must be wanting when these grounds of distraction are allowed to exist. To receive in itself the image of divine things, the soul must be undisturbed; the ruffled surface can reflect no object; and this was the very comparison of which our saint made use. Just as an image is broken into fragments when the breeze passes over the surface of the stream, so it is with the soul when any earthly solicitude or desire sweeps over it while it is striving to receive the image of God into its placid depths, that it may by meditation be transformed into His likeness. Aloysius also took extreme care to avoid any casual distraction after entering on his meditation; and for this end he avoided even making the least bodily movement. Soon he became so fixed and absorbed that all his vital powers seemed concentrated in the superior region of his soul, and when he had finished he could scarcely rise from his knees, and would sometimes remain a brief space as one who had lost his recollection, not knowing where he was. During the whole time he passed in religion, which was six years, not once did he notice the customary visit paid to the novices' rooms for the purpose of ascertaining whether they were engaged in prayer at the appointed time. This one fact is sufficient proof of his habitual deep abstraction. In the accounts rendered every six months by each member of the Company of the state of his interior—of his defects, as well as of the graces, gifts, and virtues with which the soul has been enriched by God—Aloysius had to reveal much which otherwise his humility would for ever have concealed, for it was his custom never to speak of himself. On one occasion, when questioned by his superior, he frankly and ingenuously confessed that if all his distractions during the last six months at meditation, prayer, and examination of conscience were put together, they would not have occupied the the time of the recital of one Ave Maria. His chief difficulty was in making vocal prayer, not so much from distraction, but from his effort to penetrate the interior sense of the Psalms or other holy words he was repeating; and he compared his state to one detained at a door which he cannot immediately open. Hence the great length of time which he would often spend in saying office, a custom which he had adopted out of devotion, consuming a whole hour sometimes in reciting matins alone. From this circumstance it is plain that he knew how to unite vocal prayer with contemplation; and the abundant sweetness which he experienced even at these times, would alone sufficiently prove that he possessed this extraordinary gift.

The chief subjects of his meditation were the Passion of our Lord, the circumstances of which he always vividly renewed at mid-day; the Divine attributes, in the contemplation of which he became always singularly absorbed; and the Most Holy Eucharist. To the holy angels, and in particular his own guardian angel, he had a special devotion; and we cannot doubt but that he received many lights and communications through their ministry—a conviction strengthened by the perusal of the beautiful meditation which he composed at the desire of P. Vincenzo Bruno, and which has been preserved to this day.*

It was not only at the special times of prayer that Aloysius enjoyed these peculiar favours, but during the ordinary occupations of the day his soul was visited by God with marvellous consolations, and these, not passing touches or short elevations of spirit, but overflowing torrents of joy, which would sometimes last

* This meditation has been published in the Appendix to the new edition of P, Cepari's Life of St. Aloysius put forth by the Company of Jesus.

above an hour, and were often betrayed by his countenance being all on fire with heavenly love, and by the palpitations of his heart, which seemed almost as if it would bound out of his bosom. Continually drawn inwards, Aloysius confessed he had as much trouble in turning away his mind from spiritual things as he heard others complain of experiencing in detaching their attention from earthly objects; nay, he had to put a sensible strain upon himself the whole time that he made the attempt. For his superiors, fearing for his life, wasted as they saw him to be by continual interior attention and consumed by the flames of Divine love, not only forbade him to excite his devotion by frequent mental ejaculations, as was his custom, but bade him pray as little as possible: advice which sounds strange to our ears, and which could have been safely given only to a saint. So great, indeed, was the violence he had to use with himself, that it proved even more exhausting than the attention to which his mind was drawn. "I really do not know what to do," said the perplexed youth to his fellow-novice Gaspare Alpieri; "the Father Rector forbids me to pray,* in order that I may not strain my head by attention, but I have to use a much more violent effort to distract my mind from God than in keeping it fixed upon Him, because habit has made this come natural to me; and I find quiet and repose in it, not labour. However, I

* *Fare orazione*, by which is meant mental prayer, and all prayer of that description. Without adding the word *mental*, or employing the term *meditation*, we have no means in English of signifying the difference between these and ordinary prayer, such as adoration, petition, thanksgiving, &c., incumbent daily upon all Christians. This, of course, Aloysius's superiors could never have forbidden.

will strive to do what I am commanded, as well as I can." The difficulty he found in obeying, was not therefore on the part of his will, for, although the sacrafice was the most trying which could have been required of him, yet he never hesitated to yield a cheerful assent, being, as regarded his superiors, like clay in the potter's hands. The defect was in the ability alone, for so admirably docile was his spirit that, when hopes were held out to him of procuring permission from the Father General for a daily hour of mental prayer, he reproached himself for having experienced a certain anxiety and desire for the success of this application, with a corresponding risk of disturbance of mind in the event of a denial of his request, and used his utmost endeavours to divest himself of this personal inclination. All things seemed possible to him by God's help, where the matter lay only with himself, for grace and faithful correspondence therewith are invincible in battle against nature, but it is vain to contend against God. Do what he would, turn aside as he might, God would not leave him. While labouring to think, as he was bid, of something else, gradually he was drawn away by a gentle, invisible, but all-powerful hand, and replaced as it were in the abyss of Divine contemplation. Hither his soul tended back, as the falling stone seeks the earth; the limited efforts of the creature being powerless in opposition to this ever-enduring attraction of the Creator, which made it revert every moment, by a kind of spiritual gravitation, to its central rest. To compensate himself for the prohibition laid upon him, he used frequently to go into the choir to make an act of homage to the Blessed Sacrament, but scarcely had he knelt down when he had to get up again, and make his escape, or his spirit would speedily have been rapt in God and abstracted from the senses. Yet in vain did he fly and exert himself to close every window of his soul. Light streamed in—he could not shut it out—filling him with those spiritual joys which obedience forbade him to taste. Then with all humility he would say to God, "*Recede a me, Domine, recede a me*" ("Depart from me, Lord, depart from me").

Never, perhaps, did the saint practise obedience in a more heroic degree than while thus struggling to fulfil the impossible task imposed upon him, and perpetually refusing the stay and nourishment of his soul, the wine of consolation held as it were to his very lips. But to him nothing was so dear or so sweet as obedience, because, as we have said, he saw God in his superiors. He could not remember ever having entertained a wish or inclination contrary to their known desires; rarely, indeed, did he experience even the first movement of any such inclination save, it may be, when they endeavoured to turn him from his devotions, and then, as we have seen, he used all the diligence in his power to repress the rising feeling. This reverence for superiors was unmistakably evident in his whole demeanour towards them, and in the attitude of profound attention and veneration with which he received the slightest reproof at their hands; and Cepari mentions that having himself, when acting as his superior, had occasion to chide him for one of those negligences to which his frequent abstraction made him liable, so deeply was he affected that he fainted on the spot, and no sooner had he returned to consciousness than he cast himself on his knees to beg forgiveness for the fault for which he had been reproved.

With the sanctity and perfection which we have so inadequately described, Aloysius passed the whole time of his sojourn at the house of S. Andrea, from his entrance into the noviciate until the close of October, 1586.

CHAPTER III.

THE SAINT'S VISIT TO NAPLES, AND CLOSE OF HIS NOVICIATE.

DURING the time that Aloysius spent in the noviciate house of S. Andrea, P. Pescatore, was as already noticed, the master of novices. A few passing words are due to this holy man, not only as the trainer of our saint in the religious state, but for his own intrinsic excellence. The severe austerities which he practised, and which he sedulously concealed to the best of his ability, were veiled under a countenance and demeanour of the most serene benignity. His modesty and calmness were incomparable. No accident threw him off his guard or moved him to melancholy no prosperous event elated his spirit. Never angry, never impatient, he had always a modest and pleasing smile on his face, an index of the peace and joy which are the fruits of the Holy Ghost. Nothing could well exceed his self-contempt and humility; sober and sparing in speech, not a word ever passed his lips which could hurt or wound his neighbour; all his conversation was steeped in charity, seasoned at times with an agreeable salt and graceful pleasantry, which never outstepped the bounds of religious modesty. To the novices under his care he knew well how to unite gravity with sweetness, exhibiting towards them the tenderness of father, mother, and nurse combined; patient and forbearing with faults and infirmities, not only could he reprove without asperity, but dismiss an offender at once admonished and consoled. So completely did he make himself all to all, that each was persuaded that he was the object of his particular regard; and, indeed, this was true; for that which is not possible to natural affection is one of those marvels which divine charity is able to perform. As each of us is the singular object of God's love, having been called into being in preference to an infinite number of possible souls which He might have created in our place, so also the heart which loves in and for God experiences something of this same electing preference, and bestows on each an affection which has all the positive characters of exclusiveness as respects the individual, free from those negative results which in the natural order would ensue with regard to others. Father Cepari tells us that he had been acquainted with full a hundred religious who had spent their noviciate under P. Pescatore's rule, and that there was not one amongst them but esteemed him to be a saint. The source of his holiness is not far to seek. As in Aloysius, as in all the perfect, it was prayer, unceasing prayer. Night and day he gave himself to this exercise, and wonderful things are told of the gifts he received aud the marvels exhibited in his person; Cepari himself heard from the lips of P. Bartolomeo Ricci, who succeeded P. Pescatore in his office, how one night, when all had retired to rest, he was found in the hall of the infirmary absorbed in prayer and lifted several feet from the ground. Miracles also were attributed to him, and it was believed that he was endowed with the power of reading the secret thoughts of his subjects and perceiving their occupations at a distance. It may be imagined with what love and reverence Aloysius regarded this blessed father, who was indeed a master worthy of such a disciple.

Towards the autumn of the year 1586 P. Pescatore fell ill, and began to spit blood. His superiors were alarmed, and the Father General decided upon sending him to Naples for change of air. It was resolved that three of the novices suffering from enfeebled health should accompany him, Aloysius being of the number selected, as it was hoped that the climate of Naples might afford some relief to his habitual headaches. Accordingly P Pescatore, asked Aloysius one day if he would like to go with him, to which he replied at once that it would give him much pleasure. When he afterwards learned that he had been fixed upon as one of the father's companions, instead of being rejoiced, he was much troubled, fearing that the expression of his inclinations had influenced this decision. He thought that he ought not to have manifested anything more than a simple acquiescence in the will of superiors, and this for the future he firmly resolved to do, and gave the same counsel to others. The two other novices chosen were Jean Pruinet, a Frenchman, and George Elphinstone, a Scotchman, and it was from the latter that Aloysius's biographer learned most of the particulars he relates of his journey and residence at Naples. He laments that P. Pescatore preceded Aloysius to the tomb, as from his intimate knowledge of his disciple's interior, he could, doubtless, have added much that would have been highly interesting.

Notwithstanding the great sorrow which Aloysius felt for having betrayed his inclinations, the journey itself was very agreeable to his wishes, and that for a spiritual reason, for he never entertained any other , benefit to his soul and advance in interior perfection was the measure by which he appreciated all events ; he hoped as he told one of his companions, to learn by a close observance of their master's behaviour how a religous ought to demean himself when travelling. It might have been thought that our saint had little to learn on this score, but his humility judged otherwise. P. Pescatore was ordered by the physicians to make the journey in a litter ; there was room for a second, and horses were provided for the other two. Although the advantage of near observation of this father was so highly valued by Aloysius, he would willingly have foregone so great a satisfaction in order to allow one of his brother novices to make the journey with less fatigue, but as he was the weakest of the three, it was decided that he should share the litter with P. Pescatore. Determined, however, not to be too comfortable, he folded up his outer coat in the fashion of a hard ball, and so contrived to travel less at his ease than he would have done on horseback. But while his body was suffering, his soul was enjoying much refreshment. He said office with the father, and held long discourses with him, for P. Pescatore, knowing that he was sowing on good ground, willingly opened his store of spiritual treasures to his young disciple and freely communicated the results of his long experience as master of novices. Brother Aloysius gathered up all he heard with a holy avidity, and told his companions on reaching Naples that he had learned more in those few days from the father's conversation, and from observation of his actions and behaviour on the road, than he could have done in many months at the noviciate house.

They arrived on the 1st of November, just when the studies were about to be resumed. After a little rest, the superiors judged it fitting that Aloysius, having already gone through a course of philosophy in the world, should attend lectures on metaphysics. His masters, one of whom, P. Vincenco Figliocci, was an eminent theologian, recorded their judgment of his sanctity, formed from personal knolwedge during the six months he spent at the Company's house at Naples, in the processes instituted after his death. All the different accounts of our saint combine in telling the same tale, and he left behind him in Naples a reputation for modesty, prudence, humility, obedience, and all other virtues equal to that which he had earned in Rome. So edifying was his modesty that persons used to collect in the court of the college at Naples to see him pass on his way to and from the schools, thanking God for the privilege of beholding such a model of youthful sanctity. One day in particular, news having spread abroad that a messenger had arrived from Rome to acquaint Brother Aloysius with the elevation of the Patriarch Gonzaga to the cardinalate, and was awaiting the breaking up of the schools to acquit himself of his commission, the whole court was filled with people curious to see how this modest youth would receive the intelligence of a promotion so honourable to his family. Nor were they disappointed. Aloysius listened to the messenger without raising his eyes, as if the matter were one which in no way regarded him and he were not even personally acquainted with the new prince of the Church; a faint blush alone betrayed any inward emotion, but it was a blush of confusion, not of pleasure or pride. The other novices marvelled much at such indifference for even religious will allow themselves to rejoice when their relatives are advanced to a dignity so exalted as that of the purple.

Desirous that his fellow-novices should profit as much as possible by his example, Aloysius's superiors placed him in the largest dormitory, but as he scarcely slept at all at night, and could only catch a little slumber in the early morning hours, he had lately been ordered to take longer rest than the others. It may easily be imagined—and we cannot but be surprised that it should not have occurred to those who made the arrangement—that a sensitive invalid was not likely to get much sleep while a number of persons were rising from their beds in the same apartment. The detriment to his health became at last so evident that he was removed to a separate chamber; but matters were little mended by the change, for the room allotted him was under a staircase, up and down which the domestics were continually passing, particularly in a morning; and the constant sound of feet pattering over head, now ceasing, now recommencing, but never coming to an end, disturbed the sick youth far more than the noise in his former quarters. Aloysius, however, as usual, held his peace, and thanked God for having something to endure. Possibly it was by the special dispensation of Divine Providence, thus providing him with fresh opportunities of meriting, that many gross mistakes were permitted to occur, for what has been mentioned by no means forms an exception in the treatment of our novice at Naples. He had been sent for the express purpose of restoring his shattered health; no one, indeed, could look at him and not perceive in what need he stood of the tenderest care; neither was there any lack of interest for one so valued and admired; yet matters were strangely managed, or rather, mismanaged, in all that concerned him. In the first place, the rector of the college, being himself a man much given to bodily austerities, was greatly pleased at recognizing in Aloysius a similar attraction, and accorded him larger permissions to content his desire than he had been in the habit of obtaining at Rome. This the youth esteemed a singular piece of good fortune, but whatever spiritual benefit he may have reaped, certain it is that his health suffered injury thereby. Again, it was observed that although it was winter, he was allowed to go out of doors wearing an unusually short outer coat, while what there was of this miserable habit was literally worn threadbare, where it was not torn and discoloured with age. Superiors would never have suffered any one else to appear in such mean attire; in him they did not seem to notice it. Even were we to suppose that this strange privilege was granted him at his own personal request, another oversight still more palpable cannot be so accounted for. On festival days he would repair with the other novices to the professed house to sing vespers, and often, on cold, rainy afternoons, when the father minister, standing at the door, would send the delicate ones back, Aloysius, the most delicate of all, was permitted to pass on. At last he fell ill, and had to be taken to the infirmary, but even here negligent care seemed to be his portion. For a month he kept his bed with a fever, his life was even in danger, and yet he was left one whole night without any sheets to his bed, a thing unparalleled (Cepari adds to the best of his belief,) in any infirmary whatsoever of the Company's houses. After edifying all by the patience he manifested during his illness, he was, on his recovery, recalled by the Father General to Rome, it being judged that the air of Naples did not suit him, the pain in his head having increased rather than diminished during his residence there; a result which, after the *régime* pursued, we may regard as not very surprising. Accordingly, on the 8th of May, 1587, he returned with P. Gregorio Mastrilli to pursue his studies in the Roman College.

It was at this time that Father Cepàri was brought into close intercourse with our saint, so that for the greater part of the facts related we shall henceforward have the advantage of his personal testimony.

Brother Aloysius's return was hailed with joy by the youths of the Roman College, especially by those who had known him at S. Andrea, and who looked forward to deriving great profit from the daily spectacle of his virtues. Now again was renewed the same practice which we have seen adopted at

Naples; many of the scholars would watch in the court only to see him pass, and strangers would frequent the schools for this sole purpose. We are told that so great was the impression which his modest demeanour made upon all, that not seculars alone and his young companions owned its influence, but fathers, grown grey in religion and the cultivation of holiness, felt themselves stirred to more self-observation and recollection in his presence. Aloysius pursued his metaphysical studies under P. Valle, and he was soon considered to have made so much proficiency in this branch of philosophy, and to be already so well grounded in logic and physics, as to be able to argue in the schools. Accordingly, after he had been six months at the college, he was set publicly to defend certain theses drawn from the subject-matter of his philosophical studies. As the Cardinals Della Rovere, Mondovi, and Gonzaga, who took a personal interest in him, as well as several other nobles and prelates desired to be present, the disputations, instead of being held as usual in the Theological School, were transferred to the great hall. Aloysius acquitted himself to the approval of all, and to the great admiration of the cardinals his relatives, who expressed their wonder that he should have made such progress in so short a time, with the hindrance besides of grievous indisposition. Far was it from our saint's mind, as may well be imagined, to win applause; he was not one to think of harm in taking a little honest pride and satisfaction in well-merited and hardly-earned honours. Not, indeed, that it could have beeu made matter of reproach even to a good religious if, after rectifying his intention and taking care not to allow the desire of approbation to become his primary motives, he should have felt no slight wish, in subordination to higher aims, to deserve the approval of so honourable an assembly, composed, too, of persons on whose opinion he was bound to set a special value. Yet so fearful did his humility make him of the very shadow of self-complacency, that he actually revolved in his mind whether or no it might not be well for him to assume a certain degree of dullness and embarrassment, and perhaps even make a few blunders, for his own humiliation. Unwilling, however, to act on his own judgment, he consulted P. Muzio de Angelis, one of the professors of philosophy at the college, a man of as much spirituality as learning, with whom he was in the habit of intimate communication. The father prudently dissuaded him from this project, doubtless representing that he would be bringing discredit, not merely on himself, but on the college in which he had made his studies, and so on the Company itself, nevertheless, when our saint found himself in presence of the august assembly, just as another might have felt the temptation of ambition or vanity assail him, there rushed anew upon his mind a strong desire impelling him to court mortification and shame; for a moment he paused in doubt, and it was needful for him to remember all the good and solid reasons which P. de Angelis had set before him, in order to resolve to abide by the advice he had received, and do his best in all simplicity. But God did not allow his servant to be altogether defrauded of the mortification he sought with so much avidity, though it differed widely from what he would himself have chosen. One of the four doctors who were set to argue with him indulged in some prefatory remarks of a highly laudatory character, not only personal to the youth himself, but in glorification of his noble lineage and family. Now (as has been already observed), thoroughly as Aloysius had succeeded in quelling the slightest movements of the passions, he never seems to have been freed from his sensitiveness on this one point. The blush which tinged his pale cheek revealed the pain he felt at this ill-judged compliment, and in replying to his opponent there was noticed in him a certain excitement and almost asperity of manner quite foreign to his habitual demeanour.

His metaphysical studies were followed by a theological course in which he had successively for instructors several men of eminent attainments, two Genoese fathers, P. Agostino and P. Benedetto Giustiniani, and two Spaniards, P. Gabriele Vasquez and P. Juan Azor. Their young disciple treated them with the profoundest respect; he was never heard to dissent from their opinions, he always spoke of them with praise, and never uttered a word of comment on their respective manner or methods, or made the smallest comparison between them. Every one knows how much watchfulness and self-control is implied in such systematic abstention from seemingly harmless observations. Aloysius specially loved the writings of St. Thomas, not only on account of the perspicuity and soundness of his doctrine, but from personal devotion to that great saint. His own intellect, we have seen, was singularly clear and penetrating, and his judgment mature far beyond his years; all his instructors give the same testimony on this head, and one father in particular said that amongst all his scholars, none had ever momentarily puzzled him for a reply except Aloysius, who on one occasion proposed a difficulty to which he did not at once see the solution. The great diligence with which he studied, a diligence the more surprising when his feeble health and constant headaches are taken into account, rendered all his natural powers available. Nothing with him ran to waste, all his money was at the bank, all was bearing interest; but he ever sought to render his own exertions effective by supernatural aid, and never studied without kneeling down first to pray. That done, he would limit himself strictly to the lesson set him, nor seeking out other authorities for himself. If he met with a difficulty he took a note of it for reference to the master, waiting always till others had proposed their doubts; or, after collecting a number, he would choose some time when he believed the professor to be least engaged, to consult him about them in his own room. He always put his question in Latin, cap in hand, unless bid to cover himself; and he no sooner had his answer than he retired.

Aloysius never looked into a book without the permission of his superiors; and how far he pushed this spirit of docile obedience, a single fact will show. One day, upon his referring the solution of some question on the subject of predestination to P. Agostino Giustiniani, the father, after giving the explanation, took down a volume of St. Augustine and, pointing with his finger to a particular page in the treatise *De Bono Perseverantiæ*, recommended him to read it, not noticing, however, that the subject was continued over the leaf for about ten lines. These ten lines accordingly Aloysius did not read, although they formed the completion of the passage, and most persons would have presumed that they were virtually included in the permission. This is one of those exquisite touches to which we before alluded, and which seem to escape our grosser appreciation—one of those inaudible tones beyond the spiritual gamut of the ordinary ear. They bespeak a combination of docility and simplicity of which it is not easy to conceive the possibility, and which most persons would hardly deem desirable after the period of early childhood. Aloysius was always ready to dispute in the schools when wanted, nay, he offered himself to be at call when no one else was ready. In disputing, his consideration for his antagonist was very remarkable. He never raised his voice, he never pushed a person in argument, or betrayed either eagerness or a spirit of triumph. When the question was solved or decided, he acquiesced with sweetness and ingenuousness, whatever the result. Before entering the arena, he paid a visit to the Blessed Sacrament, as also again on leaving the schools; and a venerable father, co-disciple of this angelic youth, P. Cesare Franciotti, recalled in after life the picture of holy modesty, simple cheerfulness, and heavenly serenity, which the face of the saintly novice presented, as he silently passed to and fro, the very sight of it moving him to a pious emulation to copy its lineaments in his own soul.

While scrupulously punctual in following directions Aloysius did not readily avail himself of permissions. The lessons were taken down from dictation, which required extreme rapidity, only obtained by habit; his superiors, desirous to spare him this labour, allowed him to have his task performed for him. But towards the latter part of the course, fearing there might seem some self-indulgence in his acquiescence, he begged to be allowed to do as the rest; finding, however, that he could not keep up with the master, he used to listen for awhile, then make a brief note and fill up afterwards by referring to the manuscripts of his fellow-scholars. His good memory, no doubt, helped him in this process, which, nevertheless, he found very laborious; yet he took a pleasure in it from the thought that he gave thereby a more edifying example. Once, when asked why he was reluctant to profit by these exemptions, he replied, "Because I am poor, and it is to practise poverty I act thus; the poor must only spend money on necessary things" Thus when anything was imposed by obedience he complied strictly and literally, never thinking it sufficient to acquit himself merely of the spirit of the command; but when a permissive order was given, which relieved instead of burdening him, he did precisely the reverse, and took the spirit and intention of the dispensation, not the letter, for his guide. His love of holy indifference was exemplified in one of those trifling acts which, perhaps, from their very slightness, best exhibit the faithfulness of a soul in pursuing the acquisition of a virtue. When he lent his papers to a fellow novice, which he was always ready to do, he never reminded the borrower to return them, no matter how long he might retain them. He strove as much as possible to sit loose from everything by rejecting those little accommodations with which almost all persons blamelessly seek to provide themselves. He courted inconvenience. Thus he would not keep books by him for reference, unless the necessity for reference were so continual as to render it imperative that he should have his authorities at hand. He could, he said, go and consult these works in the common library. He ended by having only the Bible and St. Thomas in his room; and even of his valued St. Thomas he at last deprived himself by permission, in favour of a scholar recently arrived, who was unprovided with a copy of the Summa. He gave as his reason for wishing to dispense with the copy specially assigned to him, that he could avail himself of that which was used by the novice who shared his room; and great was his joy in obtaining leave, not only to do an act of fraternal charity, but to make himself poorer than he was before.

He extended his love of poverty and despoilment to those pious objects in which a devout soul will often seek adornment, if in nothing else. He would not have his rosaries of any precious material, neither would he keep anything of the sort by him to give to others, nor did he like to receive such gifts himself. Some, however, there were who, from the devotion they felt for him, would try to force such things upon his acceptance, first obtaining leave from superiors to offer them. Aloysius would decline, if possible, but if the giver were one whom a refusal might offend, he would yield, and take the first opportunity to obtain permission to divest himself of what he had so reluctantly received. He was satisfied with whatever devotional objects he found in his room, and possessed none of his own, except a paper print of St. Catherine, his patroness, and another of St. Thomas Aquinas, whose works were his constant study; and these which had been pressed upon him, he pinned to the wall. His whole desire, in short, was to possess nothing and care for nothing. If indifferent even to such things as had a pious object, much more was he careless of what only concerned his personal appearance or comfort. When winter or summer clothes were made for him, he allowed himself to be dressed as if he were an inanimate block. Never was he known to say, "This is too long, or that too short;" but if the tailor asked him if the habit fitted, he would reply that he thought it did very well. In fact, everything was well with him, and best when he got the worst, which by God's Providence, as he once told his confessor (and he esteemed it a special favour), had often happened to him when a distribution was made. In the true spirit of the Jesuit rule, he used to say, "Just as a poor beggar, who goes to a door soliciting alms, certainly never reckons upon having the best clothes bestowed upon him, but only such as are shabby and worn out, and, in like manner, the refuse of everything; so also we, if we are truly poor, must expect to have the worst things in the house fall to our share, and we must be persuaded that not only will it be so, but that it is fitting that so it should be."

Aloysius had now passed two years in the Company, and (to use his biographer's simple words) being exceedingly well satisfied with religion and religion with him," after a few days' retreat, during which he went through the Spiritual Exercises, he made his three vows of poverty, chastity, and obedience, on the 25th of November, 1587, being the feast of St. Catherine, Virgin and Martyr, the anniversary, as will be remembered, of his joining the Company, In performing this act Aloysius, full of joy, saw the final accomplishment of his long-cherished hopes. He was at last a religious in very deed, and united by the closest ties to his God. On the 25th of February, 1588, he received the tonsure in the church of St. John Lateran, with many companions, amongst whom was the Maronite, Abramo Giorgi, afterwards martyred for the faith; and on the 28th of the same month, and on the 6th, 12th, and 20th of March, the minor orders of ostiarius, lector, exorcist, and acolyte were successively conferred upon them.

We conclude Aloysius's life as a novice with the letter he wrote to his mother on the 11th of December, 1587, a few days after making his vows:—

"Most illustrious Signora, my mother, and most honoured in Christ,

I have lately received a letter from you, Signora, which caused me much joy, from the good account it gave of yourself and the whole family, and not less from what it told me of my brother, whom may our Lord direct, even as I hope. This I recommend to God in my prayers, only begging you, Signora, to salute him in my name, and remind him to practise what is incumbent upon him, as well as upon his house, that is, submission to whom it is due,* as our father of happy memory enjoined. Illustrious Signora, I announce to you the donation I made of myself to His Divine Majesty by taking my vows on St. Catherine's day, for which, while inviting you, Signora, to praise the Lord, I at the same time beg you to beseech

* This passage is not clearly worded in the original; but the person alluded to as entitled to submission is probably the saint's mother herself.

Him that I may observe them, and advance in the state to which He has called me, so that, together, after this life is over, we may be united in the possession of Him in Heaven, where He is so lovingly ex-expecting all His own. I accept at the same time the offer which you made me, Signora, in your last, of some more money for defraying the expenses of letters; I will beg you therefore to let me have 25 scudi. In conclusion, I recommend myself to you in the Lord, from whom I solicit for you increase of His holy grace in all things.

"I am, illustrious Signora,

"Your most obedient son in Christ,

"ALUIGI GONZAGA, of the Company of Jesus.

"Rome, December 11, 1587."

CHAPTER IV.

THE FIRST YEARS OF HIS RELIGIOUS PROFESSION.

IT would seem as if Aloysius possessed the virtues of his new state in such perfection that they could scarcely admit of any further increase. Just as, when he entered the noviciate, he resembled rather one who was leaving it, so when he took his vows he had acquired all those perfections of the full religious state which would seem to belong exclusively to a more advanced stage, or, rather, to which few persons ever attain. Yet he was never to mount to a higher religious grade: his next upward step was to be to

Heaven. Full well did all who knew him perceive his ripeness for glory, and, coupled with the circumstance of his weak health, it must have suggested many a fear that their angelic companion would not tarry long with them. Yet, if others deemed that he had already reached the height of super-eminent sanctity, Aloysius never reckoned himself to have attained perfection in any one virtue; he was ever pressing on, and aiming at something more complete and excellent. By his very change of state many of his virtues received additional lustre. That humility which made him always seek the lowest place became the more striking when he became entitled to a higher; for, so far from abating in this respect, he was, if possible, more conspicuously lowly. Many instances are recorded of his singular love of this virtue, as displayed by his behaviour in his new position. How little he habitually spoke we already know, yet he loved to converse with the lay brethren, and at dinner would commonly go to a table at the lower end of the refectory, where those employed in the kitchen and other domestic offices used to sit. Nay, he not only placed himself on a level with them, but he strove to give them precedence, as if they were his superiors, as he was more than once seen to do in the case of the cook. Notwithstanding the man's reluctance, Aloysius had so many good reasons to urge, that he got his own way in the matter, but he was not long to enjoy it; superiors interfered, and he was even reproved, and forbidden to practise a humiliation which the respect due to the clerical tonsure rendered unbefitting. "I have seen him," said Cardinal Bellarmine in a sermon delivered after his death, "in the public places of the city walking on the left hand of the lay-brother, but I took care to admonish the latter of his duty." How minute the ceremonial of life was in those days, and how much importance was attached to its observance, it may be well to bear in mind, in order rightly to appreciate the saint's behaviour in such apparently trivial matters.

But Aloysius had a special reason of his own for thus seeking to make himself of no account. If there was one thing in the world (as we have seen) which he apprehended, it was that any distinction, accommodation, or exemption should be awarded to him on account of his birth. He would fain have concealed his noble extraction altogether, but since this could not be, he would at least endeavour that it should be forgotten, or that he should be treated as if it were forgotten. When his superiors, out of regard to the weakness of his health, bade him take his place at the table of the convalescent, and rise later than others, dispensing him also from several obligations onerous to the infirm, he entertained a secret fear that the recollection of his own antecedents might have some share in the attention paid to his comfort. He immediately set himself to do what in no other case did he ever attempt, to move his superiors to a change of will, and induce them to recall these dispositions in his favour, urging so many reasons in support of his plea that he succeeded in obtaining leave to live according to the common rule. When strongly recommended to acquiesce in what had been arranged for him, for that otherwise he was sure to make himself ill, he replied that, being a religious, he was bound to use every endeavour to live like other religious; and as for making himself ill by doing what the institute rendered incumbent upon him, so long as he was not acting against obedience, he did not give the matter a thought.

The number of persons, scholars and others, in the college rendered it impossible to allot a separate room to each; this accommodation was reserved, of course, to priests, masters, and a few others, from a regard either to their office or to their personal needs; the rest had to share their apartments with one or more companions. Aloysius's state of health made his superiors desirous to class him in the exceptional category, but although the freedom of solitude must have been so dear to his tastes and inclinations, or perhaps all the more for that very reason, Aloysius desired not to profit by this favour. He went to the rector and represented that, for example's sake, it would be better that he should have a companion allotted to him, adding—for the fear of some distinction still clung to him—that for his part he did not wish the person selected to be a theologian or remarkable in any way for his acquirements; signifying, however, at the same time his perfect acquiesence in any choice which his superiors might make. The sole requests he ever preferred were invariably prompted by a desire for his own mortification or the edification of others. For this end he courted troublesome and lowly occupations. When he had finished his theology he wished to be sent to teach in the inferior grammar school. In this office he hoped at once to satisfy his humility and his zeal for the instruction of youth in Christian piety; for he who was to be their special patron had a singular attraction to this labour of love, and even regarded with a sort of holy envy the masters of grammar, whom he used to call blessed on account of their occupation. The reason he assigned for soliciting this employment was highly characteristic of him, intended as it was to veil the humility which prompted his desire. For Aloysius was always specially ingenious in concealing his sanctity, and this not only without the slightest affectation, which would have argued some remaining vestige of self-love, but in a manner dexterous and easy. He told the rector that he was not a good grammarian, nor was he well grounded in Latin, and that to enable him to serve the Company well this deficiency ought to be supplied; and he begged the prefect of the lower schools to second his request. This father, entertaining some doubts as to the ignorance alleged, requested the rector to give Aloysius as companion in his room some one qualified to test his proficiency. As his superiors suspected, so it turned out. Our saint spoke Latin very well; however, he returned to the charge—we have had some experience of his perseverance when he had a point to gain—and again affirmed that he was not sufficiently grounded; that a solid basis could never be acquired by mere conversation, but could only be attained by following the lessons given to the lowest classes, and imprinting them on his mind by himself teaching the rudiments. However, it does not appear that he obtained what he sought. He was obliged to content himself with those humiliations which were not denied—to go out occasionally and beg in the streets of Rome, in a shabby garb, with a sack on his back, as we have already described, and to perform various domestic offices about the house; sometimes helping in the kitchen, washing plates and dishes, and collecting the scraps for the poor; indeed, when it fell to his lot, or he could obtain permission, to take them to the beggars at the door, his joy was perfect. Almost every day he had some employment of the sort assigned or conceded to him. He swept the rooms, and used to go about carefully removing cobwebs from the corners. For several years it was his office to look to the lights on stairs and in passages, and replenish them with oil, in all which he took particular delight. It was no strange thing, of course, for the members of the Company to be employed in such offices, since this is customary, and would therefore raise neither admiration nor wonder; what rendered them striking in Aloysius was the jubilant spirit in which he performed them; he seemed unable to contain himself for very exultation, so that the fathers used to tell him that it was plain from his air of triumph he had now got what he wanted. The depths of abasement, in fact, were to him the heights of his ambition, and when he had reached them then it was he gloried.

As for bodily mortifications and austerities, there can be little doubt but that, left to himself, he would have shortened his days; and to those who were acquainted with the exactness and submissiveness of his obedience in all else, it might have seemed that he even departed in spirit from his own high standard, and at the same time infringed his rule of perfect indifference, by his perpetual attempts to move those set over him to make some concession to his wishes in this matter. Some, indeed, expressed their surprise to him that he should not scruple thus to importune his superiors for penances; but he replied that, being conscious of the amount of his strength, and feeling himself also inwardly pressed to undertake these penitential exercises, he thought that by laying the case simply before those in authority over him, whatever God willed would be accorded him and the rest denied. He confessed, however, that he occasionally asked for what he was sure would be refused, but that, as he could not put his desires in execution, he at least wished to offer them to God, whereby he gained something, if it were but the humiliation of getting a rebuke for being so ignorant of his own strength or for making what he knew must be fruiless efforts. Yet sometimes, to the surprise of all, he obtained what he asked. Being questioned once how, with his wisdom and discretion, he could persevere in disregarding the counsel of pious and venerable fathers, who had so often urged upon him a relaxation in the severity of his penances and his intense mental application to spiritual things, he made this reply:—"The persons who give me this advice are of two sorts; some of them lead such holy and perfect lives that I can discern nothing in them but what is worthy of imitation, and I have more than once been minded to abide by their counsels; but when I noted that they themselves did not observe them in their own conduct I judged it better to imitate their actions than to follow their recommendations, which they gave me from a certain charitable feeling and compassionate affection. Others there are who themselves follow the advice which they give me, and are not so much addicted to penitential exercises; but I consider it better to rule myself by the example of the first than by the counsel of these last." To this he added the doubt he entertained whether, without this help, grace would continue to make head against nature, which, when not afflicted and chastised, tended gradually to relapse into its old state, losing the habit of suffering acquired by the labour of many years. "I am a crooked piece of iron," he said, "and am come into religion to be made straight by the hammer of mortification and penance." When reminded by some that perfection consisted in what was interior, and that it was more needful to discipline the will than the body, he replied, "*Hæc facere, et illa non omittere*—(These ye must do, and not leave the other undone)." The example of the saints of his order, and in particular of its great founder, weighed also much with him; he remembered how St. Ignatius macerated his body, and how he left it written in the Constitutions, that he did not prescribe to his followers vigils, fasts, disciplines, special prayers, and penances, because he supposed them to be already so perfect, and so much given to these things, as to need rather the curb than the spur.

Yet it must not be supposed that because Aloysius disregarded in this particular the advice even of many of his elders in religion, he took any such liberty with the recommendations of his superiors, whose every expressed wish or direction was received by him with the deepest respect, and followed with the most unquestioning submission. He looked upon the relaxations enjoined upon him only as temporary condescensions to physical inability, and never considered himself as dispensed from observing and reporting to his superiors his own capabilities and his earnest desire to resume the forbidden austerities so soon as they should see fit to grant him permission. Meanwhile he was diligent in seeking and solicitous in requesting compensation in other ways less trying to his bodily strength; and his ingenuity in making himself uncomfortable and in hunting after humiliations will bear a comparison with what the most delicate and fastidious will display in avoiding inconvenience and annoyance. For this end he would ask to be employed in some task which he considered he could not discharge with credit to himself, hoping thus to raise a laugh at his expense; a mortification to which many would much prefer taking a severe discipline.

His great love for his neighbour, the sure accompaniment of the burning love of God which consumed him, made him zealous to seek opportunities for exercising it in their behalf. Besides begging leave often to go to the hospitals to serve the sick, to whose bodily wants he ministered with the sweetest tenderness—making their beds, washing their feet, and cleaning their rooms, never losing sight meanwhile, of their spiritual necessities—he also obtained permission to visit daily all the sick in the college, an office which he performed with singular assiduity and charity. Consolation attended his every act and word, all felt its influence alike, and many had reason to thank him also for benefit received to their souls. So desirous, indeed, was he to be busy in some way in the relief of suffering, that, when his superiors took him off study in order to spare his head, he would seek out the infirmarians to aid them in cleaning knives and forks, and in cooking and serving up the meals of the sick and convalescent.

As long as he was engaged in his studies, and had

not attained the age at which, by receiving the sacerdotal character, he would be specially called to the care of souls, Aloysius could not make the spiritual profit of his neighbour his direct employment; but he constantly bore it in mind, and had a way of exercising a kind of apostolate the success of which, when we consider the simplicity of the machinery employed, is truly marvellous; leading us to exclaim, What cannot one single soul which has achieved high sanctification effect for others! For this is the condition, the inexorable condition of spiritual influence. Even zeal and piety of no ordinary degree may labour at the work of conversion and improvement of others with pertinacious ardour yet with scanty success, toiling and taking nothing for many a long day, because defective in close interior union with God; But the words and acts of saints are gifted with a kind of spiritual magnetism. Aloysius did not let his talent sleep. He first consulted the father rector as to whether he approved of his striving to hinder all conversation at the morning and evening recreation except on spiritual subjects. It need scarce be observed that idle and profitless talk was not tolerated even in the hours devoted to relaxation, but Aloysius desired to exclude indifferent topics, not having God or the soul's benefit for their immediate object. Having obtained the rector's assent, he conferred with the prefect of spiritual things, P. Girolamo Ubaldini, a very holy man, who had resigned a Roman prelature to join the Company, begging him to favour the work, which he took care himself meanwhile to reccommend to God He then selected from amongst his companions some of those whose spirituality fitted them to aid him in his pious design. They began by meeting occasionally in recreation hours to discourse of divine things. For these conferences Aloysius, not content with the abundance of his heart, which was a very treasury of holy thoughts and affections, used to devote daily a special half-hour to reading some spiritual book or saint's life, that he might not be barren of matter for conversation. With the assistance of his associates, he now commenced operations. His method was this. If he was in company with his inferiors in age or position in religion, he would at once introduce holy subjects, and his companions were sure to follow his lead; but with his superiors he adopted another course. He would ask a question, or propose some spiritual doubt or difficulty, like one who is desirous to learn; thus was he equally certain of gaining his point, and, indeed, his superiors were so well aware that he had no taste for any but spiritual discourse, that his very presence was sufficient to ensure his purpose; for no sooner did Aloysius appear, but they would, out of love and condescension to his known desire, drop any indifferent subject of conversation. Youths from the noviciate, or from other parts, coming to Rome to pursue their studies, were immediately caught in our saint's toils. Either he devoted himself personally, or he commissioned some companion or co-novice of the new-comer to seek him out at recreation time, and take occasion also to mention to him five or six persons whose friendship would be peculiarly desirable to assist him in keeping up the spirit of devotion. These five or six were, of course, belonging to the band of pious conspirators, and were warned to make themselves particularly accessible to the youth thus prepossessed in their favour. Or, again, if he knew of any one needing counsel or aid, he would leave nothing undone to gain his confidence. For days and weeks he would make him the object of his marked attention at recreation time, not caring what others might think of a display of apparent preference so generally discouraged in religion. When he thought he had gained his point, and could safely leave his *protége* to himself, he would gently draw off from the temporary intimacy, alleging the desirableness of avoiding too much exclusiveness in religion, where private friendships are a sort of injury done to fraternal charity, but naming a few persons whose conversation would be specially profitable, and to whom he privately handed over the completion of the charitable task he had begun. Such were the simple and innocent devices which Aloysius employed to catch souls.

In a house where all had one end in view, their own spiritual profit, our saint might reckon on favour and countenance; what could not have been reckoned upon were the splendid results which were achieved. Few weeks had passed before a palpable change came over the Roman College. The flame of divine love seemed to dart from one bosom to another, and even the coldest felt its warmth and began to kindle like the rest; so that Cepari himself, the witness of what he describes, when in summer time he contemplated these two hundred students scattered through the garden in parties of three and four at the recreation hour, could feel well assured, from his intimate knowlege of all, that there was but one subject of discourse among them, as they sat or wandered at will, like so many angels communing together amongst the trees of Paradise.

Blessed sight to one who looked on to the time when these youths, now kindling daily more and more with the love of God, and fanning mutually the holy passion in each other's breasts, should themselves become focuses of heavenly light and heat to thousands in the world! Who, indeed, could attempt to calculate the harvest of the young Aloysius's apostolate, or compute as by some spiritual arithmetic, the souls brought by him to God, long after he had ceased to aid in the work save by his powerful prayers in heaven?

Vacation time did not interrupt this process of mutual sanctification. When the youths of the Roman College were sent for a few days in September or October to refresh themselves at Frascati, a store of spiritual books, such as Gerson's writings, the Lives of St. Francis, St. Catherine of Siena, and St. Ignatius, was provided for the trip. Some took great delight in the Chronicles of St. Francis or of St. Dominic, others in St. Augustine's Confessions, or in St. Bernard's Exposition of the Canticles; again, the Life of St. Catherine of Genoa had special charms for those who had made considerable progress in the inner life; while such as felt a peculiar attraction, like their angelic apostle, Aloysius, for contempt of self, might be seen buried in the study of the Life of the Blessed Giacopone and Giovanni Colombini. From this spiritual refection they would rise and go forth, morning and evening, by twos or threes to wander over the hills, and how could they talk of anything but what their hearts and minds were full of? Sometimes ten or twelve would meet in the recess of some shady wood, and there, sitting down, hold conference together, with such fervour and jubilee of soul that it seemed as if heaven had begun on earth. And this was the work of Aloysius, and they all knew it. Hence he was the object of general love and admiration, which made each one eager to follow and listen to him, moved thereto, not only by the appreciation of his holiness, but by the charms of his gentle and gracious conversation; for Aloysius knew how to relax the bow, and with prudence and sauvity accommodate himself to time and place; nay, he would on occasions season his discourse with some playful anecdote or modest pleasantry, which helped to win his hearers' hearts, rendering his very perfection more lovable by an attractive familiarity.

Such was the life Aloysius led for the first two years and a half of his abode at the Roman College. Happy days! dear to the many who shared their joys, and who, later, were to go forth to labour in the Lord's vineyard, carrying with them the memory of their fragrance and the blessed fruits in their own souls.

CHAPTER V.

Aloysius's Mission of Peace to Castiglione

Once and once only was Aloysius to emerge from his retirement and appear publicly before the world; to revisit the land of his birth, the home of his youth, and the castle of his ancestors; once again was he to be seen in the bosom of his family and surrounded by his noble kindred. This episode forms not the least striking or interesting passage in his short life.

Discord and confusion reigned in the house of Gonzaga. One day in the Lent of the year 1587, Ridolfo of Castiglione was seated in the collegiate church of that place assisting at a sermon, when a gentleman of his household entered the sacred edifice, approached the young marquis, and whispered something in his ear. They were few words, but they had the power to move and to disturb. Orazio Gonzaga, lord of Solferino, was dead. Scant attention, we may conceive, did Ridolfo give to the remainder of the preacher's discourse, but he kept his place till its conclusion, then hastened forth, and soon the beating of the drum through the little town of Castiglione called the retainers to arms. Two hours sufficed to collect a band of six hundred stout vassals, ready to march with their lord to take possession of his deceased relative's castle. It will be remembered that by the will of their common grandfather, Aluigi, Solferino was to revert to the marquisate in the event of the failure of male heirs, but such arrangements in those days were not unfrequently disregarded where other interests were involved, unless there was some display of the capacity to enforce them on the part of the legal claimant—not always even then did they pass undisputed, as the event proved. His serene highness, Duke Guglielmo of Mantua, put in his claim: Signor Orazio had made a will, bequeathing the fief to him; he politely signified therefore to the lord of Castiglione that he should vacate the castle. Ridolfo replied that he was the very good servant of his highness, but that Solferino was a free Imperial fief, and that his uncle had not the power of willing it away. The possession reverted to him as his own rightful inheritance. This argument did not convince the duke, who was not a little offended that his cousin should take on himself to decide the question in this off-hand way; so he also armed and prepared to take the field. However, more moderate counsels prevailed, and it was agreed to abide by the Imperial award. The troops were accordingly disbanded, and the two parties awaited the decision of this ultimate court of appeal. Duke Guglielmo might hope that his close connection by marriage with the Emperor would secure a favourable leaning to his interests in that quarter. But while the case was being carried to an earthly tribunal, he was himself summoned to appear before his Heavenly Judge. He died on the 14th of August, and was succeeded by his son Vincenzo, who was fully determined to prosecute with vigour his father's claims. A certain captain of the duke's, opining perhaps that possession formed nine-tenths of the law, and at any rate judging it more for the honour of his master that, while the matter was pending, the disputed property should remain in his hands, made an unexpected night-attack on Solferino, scaled the walls, and secured the castle. It does not seem that his highness of Mantua disavowed this discreditable act by which his honour was considered to be promoted. Donna Marta, when she heard of the occurrence, left Castiglione and hurried to the Imperial presence at Prague with three of her sons, the eldest of whom, Francesco, was at that time but nine years old. Yet the little boy acquitted himself with so much grace and propriety of a long speech addressed to his Cæsarian majesty, as quite to win the good graces of the sovereign. He took such a fancy, indeed, to the child that he begged him from his mother to make him a page about his person. Meantime an Imperial commissary was despatched to assume the government of Solferino in the Emperor's name while the cause was under consideration. It was finally decided in Ridolfo's favour, but although the original matter of dispute was thus settled by superior authority, minds had become so much embittered, chiefly, as usual, through the malicious interference of busy designing persons, who make capital of the dissensions of the great, that the old quarrel formed now the least portion of the causes of offence, real or supposed, existing between the duke of Mantua and his cousin of Castiglione. So many imputations in particular had been cast upon Ridolfo, that the whole family and all the friends of the house were in daily fear of some violent explosion. Many great personages, amongst others, the arch-duke Ferdinand, brother to the emperor Maximilian, tried their hands unsuccessfully as peace makers: it was reserved for two women, who on these occasions have sometimes the best wit, to be the instruments of restoring concord. Madama Eleonora of Austria, mother of the duke Vincenzo, and Donna Marta, mother of the marquis Ridolfo, had the happy thought of sending for an angel of peace, who, if any one were able to effect so desirable an object, could calm the troubled waters and restore union to their divided house.

Aloysius was much beloved by the duke of Mantua, and his brother, of course, who owed his position to him, must needs hear him with favour and respect; and then the words of saints, the very sight of them, are in themselves so potent. These pious women quite appreciated the value of such influence, and so, without communicating their purpose to their sons, they had recourse directly to Aloysius, beseeching him to come and mediate between the disputants. As it may well be supposed there was little inclination on his part to mix himself up with these worldly affairs, and take part in the strife of human passions and interests, from which he had fled to the sanctuary of his God, to repose under the shadows of His wings. "Woe is me!" must he often have mentally exclaimed in former days, "that my sojourning is prolonged with the inhabitants of Kedar." * He dreaded even a temporary return to their tents, as an inrode on that peace which he so valued; nor was this a mere natural love of quiet· the peace he loved was that peace which must be cultivated in the soul, if we desire that God, whose abode is in peace, should dwell therein. Accordingly when the application was made to him, he returned an unfavourable reply; yet, ever fearful of being influenced by his own inclination, he referred the matter to God, and begged the prayers of others especially those of his confesser, P. Bellarmino. The latter after seeking Divine light, said, "Go, Aloysius, I hold that God will be served thereby." Our saint received this communication as an oracle, and, placing himself in a state of indifference, immediately prepared to do as he should be desired. Meanwhile the arch-duchess Eleonora, hearing of the difficulties he had raised, and believing that he alone

* Psalm CXIX, 5.

by his intervention could avert the dreaded danger, had applied to his superiors, entreating them to send him on this pacific mission to Mantua. Her request was granted, and so the question was decided.

It was the month of September, and our saint was spending the vacation time at Frascati with his companions. We have already described the sweetness of those days, and how Aloysius's presence made this recreation time like a foretaste of heaven. Great, then, was the dismay of the little band when one day Padre Bellarmino arrived with orders from the Father General for Aloysius to return immediately to Rome in order to start at once for Mantua and Castiglione; but he himself was calm and impassible as ever, and took but a quarter of an hour to get ready to fulfil his superior's behest. They all (as Cepari, who was of the party, relates) accompanied him on his way beyond a *vigna* of the college; and as they returned, P. Bellarmino discoursed of the virtues of their angelic brother, the loss of whose example for so long a time every one was deploring. He related many instances of his marvellous holiness, adding that when he endeavoured to picture to himself the life of the great St. Thomas Aquinas in his youth, he could not form a more perfect idea of it than by looking at Aloysius. It was upon this occasion that Bellarmine expressed his decided conviction that this youth was already confirmed in grace, an opinion which, as coming from Aloysius's confessor and a man of such high spiritual attainments and discernment, possessed peculiar force and authority.

Meanwhile the angel of peace was on his road. He only tarried at Rome for a sufficient time to take leave of the cardinals, his relatives, to whom on this occasion especially it was fitting to pay respect. So great was his exhaustion that, while visiting the Cardinal della Rovere, he fainted, and had to be laid on his Eminence's bed to recover. When he came to himself the cardinal remonstrated with him for his excessive mortifications, and exhorted him to take more care of his health. Aloysius replied that, so far from practising excessive austerities, he did not even fulfil his obligations. Ill fitted, indeed, did he seem to undertake the fatigues of a journey; and journeys were veritable labours to the weak in those days. His superiors, aware of his debility and unsparing severity to himself, had empowered a discreet lay brother, whom they had assigned to him as his companion, Giacomo Borlasca by name to take charge of his health, Aloysius being enjoined to follow his recommendations. Old Padre Luca Corbinelli, who tenderly loved our saint, and knew how acutely he suffered in his head, did his best to induce him to take an umbrella, to shade him from the burning heat of the sun, in which he was seconded by many other fathers, but as they had no authority over the youth, they failed in gaining their point. Aloysius could never be brought to consent to this alleviation, and with equal firmness, at all seasons of the year, rejected gloves, because the members of the Company were not in the habit of wearing them, although the delicacy of his skin and his sensitiveness to cold rendered him a peculiar sufferer from such self-denial. Yet he did not blame those who accepted a dispensation, especially priests, whose hands had to minister at the altar.

Aloysius now took leave of his fathers and brethren.

There was a singular grace in his demonstrations of affection: never redundant, always spiritual, they were at once touching and edifying. Before setting out, he sought P. Muzio Vitelleschi in his room and gave him a little crucifix, saying that he was leaving him that on which the eyes of his mind were ever fixed, and all his love and all his desires intent. Could he more tenderly have expressed at once his love for Jesus and for him who was so dear to him in the Lord? Another characteristic anecdote is related of him at starting. Were we not persuaded that in him all was well regulated and balanced, and nothing overcharged or exaggerated, we might be tempted to suspect him of a sensitiveness almost excessive in his fear of distinction. If any will still esteem it a weakness, they must at least confess that it was a magnanimous weakness. When preparing to mount, a pair of riding-boots were brought to him, but some one unfortunately observed in his hearing that their former possessor was a certain lord. Immediately Aloysius suspected that it was on that very account they had been selected for him; he looked at them, and turned them round and round, apparently seeking some fault, and desirous of an excuse to have them changed. To humour him, his companion, who guessed the cause, said, "What's the matter with the boots? Don't they fit you? Aloysius was silent, and the brother, telling him he would look out a pair which would suit him better, returned to the harness-room. There, making some trifling alteration in the offending articles by bending them into another form,* he brought back the identical aristocratic pair

*Boots in those days were commonly made of some kind of cloth. Princes wore them of velvet or silk, embroidered in gold and silver.

which had alarmed Aloysius's humility, who now put them on unsuspiciously, and said, "I think these will do very well;" and so they mounted, and proceeded on their way. Bernardino Medici, who was going to lecture on Sacred Scripture at Milan, and with whom Aloysius was in habits of intimacy, was his welcome companion. From him we learn a few incidents of the road. It was very striking, he says, to witness the devotion shown by the *vetturini* to this young Jesuit father. The common sort of people, ignorant as they may be, will often, even when no way remarkable for attention to their religious duties, recognise holiness in others with a marvellous instinct. These men would come and open their whole heart to him, seeming as if they could not prevail on themselves to leave his side as long as they remained with him. Nor did Aloysius chide or repel the simple, loving veneration of these poor people; but he evinced considerable mortification at the attentions he received at the Company's house at Siena, where one priest in particular was most enthusiastic in the expression of his feelings. Our saint may have thought that his behaviour was referable to some deference entertained for his former position in the world; anyhow such exuberant displays of affection and complimentary expressions he considered to be contrary to the moderation and decorum of the religious state, which forbids all exaggerated marks of personal respect and consideration. In this instance his sensitive humility probably deceived him; the fame of his virtues, as we have seen, had travelled to Siena, and the good priest was but honouring the saint in his young brother in religion, with, it may be, a little deficiency of tact and disere-tion in its manifestation.

At Florence, which he always rejoiced to see again, he had to part with P. Bernardino, who was detained in that city for a few days by his relatives, the Medicean lords, he himself proceeding on his way to Bologna without delay. Here he was soon surrounded by the fathers of the Company, who, like those of Siena, had heard of his sanctity and were eager to converse with him. There was nothing, however, in their cordial reception to pain his retiring modesty, for all fell at once to conversing of the things of God, the subject, indeed, upon which the fathers longed to hear the young saint discourse. Here Aloysius spent a day, and the rector sent him out with the sacristan to see the beauties of that fair city, so glorious for its churches and religious monuments, and so rich in works of art. When they left the college together, Aloysius begged his guide to take him only to some of the churches most noted as places of devotional resort; for all the rest he did not care. Between Bologna and Mantua an incident occurred illustrative of his equanimity and patience. The host showed the two travellers to a room containing but one bed. Aloysius made no comment, but the lay-brother, drawing the inn-keeper on one side, told him that they were religious, whose custom it is always to have separate beds. Mine host bluffly replied that he could not spare a second bed, as, later in the evening, gentlemen might arrive re-quiring accommodation. The brother waxed a little warm at this refusal, and was insisting, when Aloysius, whose ears the altercation had reached, called him away, and bade him be quiet. "That inn-keeper," said brother Giacomo, who thought he had good cause to be somewhat irate, "wants to keep all his beds for gentlemen, as if we were a couple of clowns; you, at least, ought to be treated with more respect." Then Aloysius, looking at him with a countenance of sweet serenity, replied, "Brother, do not excite yourself, for indeed you are wrong; we make profession of poverty; so, if he treats us conformably to our profession, we cannot and ought not to complain." However, no fresh arrivals occurring in the evening, they were accommodated without further difficulty.

As soon as he had reached Mantua, Aloysius visited the dowager duchess Eleonora; and great was the joy at beholding him of this pious princess, who embraced him with motherly affection. Meanwhile word was sent to the marchese Ridolfo of the arrival of his brother at Mantua, but Aloysius, desiring to avoid the honours sure to await him on his reception, if the day were announced, set off for Castiglione without giving any notice to his family. His hopes of avoiding any public demonstration were, however, frustrated. Just as he was on the point of entering his natal place, he requested a chance passer by to go forward and tell the marchese that his brother had arrived. The man immediately set off as fast as his legs could carry him, shouting the glad news as he went to every one within ear-shot. "Padre Aluigi is coming! Padre Aluigi is coming!" flew from mouth to mouth; streets and windows were soon crowded, church-bells ringing, and bye and bye salvos of artillery gave evidence that the tidings had reached the rock fortress. As Aloysius passed along, he encountered a prostrate multitude, kneeling to implore his blessing with as much devotion and veneration as if a canonized saint had descended to revisit this mortal scene. Great was his confusion at the sight of these demonstrations of reverence; he had feared and shrunk from honour and respect, now he had to endure almost worship. At the foot of the rock he found Ridòlfo, who had hastened down to receive him. The marchese had alighted from his carriage, and as he was stepping forward to welcome his brother, a vassal who for some offence had fallen under the displeasure of his lord, encouraged by the presence of Aloysius, threw himself at Ridolfo's feet, begging forgiveness. The marchese replied that for the love of Padre Aluigi he granted him his pardon. Such were the first fruits of the coming of this angel of God, acts of compassion and of mercy. The two brothers entered the fortress together, where the whole household, gentlemen, officers, servants, were ranged in file as they passed. Aloysius had now to suffer the pain of hearing applied to him on all sides the old titles which he had so gladly renounced for ever. Old habits and associations were too strong, and the *Illustrissimos* and *Excellentissimos* with which he was besieged filled him with confusion. But he could not remonstrate at that moment, when all were vying with each other in giving him a welcome expressive of their heartfelt attachment.

Donna Marta was not at Castiglione but at the castle of San Martino, about twelve miles distant, which together with a palace of the marquises of Castiglione in the town, formed part of her dowry. Aloysius accordingly despatched a messenger to apprise her of his arrival, and she came the next morning to Castiglione with her two infant children. Hither Aloysius immediately repaired, accompanied by the lay brother his companion. The meeting between the mother and son was very striking. The venerable duchess of Mantua had claimed the privilege of age and relationship to embrace the young religious, whom she looked upon almost as a son; but she who was indeed his mother regarded him as something so sacred, so deeply reverenced the sanctity which dwelt within him and made him like a tabernacle of the Most High, that she did not dare to fling her arms around him or to imprint a kiss on that cheek which had so often lain on her bosom, but cast herself on her knees as he entered, and bent her face to the ground. The sentiment which inspired this remarkable behaviour was not new to her, although it was enhanced by her son's religious profession, and found in this his holy calling a justification for its display; for she had ever honoured him in her heart as a saint, and the name she had habitually given him of her "angel" was, in her mouth, not an expression of passionate endearment but of reverential love. Aloysius spent the whole day with her; he had given directions to the lay brother never to leave him on any occasion, but as he and Donna Marta sat conversing of their family affairs, the good brother felt that his presence must be a constraint to the marchesa, so he retired to say his rosary and occupy himself with other devotions. After a long absence he returned, and found mother and son engaged in prayer. Being questioned afterwards by Aloysius as to the motive of his withdrawal, he replied that the Signora Marchesa having prevailed with the Father General to send her son from such a distance to see her, he did not think it proper to hinder her from freely opening her heart to him. In the case of any other lady but his mother he would willingly have obeyed him by remaining present. In this arrangement our saint acquiesced. Perhaps Aloysius had feared that Brother Giacomo was going to exercise the like delicate consideration with all the other members of his family, and did not desire (if we may use the expression) to be domesticated even temporarily. He was forced to leave his holy retreat, but he would carry its atmosphere with him as much as possible, and the constant accompaniment of the lay brother operated as a continual though silent assertion of his resolve.

In the same spirit he would, had he consulted his own inclination, have lodged at the arch-priest's house while he remained at Castiglione, but his superiors had ordered otherwise. He refused, however, every accommodation offered to him, such as horses and carriages which had been provided for him, and always went out on foot. But he was unable to escape the spontaneous honours which waylaid him at every step. His humility, however, disclaimed what he could not reject. While the great ones of the earth content themselves with condescension, and are even praised for deigning thus to stoop from their elevation, Aloysius vied with those beneath him in respectful courtesy; nay, he seemed to return them the homage which they proffered to him. Such was his lowliness of demeanour that he might have been supposed to be the inferior of the meanest who addressed him. In the house he declined all assistance, receiving what he absolutely required from his companion; but, indeed, he seldom accepted, and never asked for, the service of any one; his custom, even cases of real need, being to leave it in God's hands, if He saw fit, to move others to help him. On the first night of his arrival he dismissed all the pages who came to help him to undress, telling them he should never go to bed as long as they remained. When in his mother's house, where he had more freedom, he always made his own bed, and loved to help Brother Giacomo to make his, which when the servants discovered they did their best to be before-hand with him; in the marchese's castle he endeavoured, when he could, to perform the like offices. He never gave an order, he never made a request, but dwelt in the palaces of his ancestors like some poor traveller who has been taken in and housed for the love of God. When he had any business to transact with Ridolfo, he waited in the antechamber with the rest for his turn, permitting no one to inform the marchese that he was there. At his brother's table, it is true, he suffered himself to be waited on like others, but when with his mother, who had no desire but to content him, he was able to gratify his love of simplicity and have his own way in certain little things, such as having his beverage set upon the table by him, thus getting rid of the attendance of the butler with his wine-cup. Donna Marta, however, with that maternal tenderness which can never be altogether repressed, could not refrain from offering him sometimes of this or that dish: "Have some of this, Padre Aluigi; I think this is good, or this is better." To one whose daily bread was mortification, the good and the better was small recommendation, but he wished to please his mother, and so he took what she pressed upon him and thanked her sweetly; yet it was remarked that, in fact, he did not eat it. These dinners were a severe penance, and he used to say to his companion, "O how well was it with us in our house, and how much more sustenance did I find in one of our poor dishes than in all the meats which are set upon these tables!"

His determination to accept as little as possible from the world in which he was sojourning was exemplified when, winter approaching before he left Castiglione, he and the brother found themselves unprovided with anything but the summer clothing they had brought; declining all the offers of his family, he wrote to his superiors, who sent him and his companion some warmer apparel, which, however, had seen considerable service, for Aloysius would have no other. The marchese made two Mantua shirts, one for her son, the other for the lay brother, and this gift also he would have refused, but for Brother Giacomo, who made his appearance early one morning with the rejected vestment in his hand, and said, "Take this, for it is an alms your mother bestows upon you for the love of God." Aloysius still objecting, the brother waxed bold, and exerted the authority which had been delegated to him in matters affecting health: "You need it," he said, "I desire you to take it;" and so, without further ceremony, he began to put it over Aloysius's head, who at this mention of alms and the appeal to obedience meekly acquiesced.

He sought solitude as far as was compatible with circumstances, but with his mother, who, as we have seen, was a person of high spirituality, he was always willing to converse, and to afford her all the consolation in his power. Besides performing punctually his regular devotions—and how large a portion of time these must have occupied we already know—he would be on the watch to snatch stray moments for prayer, as some schoolboy, tired of his books, might steal opportunities for play, and would say to his companion, "Brother, let us go and have a little prayer." At the close of the day he had three good hours of meditation in retirement, followed by the litanies and examination of conscience, before lying down to rest. Good and pious as was Brother Giacomo, he could not always keep pace with Aloysius's avidity for spiritual discourse. The business in hand obliged Aloysius to make several journeys to Brescia, Mantua, and other places, and on the road he would begin to converse at great length on divine things. His companion after awhile, desiring a little change, would try to start a fresh topic, but all in vain: there was no getting Aloysius to attend to anything else. With this exception, Brother Giacomo had nothing to record but the most undeviating attention to his every wish: never did our saint say a quick word to him, never did he complain of or object to aught that he did or did not do; nay, even in conversation he deferred to the brother's opinion, accommodating himself in all things to one who was in situation his inferior, as also by appointment his attendant. In matters of health he obeyed him as his superior. And well indeed, it was that some one was intrusted with that charge, for Aloysius simply took no notice whatever of his body and its requirements.

Amongst his other journeys was one to Castel Goffredo, which belonged to Alfonso Gonzaga, our saint's uncle, with whom it was desirable he should negotiate, and who had reasons of his own for not feeling wholly satisfied with Ridolfo at this moment. There was the usual attempt made at starting to press attendants upon Aloysius. Unable to oppose Ridolfo in his presence, he allowed the servants to follow the carriage, but when he was fairly outside the city walls he sent them all back, and pursued his journey without an escort. On the road the coachman lost his way, and so they wandered about and did not reach Castel Goffredo till two o'clock in the morning. Of course they found the drawbridge up and the gates of the fortress closed; nor at that undue hour was it easy to get them opened. It was necessary to explain who they were, and what was their errand, before the sentinel would take even the preliminary step of sending a message to the count. At last, after long delay the great gates swung round on their hinges, the drawbridge sank, and at the same moment a blaze of red light streamed forth into the outer gloom. Then sallied out a number of gentlemen bearing torches, to escort Aloysius into the place; within, a file of soldiers lined the way on either hand from the gate to the palace. It had taken time, of course, for this guard of honour to accoutre itself, all the men being in their beds when summoned to service. Patiently would Aloysius have waited all night long at the gate, but so pompous a reception was a considerable trial to his equanimity. On the threshold of the palace his noble uncle met him with demonstrations of the most marked affection and respect; and at once conducting him to his apartments, left him to take the repose he so much needed. But what apartments!—rooms luxuriously furnished and regally adorned; couches whose splendour made them resemble thrones rather than beds.

"O my brother!" exclaimed poor Aloysius, after casting a look of consternation at the magnificence which surrounded them, "God be our help this night, for what a place for our sins have we got into! See these rooms, see these beds! O how much better should we be lodged in the naked chambers of our house and on our poor pallets, than amidst all these honours and luxuries." And it seemed like an age to him, albeit but a few hours, till he could dispatch his business and get off.

Having made himself thoroughly conversant with all particulars relating to the affair in hand, he now proceeded to Mantua to treat with the duke. From a letter to his mother, which has been preserved, it appears that he did not immediately obtain an audience, his Highness being apparently much engaged. He tells her that he is adopting all the measures which prudence appeared to suggest, having engaged Fabio di Gonzaga, the duke's nephew, and Prospero di Gonzaga, his cousin, to interest themselves in forwarding the affair; adding, however, that he did not like to be too urgent with them for fear he should have seculars recommending patience to him, which he ought rather to preach to them.

But while he did not neglect to secure the influence of worldly friends, Aloysius was seeking aid in a more powerful quarter. One may say, indeed, that the business was already concluded with the King of Heaven, before our saint had his interview with the earthly potentate with whom the matter, humanly speaking, rested. The delay seemed to be providentially ordained that this holy youth might embalm another house of the Company with the fragrance of his virtues. The fathers thought they saw in Aloysius a living image of the great St. Charles Borromeo, and even traced some personal resemblance to the great archbishop in his features. The venerable rector of the college of Mantua, P. Prospero Malacotta, who had been received into the Company by St. Ignatius himself, so exceedingly admired the matured sanctity which shone in every word and look of Aloysius, that he bade him one Friday deliver an exhortation to the fathers of the college, an office which none but priests were ever selected to fill, and that, too, generally superiors of the order, or grave veterans from the sacerdotal ranks. Obedience made all things possible to Aloysius, and softened the pain which his humility endured from having to make so public a display. He took for his subject fraternal charity, choosing as his text, "*Hoc est præceptum meum, ut diligatis invicem, sicut dilexi vos.*" * It was as if a seraph had come down to discourse of the love which is the element he breathes, and in which he dwells. All departed deeply edified and full of consolation

When we consider that the duke Vincenzo was much irritated against Ridolfo, and that the quarrel had continued long enough to acquire all those complications which seem to render the task of reconciliation well-nigh hopeless, each fresh cause of offence, real or supposed, raising an additional obstacle to mutual concession and forgiveness; when, too, we remember how strongly pride and self-love become interested on such occasions, we may well marvel that

* "This is my commandment, that you love one another, as I have loved you."—John, xv, 12.

an hour and a half's conversation with Aloysius, the brother of his opponent, and, as such, liable to the suspicion of partiality, should have completely pacified Vincenzo, and obtained from him what he had refused to kings and potentates no less than to his nearest relatives and dearest friends. Vincenzo, it is true, loved Aloysius, but that alone could not have sufficed where others equally or more beloved, not to speak of those whose position conferred on them a high title to consideration, had signally failed. It was the duke's conviction of Aloysius's pure and holy intention, his reliance on his goodness and rectitude, which gave him a power to move which no one else possessed; and then there was the look, the voice, and the inexplicable charm which hangs about a saint! Have we not said, too, the matter was concluded before they met? Aloysius had prayed: that was sufficient. Vincenzo could refuse him nothing. He granted all; he restored Solferino, he renounced his claim, and, more than this, he gave back the heart of fraternal affection so long withheld from his cousin. Aloysius however, obtained, in writing, from the duke's secretary, all the grounds of complaint and offence which had been alleged against Ridolfo; and after engaging that his brother should justify himself and give satisfactory answers to his Highness on all these points, he hastened back to Castiglione.

There were not wanting those who endeavoured to hinder the reconciliation now in such fair progress, or at least to retard it; one important personage in particular, whose name Cepari does not give, suggesting that since his Highness had made up his mind, it would be as well not to appear to yield solely to

Aloysius's representations, but to let some little time elapse, that the nobles and princes who had previously negotiated with him might have the satisfaction of believing that they had some share in determining his decision. But the duke replied that he would dispatch the matter at once, because what he was doing was wholly and entirely to please Padre Aluigi, and no other motive would ever have induced him to give way. Men marvelled, but held their peace. Aloysius speedily returned from Castiglione with the desired explanations. with which the duke of Mantua expressed himself fully satisfied. Immediately the angel of peace hastened back to fetch Ridolfo, who was affectionately received by his noble cousin, and the two rivals dined and spent the day together as if nothing had ever disturbed their amity. Vincenzo would fain have induced Aloysius to be of the party, but he was not to be persuaded. Turning to the marchese, the duke then said that he must at least prevail on his brother to be present at the little play which was to be acted in their presence, but Aloysius, smiling, observed that his companion would not agree to that; aud so having accomplished his work, he returned to the Company's house. Our saint had yet, however, one affair at heart, which he must arrange ere he retraced his steps to his much longed-for home.

CHAPTER VI.

Aloysius's Conduct in the Affair of his Brother's Marriage.

It will be remembered that the fief of Alfonso Gonzaga was to revert, at the death of its possessor, to the marquisate, in the event of his leaving no son; in order therefore to secure the succession to his only child, a daughter, it had been agreed between the brothers that she should marry the heir of Castiglione. When Aloysius resigned his inheritance, it was expected that Ridolfo would fulfil this family arrangement; but hitherto the young marquis had given no signs of any such intention, though neither, on the other hand, had he ostensibly withdrawn his consent. Anyhow, his uncle Alfonso reckoned, or affected to reckon, upon his acquiescence; and as his daughter was now grown up, he designed applying to Rome for the needful dispensations. Meanwhile Ridolfo's backwardness in no way surprised such as were acquainted with the situation in which he was placed, a situation which was the source of much pain to all who were interested in his soul's welfare, or who had the honour of the house of Gonzaga at heart. The marchese had become deeply enamoured with a young lady of Castiglione, named Elena Aliprandi, only daughter of his director of the bank. Beauty, merit, and money were none of them wanting to make her a fitting partner for Ridolfo, but by birth she did not belong to the high nobility of the land. The family of Aliprandi possessed, it is true, senatorial rank at Mantua, and a fief dependent upon Castiglione; but to one who owed homage to the Empire alone, it was derogatory to seek union with any save the great families of his own class. It does not seem, however, that this disadvantage in the world's eyes would have weighed with Ridolfo; but the engagement by which he was hampered, and his fear of rousing his uncle's wrath if he espoused any one except his cousin Caterina, deterred him from taking Elena openly to wife. They had accordingly been privately married the previous year, in presence of the archpriest of Castiglione, who had received the necessary faculties from the bishop, and with the proper witnesses;* but so strictly had the secret been kept by the few who were acquainted with the fact, that even Donna Marta was entirely ignorant of what had taken place, and Alfonso of course equally so. The secrecy, however, with which the marriage was shrouded could not altogether conceal the connection which subsisted, and which the unhappy mother consequently believed to be of an unlawful character. Hitherto she had been spared anxiety of this afflicting character; and indeed, whatever may have been his faults, neither levity nor irregularity of conduct seems to have been chargeable on Ridolfo, who is described as a man of good morals and grave manners, although inordinately fond of sports, games, and martial exercises. Yet the

* Cepari is particular in stating that the *parochus* and witnesses were present, in order to show that the marriage, although secret, was not *clandestine*, in the ecclesiastical sense of the term; clandestine marriages (which had been previously *illicit*) having been pronounced *invalid* by the Council of Trent —provided that its decree had been published in the parish where the marriage took place.

evidence against him seemed too clearly condemnatory for even his mother to believe him innocent. Many tears had she shed and many prayers poured forth before God for her erring son, and the subject had doubtless been one of frequent and sorrowful discourse with Aloysius. To him she now looked with confident hope: even as he had succeeded in moving Vincenzo to sentiments of charity and peace, so, also, with God's blessing, which attended all he undertook, would he win his brother back to the paths of virtue.

Aloysius had several times entered upon the subject with Ridolfo, and had earnestly exhorted him to break off this connection and content the whole family by agreeing to the proposed marriage. But the marchese, unwilling to tell the whole truth, and reveal what he believed his interest required him to conceal, evaded the subject, and put off his brother with fair words. At last, as the time of his departure drew nigh, Aloysius redoubled his instances, and pressed Ridolfo so urgently that he passed his word and even solemnly swore that he would give him satisfaction. Yet he entered into no explanation, but deferred the disclosure to a future time; nay, he took leave of Aloysius and allowed him to set out without the slightest intimation of the truth; promising, however, to see him at Milan, and renewing his assurance that he would faithfully abide by his counsels.

To Milan, accordingly, by the direction of his superiors, Aloysius proceeded on the 25th of November, 1589, and here he remained during the winter. He had to wait some time for his brother's promised visit. It was on a feast day towards the end of January of the ensuing year, when, our saint having communicated and being engaged in offering his thanksgiving in the choir, the porter came to tell him that the most excellent Signor Marchese, his brother, was at the door desiring to see him. Aloysius heard but did not stir; he had received the King of Heaven, and was entertaining Him in his soul; and so Ridolfo had to wait two hours while the saint continued immovable at his devotions. When the brothers met, after the first greetings were over, Ridolfo acquainted him in confidence with his marriage with Elena Aliprandi, which, although it had taken place fifteen months, he feared to acknowledge on account of his uncle Alfonso. But Aloysius, to whom there was but one evil or misfortune in the world, when he learned that his brother was not living in sin, and had moreover the fear of offending God before his eyes, returned thanks to Heaven, and rejoiced exceedingly. To him embarrassments, difficulties, family complications, were as nothing compared with what he had had cause to apprehend; but as regarded the secresy enjoined on him, he replied that he could only observe it so far as conscience permitted; he would write to Rome, and would also consult some of the fathers at Milan. These religious concurred with Aloysius in holding that Ridolfo was bound in conscience to declare his marriage, on account of the scandal given to the world by its concealment, and the injury it inflicted on the lady's reputation. Ridolfo consented, and Aloysius on his part engaged to pacify the relatives. Some little delay, however, appears to have occurred; Ridolfo, like most men who have got themselves into an awkward position, and have to face what is unpleasant, being disposed to find reasons for procrastination. He wished to put off the declaration of his marriage till after his return from Germany, whither he was about to repair, probably to thank the Emperor for his decision in the affair of Solferino. The following admirable letter, written by Aloysius to his brother, will throw sufficient light upon what passed on this occasion:—

"Illustrious Signor, and most honoured brother in Christ,—Pax Christi.

"I thank your lordship for the messenger you have sent me, to whom I fully explained all that, according to the judgment and opinion of competent persons, and, amongst them, the same you consulted when in Milan, I feel, *in Domino* (in the Lord), you are in conscience obliged to do under pain of mortal sin. I have therefore nothing to add to your lordship, save to beseech, nay, supplicate you, for the love of God, and by the bowels of Jesus Christ and of the Blessed Virgin, not to defraud me of the expectation I have hitherto entertained, and which on oath you promised to fulfil; namely, to put in execution one or other of the two plans I laid before the archpriest. If you will do this, then shall I rejoice that I have a brother in Christ, whom, as I have ever desired to aid and serve him, so henceforward shall I never cease to aid and serve, desiring that I may have the opportunity of exposing even life itself for your soul's welfare. It was this desire which prompted me to leave Rome, and to come and spend the winter in Lombardy, to the detriment of my studies; but all seems little to me so as (I may win to Christ thee, a brother most dear to me in Him) *acquiram Christo te fratrem in Illo carissimum*. If I do not obtain this, then as a brother only (according to the flesh) *secundum carnem*, I neither know nor wish to know you, having died to you as such more than four years ago; and, indeed, I should feel that I ought to take great shame to myself if, after having renounced every other thing, and even myself, for the love of Christ, I should now, for the sake of carnal affection (be ashamed of Him) *erubescerem Christum*, and seem blind to the offence committed against him: for the same Christ has said, " *Vade et corripe fratrem tuum; si te audierit, lucratus es fratrem tuum; sin minus, sit tibi tanquam ethnicus et publicanus.** Such is my intention; however, I will wait twelve days, counting from to-morrow, for an answer, and if it be conformable to your duty, to the fulfilment of which the example of the duke of Mantua and of your uncle Signor Alfonso ought to be sufficient to excite you, not to speak of some service received from me, but principally your obligation to the Ever Blessed God—if, as I say, you shall act thus, then shall I return consoled to Rome; but if you shall deal otherwise with God and with me, I will conclude the business in the manner I told the archpriest, and deploring my bad success with you, will leave it to God to remedy the evil with His holy and powerful Hand. But again I entreat your lordship to give heed to this, because everywhere you will find God, whether awaiting repentance or punishing the offences committed against Himself, as also against those who desire to serve Him. Wherefore do not fail in your duty, do not fail, *et iterum* (again) I repeat, do not fail; and I warn you that I say it three times, in order that you

* Matt. xviii, 15, 17.

may be assured that if you fail you will repent it. In the meantime I shall pray the Lord to dispose your heart, and grant you in the end that happiness and abundance of grace which with all my heart and affection I wish you.—From Milan, the 6th of February, 1590.

"Your illustrious lordship's most affectionate brother in the Lord,

"ALUIGI GONZAGA, of the Company of Jesus."

It would appear that Aloysius had set before his brother the alternative of either declaring his marriage or removing Elena at once from his palace, where she occupied some private apartments. In a letter dated three days later, he seems to have so far relaxed, as not to insist upon her being sent away before the journey to the Imperial court which Ridolfo said he was on the point of undertaking, allowing him to defer the public disclosure of his marriage until his return. He still, however, suggested that the holier course would be to make this declaration at once. The postscript of this letter, in which he reiterates part of what he had just said, reveals all his tender solicitude for his brother's spiritual welfare. "We must absolutely be friends," he says, "(*Io voglio in ogni modo che siamo amici*) and that (in the Lord) *in Domino;* wherefore from Him I must obtain the strength to gain my point, even at the expense of exercising a kind of religious violence." We know well what those means were by which he was used to take Heaven by storm and get all he wished; who could resist the moving exhortations and touching entreaties of the saint, not to speak of the inward pleadings of grace which were the fruit of his prayers? Ridolfo yielded, and granted all his brother asked; and Aloysius, on his part, performed all he had engaged. He now repaired again to Castiglione accompanied by a Jesuit father, to whom he said that the first time he had gone there it was to settle the affairs of the world, the second time, the affairs of God. He had already prevailed on Ridolfo to make known his marriage to Donna Marta, and beg her to receive Elena as his wife and treat her as her daughter-in-law. This preliminary step having been accomplished, Aloysius undertook himself to make the necessary declaration to the people. He then lost no time in writing to the different members of the Gonzaga family; and so powerful was the gentle influence he exercised over his kindred, that he received satisfactory answers from all, and even the aggrieved uncle was reconciled to a union which disappointed all his hopes. The good effect of Aloysius's interposition did not end here, for many who had probably been encouraged in a life of sin through the scandal given by their young lord, were induced to make amends for the past, and enter into the bonds of Christian matrimony. Donna Marta was desirous that her son should not depart without preaching a sermon in the church; and after taking counsel with his companion he agreed to comply with her request. But to avoid that publicity which he so much deprecated, he delivered his discourse, not at S. Nazario, but in a neighbouring church known as that of the Company of Discipline, and would not even allow the bell to be rung to summon a congregation. Notwithstanding, however, all his precautions he found the church full to overflowing. It was the eve of Quinquagesima Sunday, and he took occasion to invite all present to come and receive their Lord the following morning. So earnest and persuasive was the invitation, and so fervently was it accepted, that the priests and religious were kept all night hearing confessions, as if it had been the eve of a great jubilee. And a jubilee, indeed, it was of reconciliation and holy love and family joy in Castiglione. Donna Marta, the happy mother of a saint and of a son newly reconciled to God, Ridolfo himself and his wife Elena, with seven hundred other persons, together partook of the heavenly banquet; Aloysius served the mass and gave the ablution to the communicants; and after dinner they all went to the Christian doctrine. To the other successful results of his mission of peace, we must add that during the course of his stay at Castiglione he composed many differences, some of an embittered character and long standing.

Aloysius had now finished his work, and like another Raphael, the world could retain him no longer. Accordingly, after exhorting Ridolfo to behave well to his wife, he took leave of his family, never on earth to behold them again, and on the 12th of March set out for Milan, having on the 9th of that month completed his twenty-second year. He passed through Piacenza, where, it is related, one of the fathers having gone to his room to welcome and embrace him as soon as he reached the college, and finding him with a brush in his hand cleaning his shoes, was moved to much devotion, both from the angelic holiness of his aspect, and from the sight of his humble employment; remembering how in former days he had seen him at Parma attended by a princely retinue of servants. When Aloysius at last found himself within the walls of the college of the Company at Milan, great was his joy, for now he had finally closed with the world and shut the door upon it; the last time he was at Milan it was not so, for he still had about him a chain which was to drag him back within its circle. "O what consolation do I feel," he exclaimed, "at beholding myself at last restored to our house! I feel like one who, cold and frozen in mid-winter, finds himself laid in a downy, warm bed: even such was the cold from which I suffered when away from our houses, and such is the comfort I experience on finding myself once more within them." This was the only warmth he coveted, this the only cold from which he shrank. To the bitter chill of the Lombard winter he seemed insensible, as usual refusing alike precautions and alleviations.

After his arrival at Milan, he wrote the following letter to his brother:—

"Illustrious lord, and most honoured brother in Christ.

"The desire I have ever had for the spiritual welfare of your lordship, and the consolation you have lately afforded me at Castiglione, moves me in this letter to suggest to you, according as the Lord shall inspire me, what in the same Lord appears to me most useful and expedient for the security and preservation of your soul's well-being; and that is, that, before your departure for Germany, you should, during what remains of this season of Lent, prepare yourself for making a general confession at Easter, or, at least, a confession which shall include the time elapsed since the one I know you made at Mantua five years ago, because you will thus render certain, as far as is possible in this present life, that none of the offences of which you have been guilty against the Divine Majesty—and which possibly you may have omitted in those furtive and private confessions which you made during the period when from human respect you did not dare to show yourself the servant of Christ—shall remain in you. And this I believe will be the more easy to you, because the difficulties which you have already surmounted no longer stand in the way, leaving only the fruit of hope and the sure pledge which the adoption of such a measure may be presumed to give of being in God's grace. I recommend this very strongly to your lordship.

"Then, as regards the preservation of this grace, although it is the Lord who has been pleased to move your heart, rather than my words and good offices, as also it is He who must instruct and guide you, nevertheless, to satisfy those claims of relationship which bind me to you, and to co-operate, as I have hitherto done, with the Providence of the same Lord, I propose to you two means in particular which occur to me.

"The one is to entertain within you such a high esteem and value for the grace of God, as all I might say to you could not in the smallest degree adequately express; neither is it possible for any one fully to make you comprehend it, save the Ever-Blessed God alone; to Him therefore I leave it to teach you this. I will only say that, inasmuch as God transcends all created things, honours, possessions, and all else whatever, so in the like measure ought our inward esteem of His Divine Majesty to surpass all other esteem or conception. But as the finite capacity of our heart does not admit of this, at least we ought to strive that the esteem in which we hold Him be the highest that is possible to us.

"The second means is to act conformably to this state of grace, '*Providendo bona non solum coram Deo, sed etiam corem hominibus.*'* As regards our Blessed God, I will here remind you of what by word of mouth I recommended to you concerning His worship and service. And since the recommending of the virtue of religion, which we owe to God, seems peculiarly to belong to religious, I will descend to some particulars, which you can put in practice according to the measure of grace which the Lord shall deign to communicate to you. Amongst these, one is that you should commend yourself to the Lord every morning, making use of the 'Daily Exercise,' or other such-like prayers, during which you might meditate on some of the points which you may find in the 'Daily Exercise' at the end of the little work I send you, which was compiled by the direction of Monsignor the Cardinal Borromeo, of happy memory; and as your lordship will there meet with suggestions which you can yourself read, I will not enlarge on this subject any further; only I would remind you besides to hear mass, according to the agreement between us.

"Moreover, I would not have you lie down to rest at night before examining yourself as whether you have offended God, so that if you should have any mortal sin on your conscience—from which may the

* "Providing good things, not only in the sight of God, but also in the sight of men."—*Rom.* XII. 17

Lord preserve you!—you may as soon as possible efface it by means of penance; bearing in mind that this is always needful whenever you have anything to repent of, and never waiting for a specific time, such as Easter or some other season; for no one can assure you of being then alive.

"Next, as regards providing good things before men, I recommend to your observance the respect which you owe to your relatives and lords, upon which point I shall say nothing, as presuming how much you have this at heart; only, from my own personal obligation, and not from any idea that you need to be reminded thereof, I recommend to you the reverence you owe to the Signora Marchesa, your mother, as being your mother, and such a mother.

"Moreover, as the head of your brethren, you know how much it behoves you, both to have them united to you, and so to behave towards them as to endear this union to them. As for your vassals, I will simply observe that God has perhaps given them into your charge in a special and peculiar manner, only in order to signify to you the special and spiritual care which you ought to have of them, recognizing in the Providence of God towards yourself a pattern of the manner in which you ought to provide for them.

"For the rest, I commit it to God to instruct and guide you to our blessed country; to the which that I may attain with you and others, I have embraced my present state of life. In the meantime, for the confession I spoke of at the beginning, I propose to you for your spiritual father some one of our Company, who, from the obligations of our institute, are commonly well versed in these matters. If you went to Mantua, I should strongly recommend to you P. Mattia for this office. He was confessor to the duke Guglielmo of worthy memory. But should you not leave Castiglione, I have already spoken to the father rector of Brescia, who places himself and his college at the service of your lordship, and who will speedily provide you with a confessor whenever you ask for one.

"Herewith I conclude; and as the execution of what I have recommended to you must be the work of Divine grace more than of your own efforts and my exhortations, I offer and promise ever to recommend you in my prayers, such as they are, to His Divine Majesty; and may He preserve and guide you to that happy end to which His elect shall attain.—From Milan, March 17, 1590.

"Your illustrious lordship's brother in the Lord,

"ALUIGI GONZAGA, of the Company of Jesus."

This letter may be regarded as a model of advice to a man of the world. As perfect as he is, Aloysius, with the true discretion of a saint, refrains from asking too much of his imperfect and worldly brother. Yet he never lowers the standard of holiness; he does not set before Ridolfo an accommodated Christianity; true, he presents only a sketch of Christian life and duty, the filling-in of the picture is necessarily omitted; but there is neither curtailment nor reduction.

The College of Milan, known as Santa Maria di Brera, possessed at that time a lay-brother of consummate virtue, Fr. Agostino Salombrini; Aloysius was not slow to discover his merits, and an illness, the consequence of his late fatigues, in which Fr. Agostino tended him as infirmarian, gave him special personal experience of his angelic charity. They held long discourses together on the things of God, animating each other to join in the Divine praises, after the pattern of the seraphim whom Isaias saw in vision throwing one to the other, like so many fire-brands of love, lauds and benedictions to the Ever-Blessed Triune God. Aloysius so highly esteemed this holy brother, that he consulted him in all the difficult matters he had in hand during his sojourn at Milan, and by permission of superiors was accompanied by him on several of his journeys; he even begged to be allowed to take him to Rome when he returned, and to this request, although reluctantly, they acceded. No one could resist Aloysius.

CHAPTER VII.

Aloysius's Life at the College of Brera, and Return to Rome.

To speak of Aloysius's life at Milan, and of the edification he gave, is almost to repeat in another form what has been already described. He seemed more than ever insatiable of mortifications, as though to make amends for the late compulsory relaxations which intercourse with the world had imposed upon him; relaxations, if such they could be called, which were to him more trying than the most rigid austerities. He pursued his theological studies assiduously with the other scholars, as usual shunning all distinction, refusing exemptions, courting poverty and humiliation in every form, and, whenever he could economize an hour from his studies, hastening to his favourite avocation of helping in refectory or kitchen. It was one of his pious fancies to give names to the different tables. Thus the superiors' was the table of our Lord; the nearest to it, the table of the Madonna; and so, in a graduated scale, followed those of apostles, martyrs, confessors, and virgins. When engaged in preparing for the repast he would say, "Let us go and lay the cloth for our Lord or for the Madonna,"—imagining to himself that he was actually waiting upon Jesus and His Blessed Mother; and all this in order to maintain in his commonest actions a more perfect and fervent union with God, and to acquit himself of them with greater merit. We must not forget to notice amongst his favourite employments that of diligently removing cobwebs, to which allusion was before made. Even this humble work he desired to make an occasion of extra humiliation; no sooner did his eye, which could be quick enough in discerning opportunities of mortification, catch a glimpse of some senator or person of distinction entering the cloisters, than immediately he was out with his broom, delighted to be taken, though but for a few moments, for one of low condition and of small account. So thoroughly were the fathers of the college aware of this device, that when they saw Aloysius emerge with his broom, it was a sure sign to them that there was a stranger of some importance in the house.

Here, as elsewhere, the lay-brothers were his chosen companions; not only from motives of humility, but on account of the greater liberty he could allow himself in conversing on the things of God, coupled with his longing desire to impart spiritual aid to others. The exquisite delicacy of his charity and lowliness exhibited itself continually in all these little passing incidents and slight occurrences which are the touchstones of sanctity. For just as genuine courtesy is shown in the considerate fulfilment of the minor civilities of life, so it is with that true civilization, the refinement of the heart, which grace only can effect; it is the trifles, the minutiæ, which test and prove it. If he found himself among a group of persons standing engaged in conversation, he would step behind, and remain a listener; but if the party were seated he would be sure to secure himself the last or most uncomfortable place. The same deference to others, the same eclipsing of self, was always observed in him; his preference of others being evidently neither a deliberate compliment nor a formal ceremonious act, but proceeding from a genuine sentiment of humility, the acts of which had become, so to say, instinctive with him. His gratitude, on the other hand, to others for the least service done him was manifested with the most unaffected cordiality. He seemed as if he could not be thankful enough.

How completely he kept himself separate as much as possible from all worldly affairs, even while of necessity brought into contact with them, the following little incident will show. One day, as he was on his way to the church of S. Fidele, he heard himself accosted as "Your Excellency," and was approached with demonstrations of profound reverence by an individual whom he recognized as a vassal of the house of Castiglione. The man had come with the hope of obtaining the redress of certain grievances through the influence of Aloysius. But the humble religious, although at the command of superiors he had undertaken to mediate between the divided members of his family, in all other things followed the pattern of his Lord, who, though God over all, refused during His earthly ministry to accede to the prayer of one who said, "Speak to my brother, that he share his inheritance with me" Returning the applicant's salutation with modest lowliness, and uncovering his head, he replied, "I am no longer anything but Aloysius of the Company of Jesus, and can only help you by praying to God for you, and advising you to go and state your grievance to my brother." He said these few words with such simplicity that his petitioner left him edified, if not satisfied, at the manner in which his request had been refused.

A few sayings of our saint during his sojourn at Milan have been recorded. P. Cosimo Alamanni, one of the fathers of the college, sought our young saint one day, sorely troubled in mind at the thought of his own imperfections, and begging for spiritual counsel. Aloysius for his consolation quoted those words of David, "*Imperfectum meum viderunt oculi tui, et in libro tuo omnia scribentur*,"* giving them one of those manifold applications of which Holy Scripture, and the Psalms especially, are susceptible, and which prayer and meditation render familiar to the contemplative soul. He said that although our imperfections be a

* "Thy eyes did see my imperfect being, and in Thy book all shall be written."—*Ps.* CXXXVIII. 16.

great cause of sorrow to us, yet we ought to draw much consolation from reflecting that, imperfect as we are, we are written in God's book, who beholds our imperfections, not to condemn us, but that He may humble us, and that we may derive the greater good from them. With such devotion did he develop this practical interpretation of the passage as greatly to cheer the father's depressed spirit. Having obtained by earnest entreaty leave to accompany one of the brothers who, being on the point of making his vows, was sent to beg alms about the city, a mortification customary on these occasions in the Company, such was the exuberance of his joy, that ever and anon he broke forth in these words, "Christ our Lord also went about thus begging alms, particularly during the three days when He was absent from His Mother." Another day, being similarly employed, he was accosted by a lady showily dressed, who inquired if he belonged to Santa Maria di Brera, for that she had an acquaintance among the fathers there, at the same time mentioning his name. Having received a reply in the affirmative, she added, "Miserable man! and whither has he gone to die?" "That father," replied Aloysius with holy animation, "is blessed, not miserable; he is not dead, as you say, but lives a life of perfection; it is you that are miserable, living in the world, and in danger of eternal death, given up to vanity, as your appearance bespeaks." With such power of divine grace were these words accompanied, that they moved the heart of this worldly creature to compunction, as her subsequent life testified.

Aloysius would volunteer to go and teach Christian doctrine in the streets on Sundays and holidays, and this notwithstanding the bitter cold, from which he always suffered extremely. So, too, he would beg to accompany the scholars sent to preach in Carnival time in the open places of the city, and would himself take the humble office of collecting an audience for them; the modesty and charity with which he solicited those he met, making him, it was observed, singularly successful. Sometimes, however, offices would be committed to him not so consonant with his inclinations; for instance, when he was ordered by the superior to preach in the refectory before certain bishops and prelates. Perfect obedience never admits of excuses; and so he submitted, and delivered a discourse, both learned and impressive, upon the office of a bishop. When congratulated afterwards on his success, he playfully observed that he was not aware of having had any other gratification that morning except that of displaying in public the impediment in his speech; alluding to his imperfect articulation of the letter *r*. He resumed at Milan the practice of asking for public reprehension, which he had discontinued at Rome, because he found that he obtained praise where he sought blame. Here he was more successful, at least on one occasion. Owing to his continual absorption in God, it would sometimes happen that he did not observe when others saluted him. He was charged with this fault; upon which he humbly accused himself of pride, and was ever afterwards most exact in this particular, putting a constraint upon himself in public, so as not to allow his union with God to hinder him from fulfilling the obligation of courtesy to man.

P. Bernardino Medici, a Florentine father, who

had lived on terms of much intimacy with Aloysius while at Milan, writing to P. Cepari after the saint's death, notices the special estimation in which he held perseverance in little things. This constancy he considered as essential to progress in virtue; accordingly, he always followed the same order in his daily actions, performing them at their appointed hours. He feared nothing so much as acting through affection or inclination; the safe course, he said, was to be guided by light, by knowledge, and by reason. Where he sought this light we well know, as well as the abundance in which he received it; an abundance so great, that he said he seemed never to act up fully to what it manifested. This was because the light accompanied as well as preceded his acts; as he advanced, therefore, he always discovered something beyond upon which the illuminating ray fell. But if he did not satisfy himself, others, at least, could perceive no shortcoming, and this same father affirmed that he had never seen him commit a wilful fault in the smallest thing, nor infringe the minutest rule. Yet, while thus distinguished in the practice of every virtue, it was remarkable that he did not appear singular in anything; "and this freedom from peculiarity," P. Bernardino adds, "I esteem in itself a great virtue."

Much as Aloysius endeavoured to conceal the favours which God lavished on his soul, they could not remain hidden, and it was rumoured in the college that he had a supereminent gift of prayer, and never suffered from the smallest distraction. P. Achille Gagliardi, a father of much learning and authority, with whom we have already made acquaintance, when called upon to test Aloysius's vocation, being desirous to ascertain whether there were any exaggeration in these reports, engaged him one day in conversation on the subject of mystical theology discoursing of the union of the soul with God by perfect charity. The result was the discovery that this saintly youth had a deep experimental knowledge of the unitive way, being privileged to enter daily into that cloud of divine obscurity, of which Dionysius the Areopagite speaks, and which was typified by the thick darkness on the top of Sinai, shrouding the presence of the God who is Light Ineffable, into which Moses entered. P. Gagliardi described himself as quite astounded at the heights of grace and perfection of consummate virtue to which one who was barely four years old in the religious life had already attained. Finding him so perfect a contemplative, the father marvelled if he experienced any difficulty or repugnance in general intercourse with others, as finding it to withdraw him from his sweet repose in God. To try him, he proposed, as a difficulty, whether he had not cause to regard with suspicion exercises which must needs have this effect, and as such appeared to be contrary to the spirit of the Company and to one of the main objects of its institution. Aloysius replied, "If I recognized in myself the effects your Reverence describes, I should regard this way with suspicion, and hold it as not good for me;" from which answer the father concluded that Aloysius possessed the high and rare gift of uniting the contemplative and active lives without prejudice to either.

Our saint was ripe for glory, but God would not call him to Himself without warning. Little more than a year before his blessed death, while engaged in his morning meditation, and rapt in sublime contemplation, he received a supernatural intimation that his days on earth would be short. The same interior voice which made this communication to him, bade him apply himself to the service of God, during the time that remained, with still greater perfection and detachment of spirit. This inward illumination seemed to transform him into another person. The room in which he received this revelation—if room it could be called—was a little dark chamber in a remote part of the house, formed by the vacant space under a wooden staircase, up and down which the servants were continually passing. Not that this receptacle, which was a fitter abode for rats and mice than for a human being, had been allotted to Aloysius on his arrival; the College of Brera had received him as an angel of God, and, in consideration of his delicate health, had assigned him a room to himself; but, soon perceiving that the other young men, not priests, did not enjoy this advantage, he requested the superior so earnestly to allow him to occupy these dingy quarters under the stairs, that he obtained his wish. The father who related this circumstance said that, even as on the Aventine at Rome the receptacle under a staircase, inhabited by the pilgrim Alexius when he lived unknown in the house of his parents, became afterwards glorious and honourable, so also was it with the little lumber-room in which Aloysius had lived and prayed while at the house of Brera. It was soon after converted into a chapel, and, as a memorial of the revelation which the saint had received of his approaching death, an angel was depicted presenting to him a skull.

Aloysius did not acquaint any one at the time with the divine communication that had been made to him, except P. Vincenzo Bruno, though after his return to Rome he disclosed it to a chosen few. He continued his theological studies with the same assiduity, but he could no longer feel the same interest in them, or the same affection for them, his heart being continually drawn to the pure and exclusive love of God. If he had an earthly desire, it was to return to Rome. "*Si nobis est patria super terram*," he said in a letter to a co-novice when about to leave Milan, "(if we have a country on earth) I know none other than Rome; *ubi genitus sum in Christo Jesu* (where I was begotten in Christ Jesus)." There it was that he had taken his first steps in the religious life; there also he had many friends and companions, dear to him in the bonds of spiritual affection; and there, too, were his much-loved patients whom he had left in the infirmary, particularly two sick old fathers, P. Corbinelli and P. Pedro Parra, a Spaniard, who had lost the use of his hands, and whom Aloysius used to delight in feeding, putting bread into his mouth like a tender nurse. Everywhere, indeed, was Aloysius noted for this attraction to the sick, which is the exclusive mark of gentle and loving hearts. It extended to the sick in heart and mind, and he considered it a favour to be entrusted with the charge of those who were disposed to peevish impatience and fastidiousness.

Out of a love of holy indifference he did not manifest to any one his wish to return to Rome; and when the summons at last arrived, he feared that he had felt too much joy, and begged P. Bernardino Medici to offer mass with the intention, if it were for God's greater glory, that this desire of his should be mortified. P. Rossignoli, rector of the Roman College, was anxious for Aloysius's return, on account of the edification he gave to the other youths; the winter therefore now being past, and the business concluded for which he had left them, he begged the Father General to recall him from Milan. He set out in the beginning of the month of May of the year 1590, in company with several of the fathers. It was a year of great scarcity in Lombardy, and the roads were full of miserable starving people. "How great a blessing has God vouchsafed us, Brother Aluigi," said P. Gregorio to him one day, "that we have not been born to the lot of these poor creatures!" "A greater," he promptly replied, "that we were not born Turks." With our saint nothing was ever measured by a natural standard; with him there was no good but the love and favour of God, no evil save the deprivation of these treasures "*Quid ad æternitatem?*" was a frequent saying of the holy youth.

The fathers who accompanied Aloysius treated him with the greatest respect and care—too great indeed, as the saint considered, who, although he referred it all to their exceeding charity, would have preferred, as he afterwards told one of the Company in confidence, travelling with those who held him in no consideration. But where were these to be found? At Siena, his devotion was satisfied by hearing and serving mass and communicating in the very room which St. Catherine had inhabited. He was requested, while here, to preach to the youths of the Congregation of

Our Lady. His preparation was to go and pray before the Blessed Sacrament, then, retiring awhile to his own apartment, he made a few short notes of what had suggested itself to his mind, and delivered a discourse full, as might be expected, of that grace and persuasive unction to which human industry can never attain, and which fails to accompany the highest gifts of mere natural eloquence. That sermon proved the germ of religious vocation in the hearts of many who heard it. In the afternoon of this very day the party were once more on the road, and reached the inn of La Paglia, but on the morrow they found the stream which they must cross swollen prodigiously by a sudden storm of rain. The waters, unable to discharge themselves by the usual bed, had overflowed their bounds, and made for themselves fresh courses, along which they impetuously hurried. Several of these rushing streams were passed by the party, with much difficulty and peril, but they were brought to a stand on the banks of a broader and deeper branch of the torrent. "Father," said Aloysius, turning to P. Mastrilli, "don't let us cross here;" and, in fact, eighteen rash persons who attempted the ford at this spot were almost all of them drowned. As they stood upon the bank uncertain how to proceed, Aloysius remained absorbed in prayer, then, lifting up his eyes, he beheld at some little distance a youth passing from one side of the torrent to the other, calmly wading through the waters, like one who is fishing in a quiet stream. "*There* is the ford," said Aloysius, and all following him to the spot he indicated, they crossed with the greatest ease, their example being imitated by forty other persons. The experienced guide, to whom this ford was quite unknown, was amazed. But where was the mysterious pioneer? He had disappeared from view, and not a trace of him was visible. No one ever saw him again, which led P. Mastrilli to the conclusion that it was the saint's guardian angel who had pointed out the road, nay, indeed, had made one where none before existed.

Aloysius on his arrival at Rome said these significant words to P. Cepari: "I have buried my dead, and need think no more of them; it is time for us to prepare for another life." To all who knew him, and especially to those who were his companions during this last year of his mortal sojourn, that preparation seemed already accomplished. He appeared no longer to tread the earth; his existence might be compared to one long ecstasy, so entirely were his thoughts and affections transferred to Heaven. Very shortly after his return he handed over to the Father Rector all his spiritual and theological writings, and when the father asked him why he deprived himself of his compositions, he replied that it was because he felt some remaining affection for them, as though they were a portion of himself, being the product of his own mind; to nothing else in the world had he any attachment, and so he would rid himself of these, that he might sit loose to all things. Few, perhaps, however much disengaged in affection from the world, become altogether freed from that love of sympathy which is so strong in the human heart, and from a certain pleasure felt in receiving demonstrations of kindness and regard; but Aloysius loved not to be the object of special affectionate attention, or to be particularly considered by superiors; and of this they were so well aware that, to please him, they concealed the esteem in which they held him. Meanwhile his own most engaging sweetness and exceeding charity constantly more and more attracted hearts towards him, and at the same time towards God, who manifested Himself so wonderfully in His servant. For as he walked continually in the Divine presence, with his eve and ear intent upon God, so his whole countenance, his whole bearing, reflected the Eternal Light on which he was always gazing, while every word he uttered was an echo of the voice of the Beloved, to which he was ever hearkening. Every one could perceive how the fragile vessel was, so to say, filled to the brim with the love of God, so that it needed but the slightest allusion to what was ever glowing in his heart to make the burning stream overflow, raising such a commotion in his breast as to deprive him of the very power of speech. He would be thus affected during the spiritual reading in the refectory; his face would become all inflamed; he would cease eating, and remain fixed like one who is struck with a sudden illness, but the tears which bye and bye gently welled from his eyes, cast down with shame at the notice he excited, would reveal the nature of the malady from which he suffered. Fears were entertained by some that he might break a blood-vessel in his chest in one of these ecstatic seizures, so that, though there were persons who would purposely introduce the subject of God's love for man in order to witness the blush which was sure to crimson the youth's cheek, others, more considerate. would immediately turn the discourse to some other topic, dreading the effects on his delicate frame. His abstraction daily increased, and was now beyond his control. While pacing up and down the galleries and passages, as he was wont to do, engaged in saying the rosary or in other devotions, he plainly saw no one, as Cepari himself ascertained by often passing before him and saluting him. Nor did he so much as retain the consciousness that he *might* be seen, for occasionally he would kneel down for a considerable time, then rise and kneel again,—acts from which his desire to avoid singularity would otherwise have deterred him.

When, in November, 1590, he commenced his fourth year of theology, his superior obliged him to accept a room to himself; but Aloysius defeated the intention as respected his own accommodation, by obtaining, after earnest solicitation, a little garret at the top of a staircase, dark, low, and narrow, with a window in the roof. This wretched apartment, which was never used for the students, would barely hold his bed, a wooden chair, and a kneeling-stool which served him also as a writing-table; in short it resembled a prisoner's cell rather than a room. These qualifications were sufficient to make our saint esteem it a palace. "We used to joke with him about it," says Father Cepari, "and tell him that as St. Alexis chose to live in poverty under a staircase, so he had chosen to live in a similar miserable tenement at the top of one." We have seen him at Brera in the former situation. The united testimony of his brethren and fathers at this time establishes the consummate perfection to which Aloysius had attained. All eyes were upon him, and yet no one could detect in him the shadow of a venial sin. P. Vincenzo Cigala, who for two years shared his room at the Roman College, and lived on terms of the closest confidence with him, deposed upon oath that, each having been charged by the rector to watch the other, with a view to fraternal admonition, he never could discern any fault or negligence in Aloysius, great or small; while from the lips of the great Cardinal Bellarmine we learn that never did he hear his confession without feeling himself spiritually illuminated. What wonder if the admiration he inspired in those around him partook of the character of religious veneration? Nay, we are told of a certain father and preacher in whom this feeling was so strong, that he never could summon courage to converse with him, although he greatly desired it, and had frequent opportunities.

A presentiment of death is perhaps not uncommon, the shadow of the grave is said sometimes to fall upon those who are drawing near their end; with Aloysius, ripe for glory, it was no vague or dark impression which enshrouded his mind, it was the light of the Eternal Day which seemed to be beginning to irradiate his path. It was as if he had a sight of the everlasting hills; and a few months before his last illness a longing desire for his celestial country filled and ravished his soul. He often talked of death, and used to say that the longer he lived the more doubtful of his salvation he became; he dreaded the increasing charges and corresponding responsibilities of a more advanced age, and especially he looked with awe upon the sacerdotal office. Priests, he said, had to render a strict account to God for the manner in which they have recited office and offered mass; and heavier still were the obligations of those who heard confessions and had the care of souls, who preached and administered the sacraments. As yet he had no weighty affairs entrusted to him, so that his shortcomings were less serious and perilous to his soul. For this reason, he added, he would willingly accept death in his present state, if so it should please God. And God heard the desire of His servant's heart, a desire not the result of any timorous shrinking from the burden and heat of the day, but of an ardent love for his Lord and an intense horror of sin.

In the following chapter we shall relate how his soul's aspiration was fulfilled; we conclude the present with a letter written at the close of this year to his mother:—

"Illustrious lady, my most honoured mother in Christ, *Pax Christi.*

"Knowing, Signora, how much you desire the satisfaction of letters from me, and what consolation you derive therefrom, I take occasion of these holy festivals of the Nativity to salute you and wish you a happy *Pasqua*,* as I have also in my prayers, such as they are, besought the Lord with special affection at this sacred season, which gives me leisure to write to you, a thing so much the more grateful and agreeable to my taste, as all temporal affairs and everything else which I have left are wearisome to me, and what I least care to hear about. May God Himself, then, through the universal joy of Holy Church, and the complacency with which He regards the temporal Birth of His Only-Begotten Son, console you, illustrious Signora, and fill you with all grace, and this

* At this period the name of *Pasqua* (Easter) was, in common parlance, given to all the great feasts of the Church.

through the intercession of His Blessed Mother, who as you, Signora, will well imagine, experienced at this time so much suffering and joy united; suffering from the temporal poverty which she endured in a stable, where she had no means of protecting her new-born Son, Christ Jesus, from the cold, or withal to provide for His most urgent needs, and this we may believe to have been in lieu of the pains of child-birth, from which she was by privilege exempt; while, on the other hand, she experienced great joy from the visit and presence of God, her little Son, whom she beheld before her. Hence, as the wise man says, speaking of other women, that when they bring forth they are in sadness, but after the birth of their child are so full of joy that they forget all their past trouble, because a man is born into the world, so it seems to me that the most glorious Virgin, considering the temporal needs of her Son, had sorrow and trouble like one in labour because she could not provide for Him according to her desire, nevertheless, gazing at this same Son of hers, she was so filled with consolation as to forget every trouble, not merely because a man had been born to her, but because a God-Man had been born into the world. And so, I venture, in consideration of my state, to give you this advice, illustrious Signora, to view yourself in the light of Mary's example, and if the temporal cares and solicitude which the charge of providing for your young children entails, sometimes bring weariness and trouble upon you —even as the thought of providing for the temporal wants of her Son Jesus gave concern to the glorious Virgin—so do you also console yourself, on the other hand, even as she did, and let her example be your solace. She is our true Queen, from whose example we ought to derive far greater comfort than were we to behold any earthly sovereign thus situated—the queen of Spain, for instance, whom you, Signora, once served. If, moreover, it is a consolation to the afflicted to have companions in their sorrow, what greater solace can you have, Signora, than the society of the Virgin Mother, considering the greatness of her who bears you company, and the likeness that subsists between her cares and yours?

"I have wished to write this to you as it has occurred to me *in Domino*, to satisfy your desire and minister to you the consolation which you tell me attends my letters to you. For the rest, as respects certain family affairs, concerning which Monsignor the illustrious Cardinal della Rovere spoke to me, you will hear his illustrious lordship's opinion, to which I entirely defer, only adding that if this difference is not to be decided by a lawsuit (which neither to me seems fitting between brothers), but by arbitration, then I should think that it had better be referred to judges chosen on the spot, than here; since the distance must either interfere with their having full information or must cause what they receive to be defective. You, Signora, can appoint whom you consider competent to settle this matter, whether the Duke Vespasiano di Sabioneta, or any other whom you may prefer. In the mean time I will pray Christ Jesus that, even as the angels at His Nativity sang "*Gloria in excelsis Deo, et in terra pax, hominibus bonæ voluntutis*," so also He may deign to accord true peace and a right will to those of your house, illustrious Signora, with all the fulness of His holy grace.

"Your reverential son in Christ,

"ALUIGI GONZAGA, of the Company of Jesus.

"Rome, the last day of December, 1590."

CHAPTER VIII.

ALOYSIUS'S LAST ILLNESS AND DEATH.

IN the year 1591 Italy was afflicted with a malignant fever, which followed in the train of dearth and famine; in Rome the mortality was particularly high, owing to the numbers of poor who flocked to the Eternal City in the hopes of sharing the abundant alms always distributed there. The fathers of the Company were foremost in energetic efforts to relieve the general misery; besides serving several of the hospitals, they opened one of their own, and the General, P. Claudio Acquaviva, with his own hands ministered to the sick, not excepting lepers. The charity of our saint was sure to be conspicuous. He went about begging alms, and, hearing that Don Giovanni de' Medici, with whom he had been well acquainted ever since his childhood, and whom he knew to be piously disposed, had come to Rome to transact some business with the Pope, he asked leave to go and visit him in a patched coat and with a sack on his back; and this he said he wished to do, first of all, to obtain a more liberal alms for the poor in the hospital, and, secondly, because, this lord having always shown him particular affection, he thought it his duty to do him some spiritual good; and in order the better to impress him with contempt of worldly things, he judged it to be well to visit him in this mean attire. He attained both ends, as that noble's majordomo, Aloysius's old tutor, Francesco del Turco, afterwards assured P. Cepari. But he was not contented with the assistance he thus indirectly rendered to the sick; he earnestly requested to be allowed to serve them in person. His superiors objected, but he insisted with that holy perseverance by which he so often gained his point, and leave was given him to satisfy his desire. One of his twelve companions, Tiberio Bondi, a Genoese, being cautioned by his friends against the danger of infection, replied that it was quite impossible for him to withdraw from the work, or to spare himself in any way, how great soever might be the peril, with the spectacle of Aloysius's charity before his eyes. This youth had his reward, first in an extraordinary accession of fervour, so that all who knew him marked the change, and next by the death he had so heroically braved, for he was the first to be called away. Aloysius felt a holy envy for his companion:—"O how willingly," he exclaimed, "would I change places with Tiberio, and die in his stead, if God our Lord would vouchsafe me this favour!" alleging as his reason that at present he had some probability of being in God's grace, but, as he did not know whether he should continue therein, he would willingly die now. He had, as we have said, an abiding impression that his would be an early death, not only on account of the interior communication which he had received at Milan, but because of his insatiable avidity to consume himself in God's service. "I do not think," he said to his confessor, P. Bellarmino, "that God would give me this extraordinary desire if He did not intend soon to take me out of this life."

It was a terrible and revolting sight to flesh and blood, that hospital of S. Sisto, in which Aloysius served, crowded as it was to excess, fever-stricken sufferers arriving every moment* in every stage of loathsome disease, some in a state of almost complete nudity, and many so near their end that they would crawl into corners to die, while others would fall down dead on the very staircase: I "felt," says P. Fabrini, "as if my soul was plunged into purgatory." But, viewed by the supernatural eye, it was a beautiful scene. Aloysius and his brethren, like so many angels, ministered with a serene and loving joy to these afflicted creatures, performing for them every office which their miserable condition demanded, undressing and placing them in their beds, washing their feet, and bringing them their food. Not only were these acts of mercy performed by our saint with the sweetest tenderness and alacrity, but he seemed to take delight in what is ordinarily most trying to nature, lingering with a certain fond complacency round the most repulsive and disgustful objects. Yet by nature Aloysius was extremely sensitive to sights of this kind; for P. Decio Striverio, who as a novice had been intimately associated with him, related how,

* P. Fabrini, who was at this hospital on the last day when Aloysius served there, stated that although he was engaged from morning to night in receiving the confessions of the dying, yet on account of the great multitude he was unable to hear all who were in danger of death.

when they were together during the noviciate attending upon the sick in the hospital of Santa Maria di Consolazione, he observed Aloysius turn deadly pale as they approached the bed of an afflicted creature covered with bleeding sores; the paleness in an instant giving way to a bright colour, and a change coming over his whole aspect. Striverio augured ill from this indication of physical sensitiveness, and advised him to leave the sick man in his own charge and give his services elsewhere. But the transitory emotion had been quelled and subdued by the more powerful feeling of charity and his own strenuous effort to resist the promptings of nature, although, when questioned afterwards on the subject, he confessed that the sight of blood had always disposed him to faint. His strength seemed to bear up wonderfully, and, though several of his companions died martyrs to their self-devotion, the infection did not touch him.

His superiors, however, took the alarm, and would not allow him to remain any longer exposed to so great a risk; but at his own earnest request they permitted him to serve in the hospital of La Consolazione, which did not contain any sufferers from the prevailing virulent epidemic. In a short letter written on the 26th of February to Ridolfo, he mentions that he is in good health, and briefly recalls to his brother's memory the good dispositions in which he had left him about the same time the previous year, exhorting him to perseverance. On the 3rd of March he was in bed, struck down by the terrible malady which had carried off so many victims.* He was convinced that he had

* It would appear from one of the depositions inserted in the processes, that Aloysius caught the infection by carrying on his

received his summons, and his soul was filled with an ineffable joy. It beamed in his countenance, it was manifested in every act and gesture, and those to whom he had confided the supernatural intimation which had been given him at Milan, sorrowfully guessed the cause of his rejoicing and doubted not but that the longed-for time had come. One thing only troubled his happiness; it was its very exuberance, in which he feared there might be excess; but, his confessor having assured him that the desire to die in order to unite ourselves to God, provided it be accompanied by due resignation to His will, is not sinful, and that it is a desire which many saints had exhibited, he was pacified and gave himself with renewed affection to the thoughts of eternal life. On the seventh day the fever had so increased that he seemed to be nearing his end; he made his confession with the utmost fervour, and received the Viaticum and Extreme Unction from the hands of his rector, P. Bernardino Rossignoli, making the responses to the different prayers with deep devotion, amidst the tears of those who surrounded him, mourning the loss of so dear and holy a brother. It was on this occasion that. seeing the room full of all his fathers and brethren, after receiving the Holy Viaticum, he made the solemn declaration to which we have already alluded when speaking of his rigid mortifications. Calling to mind how many of them, from the love they bore him, had reproved him for his great bodily austerities, telling him that he would feel a scruple with regard

own shoulders to the hospital a poor afflicted creature whom he found lying in the street, and to whose necessities he ministered with the tenderest charity.

to them hereafter, and at least, in the hour of death, he was determined to leave them in no uncertainty about the matter, and begged the rector to assure them that he had none; and that had he entertained any scruple at this moment, it would have been for having fallen short of what he might have done and what holy obedience might not have forbidden. He added that he had never done anything of his own will, but always with license of his superiors, and that he felt he had no cause for self-reproach as regarded breach of the rule; this he said from his tender fear lest any should have been at times scandalized by observing that he allowed himself occasional exemptions, or in some way acted differently from the rest. These communications drew fresh tears from the eyes of all. Aloysius was to give immediate practical proof of his firm conviction that he had not exceeded in corporal mortification, by begging leave to take a discipline. P. Giovanni Battista Caminola, the Provincial, of whom he made this request, told him he was too weak to make the needful exertion "Then," said Aloysius, "let P. Francesco Belmisseri beat me from head to foot." The father replied that this could not be done without peril of irregularity in the administrator, as there must be danger of hastening his death. "Then, at least," rejoined this passionate lover of the cross, "lay me on the ground to die." This also was denied him; but his death was not so imminent as all believed. Aloysius himself, indeed, confidently expected that this was to be his birthday to life eternal, as on that day he had completed his twenty-third year. The sun set and rose again, and not only was Aloysius alive, but the fever had abated: The crisis was past, the saint was to tarry yet a few weeks more on earth, and to die not so much of the malady itself as of its lingering effects. God willed it so, doubtless, for the edification of his brethren, and to add a few jewels more to his own lustrous crown.

While temporary joy and hope filled the Roman College there was sorrow and lamentation at Castiglione. A report of his death had reached that place, and it was so entirely credited by his family, that his mother and brother had a solemn requiem mass offered for him. When the glad news arrived that he yet lived, the Marchese Ridolfo, for very joy, took the gold chain which hung about his neck, and, breaking it into fragments, distributed it to those about him. A letter, however, which Aloysius soon after wrote to his mother must have made his family apprehend that no permanent recovery could be expected. It was but a reprieve; the sentence of death, so welcome to him, was upon him, and he knew it.

After exhorting her to patience under troubles he says, "I was on the point, a month ago, of receiving from God our Lord the greatest favour that could be granted me, that is, to die (as I hoped) in His grace, and already had I received the Viaticum and Extreme Unction; however it has pleased the Lord to defer my death, preparing me for it meanwhile by a slow fever which has been left upon me. The doctors, who do not know what the result will be, are occupied in prescribing remedies for bodily health; for myself, however, it behoves me to think that God our Lord desires to bestow on me more perfect health than any the doctors can give, and so I pass my time joyfully, with the hope of being called, before many months are over, from the land of the dead to that of the living, and from the company of men here below to that of the Angels and Saints in Heaven; in fine, from the sight of these earthly and perishable things to the vision and contemplation of God, in whom is all good. The same may be a motive of consolation to you, illustrious lady, because you love me and desire my good; I beg you to pray, and to get the Brothers of the Christian Doctrine to pray, that in the short time that remains to me to navigate the waters of this world, God our Lord may deign, through His Only-Begotten Son and the intercession of His Most Holy Mother, and the Saints Nazarius and Celsus, to submerge my imperfections in the red sea of His Most Sacred Passion, that, liberated from my enemies, I may go to the Land of Promise to see and enjoy God. May the same God console you, illustrious Signora. Amen."

In the particulars that have been recorded of Aloysius's behaviour during his mortal sickness we seem to see the crowning merits of that spotless life through which we have followed him. This constant lover of poverty made one objection to the bed on which he lay; it had curtains; and this he thought a superfluity, and requested that they might be removed. Being told, however, that they had been put up, not for him, but for a former occupant, and that they were so coarse and shabby that the use of them could be no infringement of holy poverty, he acquiesced. His spirit of mortification exhibited itself in the way in which he took his medicine; while a sick companion swallowed his dose at a gulp, and employed other devices to neutralize the nauseous taste of the potion, Aloysius sipped his glass as men do some choice wine, that they may the better relish its flavor, betraying no symptom of disgust. Some sugar-candy and liquorice were laid on a neighbouring table, that he might keep some in his mouth when the cough was troublesome. He begged for the liquorice, and when asked why he did not prefer the sugar-candy, he replied, because the other was the fittest for the poor. These may seem minute and trifling sacrifices, but being the sacrifices of sickness, a season which seems to discharge the sufferer from the practice of voluntary mortification, they have a high value, and also by their very minuteness exhibit the saint's constant study of perfection. It need scarcely be observed, after all that has been said, that the patience, equanimity, and obedience which Aloysius manifested during the languishing illness which was gradually wasting his life away, offered a pattern in which not a flaw could be discerned of the way in which a religious should bear sickness. From the moment he was laid in his bed he would give ear to no conversation but such as had the things of God and eternal life for their immediate object. All who visited him were naturally anxious to afford him this just satisfaction; but if, from forgetfulness, any other topic was accidentally introduced, he at once retired within himself and paid no attention to what was saying, until spiritual subjects were resumed, when he again joined in the conversation with evident marks of pleasure. Not that he esteemed that in ordinary cases the mention of indifferent things, provided it were accompanied with prudence and a virtual spiritual intention, was opposed to the perfect observance of the rule, but now the moments were too valuable to be employed by him on anything save what was most precious; and God, he believed, required, not only that his conversation should be formally, that is, in intention, spiritual—for such he judged it ought always to be—but that materially it should be so likewise. Notwithstanding his great weakness, he asked sometimes for his clothes and dragged himself to a table on which stood a crucifix, which he would take fondly in his hands and reverently kiss, as he would also the picture of St. Catharine of Siena and other saints which were hanging on the walls; and when Brother Rosatino the infirmarian suggested that it was not necessary that he should rise in order to satisfy his devotion, as he would bring both crucifix and pictures to his bed, Aloysius replied, "Allow me, I beseech you, allow me to rise, for these are my *stations*." He used besides, when left alone, to get up and kneel on the floor of the room, but if he heard any one coming he would return to his bed as fast as he was able. Feeble as he was, he could not be quick enough to avoid the notice of the infirmarian, who, frequently finding him in the act of getting into bed, entered one day so softly as to surprise him on his knees and reprehended him for his imprudence. Aloysius, with the meekness of a child detected in a transgression of which he has cause to be ashamed, got into bed without saying a word, and then begged the infirmarian to forgive him. He was convinced, as we have said, that he lay on his death-bed, yet God would not deprive him of the merit of heroic resolutions which he was never to perform. Hearing that apprehensions were entertained that the plague would burst out in Rome, he offered himself to his superior to serve the pestilence-stricken in case he should recover; and, receiving a visit one day from the Father General, he even solicited permission to make a vow to that effect. This was, no doubt, the more readily accorded to him, as there could be little hope that he would ever be able to fulfil it.

Two of his relatives, the Cardinal della Rovere and the Cardinal Scipione Gonzaga, came frequently to see him; and when the Father Rector, desirous of sparing them the trouble and fatigue—Cardinal Scipione, in particular being gouty and requiring to be carried—assured them that he would not fail to send them constant information of Aloysius's health, they replied that they could not resist coming, on account of the edification they received. Aloysius especially loved the Cardinal Scipione, as we have seen, for the interest he had exerted in the affair of his vocation, and one day, after discoursing with him concerning his approaching death and the special grace which God vouchsafed him in calling him thus early to Himself, as the Cardinal sat listening, scarcely able to repress the tears which started to his eyes, the saintly youth went on to speak of the debt of gratitude which he felt he owed him, calling him his father and his greatest earthly benefactor, because, after so many hindrances and difficulties, it was through his assistance that he had at last entered religion. Then the venerable prelate could no longer refrain from weeping, and said that the obligation was on his own side, and that, despite the difference of age, it was he who recognised in Aloysius a father and spiritual master, on account of the great profit and consolation he had always derived from his words and example.

But nothing, perhaps, was so touching as the mutual charity which Father Corbinelli and the young saint entertained for one another. The reader will remember Aloysius's desire to get back to Rome to nurse this old man; both were now dying, and every day they used to send each other an affectionate salutation. Eight days before his death, the old religious, feeling himself rapidly sinking, deplored the necessity of departing without once more beholding his angelic friend, but both were equally incapable of moving. Aloysius, however, weak as he was, desiring to content the dying father, begged the infirmarian to carry him. To this request Rosatino willingly acceded. He dressed him, and then taking him up in his arms like an infant, for he had no longer strength to stand, bore him to P. Corbinelli's room. The joy of the old man was inexpressible; for a while they conversed together of that glorious heavenly home to the threshold of which they were both so nigh, and mutually exhorted each other to patience and resignation to the Divine will. Then, as they were about to separate, the old man said, "Brother Aluigi, now I shall willingly die without seeing you again, but I have a favour to ask, which you must not deny me: before we part you must give me your blessing." In vain did the astonished youth urge that this was not befitting; that the less is blessed of the greater: the father was old and he young; moreover, he was a priest, and himself only in minor orders; the old man would take no refusal, and besought the infirmarian not to remove his visitor till the request was granted. The brother added his own entreaties to move Aloysius to compliance, who at last, with that exquisite tact which he ever so eminently displayed, solved the difficulty, and at once gratified the old man and saved his own humility. Taking holy water from the infirmarian, who presented it, he signed himself and the father with it, saying, "My father, may God, Ever-Blessed, bless us both, and fulfil your holy desires: pray for me, and I will pray for you." This done he was carried back to his bed, leaving P. Corbinelli consoled and satisfied. One only other earthly desire did this good father manifest; when at the last extremity, he begged that he might be interred by the side of Aloysius. This was not according to the usual order, as priests had their separate burial-place, but as the old man had requested, so was it done. He died twenty days before Aloysius passed to Heaven. It was at midnight on the vigil of the feast of Pentecost. His apartment was in a quarter of the house far removed from that which Aloysius occupied. In order to spare him all disturbing anxiety he was not apprised how near the old man was to his end; but he knew it, and the next morning, when the infirmarian, entering as usual, asked him how he was, he replied, "I have spent a very bad night, with constant disturbing and extravagant dreams, or, rather, apparitions; for three times have I seen the good Father Corbinelli with a sorrowful aspect. At his first appearance he said to me, 'Dearest brother, I am now in my agony; pray to God for me, that fortitude may not fail me in these straits; and when I am admitted into Heaven, I will remember you.' I awoke, and thinking it was a dream, said to myself I had best compose myself to rest, and not attend to these illusions; soon after, having again fallen asleep, the father appeared to me a second time, and said, 'My sufferings have become so great that I seem unable to endure them; help me, with your prayers, to bear them.' I awoke, and marvelled greatly; but I was no sooner asleep again than I saw the same father for the third time, who said, 'Know now, Brother Aloysius, that I am loosed from the body and go to a better life. Pray to God for me, and I will pray for you that he may grant you a happy passage: we shall soon meet again.' At this I awoke and could not close an eye for the remainder of the night, for which I again reproached myself, and determined to ask for a penance in the morning for not better obeying the doctor, who had ordered me to endeavor to sleep." The infirmarian, whose vocation it was to cheer his patients, and who was in hopes that Aloysius might still obtain a little rest, told him these were fancies, and bade him think no more about the matter, but try and sleep, for it was all well with P. Corbinelli. Aloysius knew the truth, but he made no reply. It afterwards plainly appeared that he not only was well aware of the father's departure, but had full knowledge of his state after death, for when questioned by P. Bellarmino as to whether he supposed him to be in pergatory, he replied with perfect confidence, "He did but pass through purgatory;" and this coming from one so cautious in assertion was taken to argue a divine revelation

Feeling convinced that nothing would be denied to his prayers, all joined in pressing our saint to beseech God to prolong his days, urging all those reasons which might have weight with him, such as the acquiring additional merit, and the opportunity of labouring in the service of religion and for the good of others. But to every one he gave the same reply, with the same angelic serenity of countenance, "*Melius est dissolvi.*" (It is better to be dissolved"). His desire to die being founded on an ardent longing for union with his Lord, he feared even the briefest separation; and in one of the frequent conversations which he now held with his confessor on the affairs of his soul, he asked him whether he thought any one entered Heaven without so much as touching purgatory. "Yes," replied P. Bellarmino, "and I believe, indeed, that you will be of the number, and go at once to heaven; for our Lord God having through His mercy accorded you so many graces and supernatural gifts, as I have learned from yourself, and, in particular, that of never having mortally offended Him, I feel assured that He will grant you this grace also, to fly straight to heaven." P. Cepari, on whose authority this incident is given, adds that so great was Aloysius's joy at this intimation, that, after Bellarmine's departure, he went into an ecstacy, during which he beheld in vision the glory of the Heavenly Jerusalem; and so he remained the whole night, which, as he told his confessor, seemed to him but as a moment of time. It was believed, that, while thus rapt in spirit, he received a revelation of the day on which he should pass from earth, for he now privately informed several persons, amongst whom were the infirmarian, Francesco Rosatino, P. Guelfucci, and P. Belmisseri, that he should die on the octave of Corpus Christi. Strong indications, indeed, manifested themselves of his approaching end, so that P. Vincenzo Bruno, the superintendent of the infirmary, and himself no mean adept in the medical art, was fain to confess to Aloysius that he had but a few days to live. Of this notification our saint availed himself to speak openly and with confidence of the day of his death. "Have you heard the good news I have received," he said to P. Belmisseri, "that I am to die in a week's time? Pray join me in saying a *Te Deum* to thank God for the great favour he has granted me;" and so forthwith they said it together. Soon after, P. Francesco Suarez, his fellow-disciple, coming into the room, he joyously exclaimed, "My father, *lætantes imus, lætantes imus,*" words which inspired the hearers with any other feelings than those of gladness. Little had Aloysius now to do with earth; he would, however, dictate farewell letters to three fathers of the Company who were very dear to him, P. Pescatore, formerly his master in the noviciate, and at that time Rector at Naples, P. de Angelis, who was studying theology in that city, and P. Recalcati, the Rector of Milan. He told them he was, as he hoped, going to Heaven, and saluting them, begged a remembrance in their prayers. In place of his name, which he had not strength to subscribe, he traced with the pen the sign of the cross, P. Guelfucci holding his hand.

His letter to his mother, written ten days before his death, must not be omitted:—

"Illustrious and most honoured lady in Christ,

"Pax Christi.

"May the grace and consolation of the Holy Spirit be ever with you, illustrious Signora. The letter which you wrote to me, Signora, found me still alive in this land of the dead, but on the point of going (*su super andare*) to praise God for ever in the land of the living. I had thought ere this to have made the passage, but the violence of the fever having, as I mentioned in my last abated at its very height, I lingered on in this state to the glorious day of the Ascension. Since then a severe cold on the chest has aggravated it anew, so that I am gradually approaching the sweet and dear embrace of our Heavenly Father, in whose bosom I hope to repose in security for ever. And thus are reconciled the diverse reports which have been received concerning me, as I am also telling the Signor Marchese. Now if charity, as St. Paul says, makes us weep with those who weep and rejoice with those who rejoice, how great, Signora my mother, must be your joy for the favour you receive from God in my person; God our Lord leading me to true happiness with the assurance of never losing it more. I confess to you, Signora, that I am utterly astonished and lost in the consideration of the Divine goodness, that fathomless and shoreless ocean, which calls me to a rest eternal in reward of such slight and brief labours; from Heaven he invites and calls me to that Sovereign Good which I have so negligently sought, and promises me the fruit of those tears which I have so sparingly sown. Do you, Signora, take heed and beware not to do this infinite Goodness the wrong, which it would assuredly be, of weeping as dead him who will be living before God to aid you with his prayers far better than he has hitherto done. We shall not be long separated; we shall meet again above, and never more to part; we shall enjoy together a blissful union with our Redeemer, praising Him with all our powers, and eternally singing His mercies. I entertain no doubt but that, disregarding all that the ties of blood suggest, we shall with facility open the door to faith, and to that simple and pure obedience which we owe to God; offering him freely and readily that which is His own, and so much the more willingly as that which is taken from us is the dearer to us; firmly persuaded that whatever God does is well done, taking away from us what first He gave, and this only to set it in a place of safety and freedom, and to confer upon it all that we ourselves should wish. I have said all this only to satisfy my desire that you illustrious Signora, and the whole family, may accept this my departure as a precious boon, and that with your maternal blessing you may accompany and aid me to cross this gulf, and reach the shore of all my hopes. I have written the more willingly, inasmuch as nothing else remained that I could do to give testimony of the love and filial reverence I owe you. I conclude with again humbly begging your blessing.

"I am, illustrious Signora,

"Your most obedient son in Christ

"ALUIGI GONZAGA.

"Rome, June 10, 1591."

During the eight days that remained to him he added some special exercises in preparation for his end, and, after privately assuring P. Guelfucci, in whom he reposed great confidence, of the certainty of his death, he begged him every evening during the week to bring the crucifix and place it on a table before his bed. Then, kneeling down, the father, by his desire, slowly recited the Seven Penitential Psalms, pausing occasionally as he observed different verses particularly affect him. Meanwhile the dying saint kept his eyes tenderly fixed on the crurifix, a gentle tear from time to time stealing down his cheek; and at this touching sight the father's own tears would gush forth irrepressibly, to check his utterance and prolong the silence. During the day, Aloysius would request to have passages read to him from some of his favourite spiritual books, as St. Augustine's Soliloquies," or "St. Bernard on the Canticles," or certain Psalms of his own selection; specially did he love those which commence with the words, "*Lætatus sum in his quæ dicta sunt mihi: In domum Domini ibimus;*" and "*Quemadmodum desiderat cervus ad fontes aquarum, ita desiderat anima mea ad te, Deus.*"* No exile, indeed, ever longed for his native land, no wounded stag ever panted to slake its thirst at the living stream, as this blessed soul sighed for its everlasting home, and burned to drink of the perennial Fountain of Life. Hence, although taking with docility whatever was prescribed to him either of food or medicine, unlike other sick persons, who will anxiously inquire whether they may expect benefit from what is administered to them, Aloysius's solicitude was all in the contrary direction. "What do you think, brother?" he would say to the infirmarian; "will this food prolong my life and retard my union with God, my last end?"

The report spreading that Aloysius had foretold that he should die during the octave, all were eager to take some opportunity to recommend themselves to his prayers, and he charged himself with all these

* "I rejoiced at the things that were said to me: We shall go into the house of the Lord."—Ps. cxxi. 1. "As the hart panteth after the fountains of waters, so my soul panteth after Thee, O God,"—Ps. xli. 1.

commissions for Heaven with a readiness which marked how strong was his conviction that he was soon to make the journey; speaking of his passage out of this world with the same calmness and simplicity as people talk of going from one room to another. Many of the fathers came in turn to attend on him as an act of devotion. One of the number, P. Piatti, who was to follow him two months later, exclaimed on leaving the infirmary, "I tell you, Aluigi is a saint; he is certainly a saint; and so much a saint that he might be canonized during his life;" alluding to the words of Pope Nicholas V., who at the canonization of St. Bernardine of Siena said, speaking of St. Antoninus, the Archbishop of Florence, then alive, "I think that Antoninus living might be canonized no less than Bernardine dead." Towards the close of the octave, Aloysius's state of contemplation deepened and became more continual, though he uttered frequent ejaculations, and from time to time would say a few spiritual words. Three days before his death, taking from P. Guelfucci's hands a bronze crucifix to which special indulgences were attached, he kept it laid upon his bosom until he expired. He several times renewed the protestation of faith contained in the ritual of the Church, and often repeated these words; "*Cupio dissolvi et esse cum Christo*" ("I desire to be dissolved and to be with Christ"), or similar aspirations expressive of his ardent longing to be united to his Lord.

The last day of the octave dawned. "This is the octave of Corpus Domini, Brother Aloysius, when you said you were to die," observed Bernardino Mizzetti, the sub-infirmarian, when he entered the room that morning and opened the window; adding, "but you seem to me to be better." "Remember that the octave is not past," Aloysius serenely replied; "I shall die this day" Bernardino went straight to the head-infirmarian and smilingly said, "Do you know, Aloysius is quite sure he will die to-day? but he appears to me to be stronger than usual." The two infirmarians afterwards went together to the sick room. Rosatino felt Aloysius's pulse, and said, "Brother, how are you?" "As God pleases," was the reply. "Believe me," said the infirmarian, "you are a little better" But he answered, "According to your opinion I am a little better; nevertheless, according to God's will, I shall die this evening." He then earnestly entreated Rosatino to interest himself for him, that he might be fortified with the Holy Viaticum that morning. To this the infirmarian replied that he had already received the Viaticum, and that it might not be repeated during the same illness. "The annointing with the holy oil cannot be repeated during the same illness," said Aloysius; "in this you are right; but the Holy Viaticum may." Nevertheless the infirmarian, intimately persuaded that, his patient being better, there was no need for the Viaticum, turned a deaf ear to his oft-renewed request, sometimes even feigning not to hear the low, gentle tones in which the entreaty was expressed. All shared the infirmarian's opinion that Aloysius was decidedly better. Padre Guelfucci, reminding him of his prophecy that he would die before the conclusion of the octave, gently insinuated that it would not prove a true one, for there was certainly a considerable improvement that morning. But he persevered in his asseveration, saying, "Be it so; but the octave is not concluded: watch with me, and assist me, for I shall die." Again, when P. Belmisseri, moved to compassion for the pain which the saint endured from a festering wound in his right heel, the result of his great emaciation, said that although they were about to lose him, yet did he desire that our Lord would relieve him from that particular suffering, Aloysius spoke with the like plainness: "I shall die to-day," he gravely said. One of the fathers had begged him to recommend to God, when in Heaven, the son of an illustrious duke, who had been inspired with the wish to become a religious, and who feared his family's opposition. Aloysius, as may be supposed, readily promised, and upon seeing him again this day, he said, in allusion to what had passed, "I remember, and will do it." He then listened awhile to the father as he spoke of life eternal and of conformity to the Divine will, and, notwithstanding his feebleness, endeavoured to add a few words of his own in reply. Not long after, on the infirmarian approaching his bed, the saint said, "I beg that I may be laid in the same tomb with P. Corbinelli;" adding, "for three times did he appear to me." The infirmarian replied that he did not think death was so very near. "This night I shall die," replied Aloysius; "This night I shall die."

All that forenoon he continued in contemplation, from time to time making fervent acts of faith and adoration; and towards mid-day he earnestly renewed the request which he had made in the morning, that he might receive the Holy Viaticum, to fortify him at his last extremity. But the infirmarian could not believe that death was so imminent. Aloysius had received communion every Sunday; it was always given on that day to the sick, and there seemed no adequate cause for a reiteration of the Viaticum. While Aloysius remained still in doubt whether he should once more enjoy the happiness of receiving his Lord before his last passage, a consolation very dear to his heart was brought him by P. Fabrini, the father-minister, who, entering the sick chamber, announced that the Pope had sent him his benediction and a plenary indulgence. But humility was ever so completely the dominant sentiment in Aloysius's breast, that it seemed almost to overshadow his joy; filled with bashful confusion at the idea of the Vicar of Christ having thought of him, he instinctively covered his face with his hands, to hide the blush which perhaps for the last time was to colour his pale cheek. The father, perceiving this, added quickly, in order to relieve his modesty, that there was no cause for wonder if the Pope, hearing as he accidentally might of his dangerous state, should have been moved to send him his blessing. As the afternoon advanced, P. Giovanni Battista Lambertini, who had formerly been his co-novice, having come from S. Andrea to visit him, Aloysius besought his intervention with the Father Rector to give him the Viaticum. P. Lambertini promised on leaving him to do as he wished. The Father Rector now came to see Aloysius, who repeated his petition, and P. Rossignoli, acceding to his desire, told him that he would return with the Viaticum as soon as they had said their office. He now begged to say the Litanies of the Blessed Sacrament with the father. He made his responses with a clear voice; towards the conclusion an extraordinary expression of joy illuminated his countenance, and when they had finished, it was with a smile on his lips that he thanked the father for his charity.

At the sound of the bell, all the members of the Company, who numbered about 150, hastened to accompany the Blessed Sacrament as it was borne by the Father Rector to the infirmary, that they might behold their beloved brother once more. It was amidst the tears of all present that Aloysius received his Lord with the most fervent devotion and an undoubting trust that he was about to behold face to face Him who now came to him under the sacramental veil. Then followed a touching scene: the holy youth would embrace each and all of his fathers and brethren, as was customary when one of their number was about to start on a long journey. Weeping, they all took their leave of him, scarcely able to tear themselves from his embrace, and renewing their petitions for a special remembrance in the presence of God. One in particular, Gaspare Alpieri, who tenderly loved and was tenderly beloved by the saint, as he leaned over him whispered his hopes that he was soon going to enjoy the beatific vision, and that he trusted that, as living he had always remembered him, so he would not be unmindful of him in glory; adding that if by his imperfections he had sometimes offended him he entreated his forgiveness. Aloysius replied, with much affection, that he confided in the mercy of Divine Goodness, and the Precious Blood of Jesus, and the intercession of the Blessed Virgin, that so it would speedily be with him, and promised that he would remember him in Heaven: of this he might rest assured, for if he had loved him on earth, much more should he love him there, where charity is perfected. So clear was his mind and rapid his utterance, that he scarcely seemed like a dying man. At this juncture, the Provincial entered the room, and said, "Well, Brother Aluigi, how is it now with you?" "Going, father," was his reply. "Whither?" "To Heaven. "How so? to Heaven?" and Aloysius added, "If my sins do not offer a hindrance, I hope by the mercy of God to go there" Then, turning to some present, the Provincial said to them in a low voice, "Listen, he speaks of going to Heaven, as we should of a journey to Frascati; what are we to do with this brother? Can we lay him in the common burial place?" They agreed that out of regard to his sanctity, an exception ought to be made in his favour.

About seven o'clock, when P. Cepari was supporting him, that he might with less effort contemplate a crucifix hanging in front of the bed, to which was attached a plenary indulgence at the hour of death, Aloysius raised his hand, and removed his linen cap from his head. Cepari, deeming it to be the restless act of a dying man, quietly replaced it. But soon he again took it off, when the father gently remonstrated saying that the evening air might be hurtful to him; but he, glancing at the crucifix, answered, "Christ, when He expired, had nothing on His Head;" so close was his imitation of his Saviour even to his last moments. At the Ave Maria, there was a little whispered discussion as to who was to remain with him for the night, when Aloysius, although immersed in contemplation, appeared to be aware of what was going on, for he said twice to P. Guelfucci, Do *you* assist me." Having previously promised P. Belmisseri that he should be with him at the hour of death, he now, as though to keep his engagement, warned him that the time was come, by saying, "See that you remain." But it was ordered otherwise. The apartment was at this time still inconveniently full of persons, and the infirmarian begged the Rector to dismiss them at once to bed, for Aloysius would not die that night. P. Rossignoli accordingly desired that every one should retire to rest with the exception of P. Fabrini and P. Guelfucci. Believing they should never more behold him alive, many earnestly begged to be allowed to sit up with him; but P. Rossignoli told them he was certain that Aloysius would not die that night: if he thought it likely, he would himself remain; and so, constrained by obedience, all sorrowfully prepared to depart. Aloysius knew their love for him; he consoled them, promised again to remember them in Heaven, and commissioned several amongst them to offer certain prayers in his behalf as soon as he was dead. Then, one by one, they all drew near to speak their last sorrowful farewell, as their hearts truly foreboded, of their dear brother, and he was left with his two assistant fathers. His confessor, P. Bellarmino,* also remained awhile, and begged Aloysius to tell him as soon as he judged the time was come to recommend his soul. After a brief space Aloysius said, "Father, it is time now;" and then the confessor, kneeling down with the others, repeated the recommendation of the dying.

For awhile Aloysius remained in the same state, his soul in continual contemplation, while ever and

* Cepari says that P. Muzio also remained, but does not mention the time of his departure. Probably he accompanied Bellarmine when he retired.

anon his lips would murmur words from Sacred Writ: "*In manus tuas, Domine, commendo spiritum meum,*" and others of like kind. His countenance was serene, and the fathers from time to time gave him holy water, or presented to him the crucifix to kiss, suggesting the while some pious aspiration or holy thought. The infirmarian still adhering to his opinion that Aloysius would survive the night, the Father Minister joined his entreaties to those of Rosatino that P. Bellarmino would go and take some rest, promising that he should be called if any change took place. So confident was the infirmarian, that his words to Bellarmino (as he himself afterwards stated in the processes) were, "He is just as near death this night as I am myself." This good man much regretted that, in consequence of the rapidity with which Aloysins sank at the last, it was impossible for him to give warning to the father as he had engaged to do, and still greater was the sorrow of the holy youth's confessor at having lost the privilege he so much coveted of assisting him in death.

P. Guelfucci, hoping that Aloysius might now take some rest, shaded the light from his bed. All was stillness in the chamber; Father Fabrini had retreated to a distant part of the room, where he was saying his office; Guelfucci sat by his darkened lamp, but occasionally he would rise and go softly to the bedside to look at Aloysius, for although there were as yet no indications that the supreme hour was at hand, still he could not forget the saintly youth's confident and persistent prediction. He always found him awake, and with his soul to all appearance closely united to God in contemplation. Two or three times he asked him how he was, and if he wanted anything; Aloysius had but one reply, the same oft-repeated words: "Watch with me and assist me, for I shall die." P. Guelfucci gazed at him, but could see no sign of immediate death on the calm and placid face before him. Yet he doubted, as he once more resumed his place what he ought to do. Should he give credit to Aloysius's assertion, and call the Father Minister to make the recommendation of the dying? Unable to decide, he returned to the bed to take a more accurate observation, and again he asked whether there was anything he could do for him. It was now that Aloysius made his last earthly request; it was not to be granted. In feeble accents he replied, "To be moved from the right to the left side." Three days in fact, had he been too weak to vary his posture, and we all know, more or less, what is the torture of an unchanged attitude. The father, apprehending that this was the desire of a dying man, immediately called Fabrini and the infirmarian. Lights were brought, and they all noted the significant change which came over the countenance of their brother: a bright flush suffused it, followed by the livid hues of death, while the big drops of sweat which burst forth indicated too surely that the last moments were arrived. The infirmarian, fearful to accelerate the end, was unwilling to comply with his wish to be moved. He, observing this reluctance, faintly said, "What harm would there be in trying?" "I grieve that we cannot satisfy your desire," said Father Guelfucci, "but there would be danger of hastening your death. Bear it; it is the last drop in the cup of the Lord which He gives you to drink." Bending over the dying saint, who had now entered into his agony, Father Fabrini whispered to him the remembrance of the hard bed of the cross to which Christ our Lord was fastened and upon which, for the love of us, He died. Aloysius did not speak, but raised his eyes to the crucifix and, fixing on it a look more eloquent than words, manifested his longing desire to suffer yet more for the love of God, a desire by which he seemed to silence and repress the last instinctive pleading of nature. He had triumphed: all was subdued to the dominion of grace; it was perhaps the crowning sacrifice of his life of ceaseless mortification. He pressed in his dying grasp, in token of perseverance in the faith, the blessed candle which Father Guelfucci placed in his right hand, and thus, with his eyes rivited on the image of his Lord, and with his left hands resting on the crucifix which for three days had lain on his bosom, he accompanied in spirit the litanies and prayers offered for his departing soul; from time to time still striving to murmur the sweet Name of Jesus, until at last his lips only moved, and he tranquilly yielded up his pure soul to God.

He had always desired to die within the octave of Corpus Christi, or on a Friday, the day of his Saviour's Passion, and he obtained both boons; for he passed from this life just as the octave was closing and Friday beginning, in the night between the 20th and 21st of June. He had completed twenty-three years, three months, and eleven days. No little grace did these two fathers deem it to have been permitted to assist at this blessed death; so many had desired this privilege, and they were the elected two; moreover, they had received from the lips of the saint a precious promise, that so long as they lived he would continually remember them before God. They seemed on the instant to experience the happy fruits of his intercession; for the Father Minister was filled with indescribable peace and consolation, and Father Guelfucci was penetrated with extraordinary sentiments of contrition and devotion, and an ardent zeal for the service of God. Nor with the latter were these impressions of a merely temporary character; they lasted for several months, and were renewed at times even when their first freshness was gone. Not daring to take anything from the venerated body, he secured for himself the shoe-strings and the pens of his departed brother: these were the first relics of the saint, and as such they were piously preserved.

The infirmarians then came to wash and lay out the body, when they found two great wounds on his side, which must have caused intense suffering, but which the saint had never mentioned. His knees were, so to say, embossed with a thick callosity, the result of perpetual kneeling from his very childhood; for it may be truly said that he had spent the greater part of his short life in that attitude. The sensitive tenderness of Rosatino for the body of the holy youth exhibits his character in a very amiable light; he had little toleration for that pious greed which was ready to dismember it while as yet scarcely cold. Having left the room for a moment, he found on his return his assistant, Bernardino Mozetti, engaged in endeavouring forcibly to extract a tooth; filled with indignation at the sight, he almost fiercely reprimanded him for what he termed his cruelty. Mozzetti fell on his knees, and exclaimed, "Dear brother, forgive me; to-morrow this body will have been borne away, and every one will take something as a relic, and nothing will be left for me." He was right in his prevision. Everything was carried off, and, had not the fathers kept strict guard, the holy remains would have disappeared piece-meal. As it was, not all Rosatino's sympathy for the passionate veneration which prompted such acts, could avail to repress the rising feeling of disgust which he described himself as afterwards experiencing at beholding the body he had so fondly and reverently tended the object of rapacious attempts which his love made him view as a species of outrage.* As soon as Aloysius had expired, one of the fathers hastened to call some of the brethren who had been specially united in holy friendship with the saint. "Our angel," they said, "has taken flight to Heaven;" with them there seemed to be no question of purgatory: as they rose from their beds they began at once to beg his intercession, and then, recollecting their promises, they turned to repeating the prayers which they had engaged to say in his behalf; but soon they again began instinctively to invoke him, whom they firmly believed to be already blessed with the vision of God in the glorious assembly of His Saints.

* "Conspiciens tam indigne tractatum à rapacis pietate populi, equidem vehementer stomachatus fui," are his very words, as recorded in the processes.

PART III.

THE SAINT IN HEAVEN.

CHAPTER I.

TESTIMONIES TO ALOYSIUS'S SANCTITY. HIS BEATIFICATION.

Scarcely had the signal for rising sounded on the 21st of June, when the room in which Aloysius lay was filled in an instant, and the floor covered with a kneeling crowd. Then followed a kind of pious scramble for his relics, every one hastening to secure for himself some portion of his clothes. His nails, his hair, were still more precious treasures; they were cut and appropriated without delay. The body was then borne into the College chapel. Here many thronged to see him, and there were those amongst his acquaintance (some of whom previously had a horror of so much as looking on a corpse) who, approaching the catafalque, embraced and kissed the cold remains of him whom they all vied with each other in calling again and again by the name of saint; "Santo! Santo!" resounding through the chapel all that morning long. In the evening the body was removed to a large hall, in which all the brothers and fathers assembled; and although it was not the custom to kiss the hand of any deceased member of the Company unless he had been invested with the sacerdotal character, no one so much as gave a thought to the fact that Aloysius had received only minor orders, but, penetrated with veneration for his sanctity, all drew near to pay him a last honour usually reserved for priests alone.

The body was then borne in procession to the College church of the Annunziata. The reader will recall to mind that it was in the Annunziata of Florence, before an image of Immaculate Mary, that Aloysius, yet a boy, had consecrated his virginity to God by vow: from his birth to his death he was a child of Mary. The office of the dead was now sung, according to custom, but none believed that the soul of the departed required their prayers; fain would they rather have asked his intercession, and many, in fact, inwardly invoked him while with their lips they were asking for him the enjoyment of light and rest eternal. The office being ended, the concourse of foreign students and other persons, many of distinguished rank, who pressed forward to the bier, to venerate the holy remains, and beg, or even steal, relics* of the youthful saint, became so great, that the fathers found it difficult to bear up against the throng or keep them back. At last the church was cleared and the doors were closed.

A discussion ensued as to the mode of sepulture. It was the habit in the Company to bury their mem-

* P. Decio Striverio says in the processes that the bier was surrounded and pressed upon by a mixed crowd of youths of the college, nobles and prelates, all animated with the most ardent devotion for the saint, many of whom came armed with scissors and knives, that they might the more speedily effect their object. One Padre he mentions, who succeeded in cutting off a finger, for which act, however, it appears he received a reprimand from his own superiors. The Abbate Paolo di Angelis himself confessed that he tried to cut off an ear, but was prevented by one of the Jesuit fathers who was protecting the body. This was the scene with which the good Rosatino was *stomachatus*. The nobles appear to have been foremost in the rapacious throng. Cepari saw a large piece of Aloysius's habit in the hands of a Bohemian baron, and witnessed other equally successful larcenies.

bers, after the manner of the poor, that is, simply to lay them in the grave; but the chief fathers of the College, and, in particular, P. Bellarmino, were of opinion that it would be fitting to deposit the body of Aloysius in a receptacle apart; since, considering his eminent sanctity, it might be anticipated that God would be pleased to make his servant as glorious before the world after death as in life he had been hidden. The matter being referred to the Father General, he immediately sent directions that the body should be inclosed in a coffin. This was accordingly done, and it was laid that very evening in the Chapel of the Crucifix, which was on the left side of the Church of the Annunziata.

For days in the Roman College there was but one topic of conversation, the virtues of this holy brother, and every day saw numbers of the students kneeling and praying at his tomb, a practice in which some persevered for months and even years—as long, indeed, as they sojourned in Rome. Hidden as Aloysius had striven to remain, and, owing to his youth, never having held any public charge or office which might have exhibited his wonderful gifts of grace before the eyes of men, nevertheless he was no sooner dead than the fame of his sublime sanctity blazed forth on every side. In the numerous letters addressed to his pious mother in her bereavement, the tone of congratulation almost overpowered that of condolence, thus bearing testimony to the light in which her son was regarded. The Father General himself told her that, from the intimate knowledge he possessed of his perfect holiness, he could assure her that she had a dear and faithful intercessor in Heaven. The letter of Signor Tommaso Mancini, who wrote after the obsequies to the marchesa, is couched in similar language: "I am doubtful," he says, "whether I have to sorrow with your Excellency or to rejoice with you." He speaks also of miracles being confidently expected by the public, who already entertained as great devotion to the blessed youth as though he were a saint well known to have wrought them. Amongst the illustrious consolers of the afflicted parent was the dowager duchess of Mantua, Eleanora of Austria, so often mentioned as a second mother in affection to Aloysius. She was herself a woman of high spiritual attainments and of singular piety; and it is said that she foretold the future sanctity of Marta's child from his very birth, saying, "This will be the first saint in the house of Gonzaga." What wonder then, having intimately known him in after years, that she should exclaim, when she heard of his death, "He was a holy youth, and he died a saint!"

But not at Mantua alone did his death revive the memory of his heroic virtues; the other Italian courts of Florence, Ferara, Turin, and Parma, to which his father had sent him to transact business with their sovereigns, had all beheld that silent, modest, self-denying boy, but withal full of the wisdom of age, and with the gift of persuasion in his very look, and in those parsimonious words which came with the power of God's spirit from his lips. His memory was still fresh in these cities, where, living, he had been gazed on as a saint; and when the news of his departure arrived he was undoubtingly invoked at once as exalted to glory. Duke Ranuzio Farnese attested afterwards on oath that he received instantaneous relief in severe bodily torture from invoking his saintly relative. Maura Lucenia, his sister, Abbess of Sant' Alessandro in Parma, had the same conviction as regarded herself, and her confidence in the power of his intercession was unbounded. Ever since her childhood she had held him in veneration, remembering how, when in Mantua, Laura di Gonzaga, the sister of Prince Prospero, pointing to Aloysius, then only thirteen years of age, had said to her, "That boy, although so young, is living the most saintly life." After hearing these words she could not take her eyes off him, and felt the very sight of him inwardly move her to devotion. But, indeed, well-nigh all the Catholic princes of Europe seem to have been stirred to a like devotion, from the day that he was taken up to glory, as their letters to the sovereign Pontiff, pressing for his canonization, abundantly testify. Charles Emanuel of Savoy lauded the contempt of earthly grandeur which the holy youth manifested when he appeared at his court in humble and poor attire, but rich in virtue and in wisdom. Mary of Medicis, now queen of France, gloried in her good fortune at having been blessed with the sight of the angelic innocence of the saintly child in her father's ducal palace at Florence. Philip III. of Spain professed a special devotion for one who spent many years of his youth in his own royal city and at his father's court; and the Infanta, Margaret of Austria, his sister, now a Discalced Clare, loved to repeat how she had heard that, when her empress mother visited Madrid and Aloysius followed with his parents in her train, all held that little boy to be a saint. Rodolph II., Emperor of Germany, who had given his consent to the renunciation of the marquisate, commended the sublime example of detachment from earth in a youth born to a princely estate, and in whose veins ran his own Imperial blood. He had one at his court who, as a child, had attracted his notice, and who must have reminded him by his presence, if not by word, of his saintly brother. Francesco Gonzaga, of whom Aloysius foretold that he would be the stay of his family, and who was always (as his frequent letters to him showed) a special object of the saint's fraternal charity, loved him in return with all the energy of his ardent and affectionate nature. "When I heard of his death" (he says in the processes), "although I ought to have rejoiced instead of mourning, my soul was so filled with tenderness, as though it took a delight in weeping, that for eight or ten days, I could not restrain my frequent tears; during all which time I admitted no one to speak to me, nor would I show myself to anyone, fearing they would deride my extravagant grief; yet otherwise I was by nature very little prone to weeping, nor, indeed, did the death of my father, or of my mother, or any of the tragical events in my family, ever draw a tear from my eyes."

But if Aloysius's relatives and friends in the world so highly revered him, much more profound, may we imagine, were the sentiments of loving veneration with which his brethren in the Company, the near witnesses of his holy life, were filled in his regard. And these sentiments were abiding. We find one great teacher of theology, P. Francesco Remondo, thus characterising the privilege of having been the saint's co-disciple "*Beneficium a Deo magnum in me collatum.*" Another, an illustrious martyr, P. Carlo Spinola, when about to be consumed on a slow fire in Japan for the love of Jesus, still remembers with joyful exultation that he studied philosophy with Aloysius at Naples. P. Paolo Comitolo, also an eminent theologian, when requested by superiors to add his testimony to the singular supernatural endowments which had distinguished Aloysius, replied that he judged him most worthy of being numbered amongst the saints, and that the gifts with which God enriched him made him appear greater in his eyes than if he had raised the dead. Such, indeed, was the universal feeling entertained by all the fathers who had known and conversed with the saint, and it was shared by the youths in the noviciate and in the Roman College, who had been used to ask their superiors as a favour to be allowed to inhabit some room near to that of Aloysius, convinced that his very person exhaled, as it were, the spirit of sanctity and especially that of prayer. Passing over the names of many grave, learned, and pious divines, names carrying much weight in their day, we may rest satisfied with the testimony of the great Bellarmine, whose high reputation for spiritual gifts and theological science is still fresh in our times. As Aloysius's confessor, we have had occasion to record his opinion more than once in the course of the saint's life. It may here be added that he was in the habit of saying that so long as Aloysius was at the college, he did not fear that any evil could happen to it; and in a discourse delivered before the whole community in the year 1608, he has left on record an attestation truly remarkable, as coming from one whose own soul was so sublimely illuminated. "When I gave," he said, the

Spiritual Exercises of St. Ignatius to Aluigi, I discovered in him such abundance of Divine light, that I must confess that, at my advanced age, I learned from this youth how to meditate." When raised to the Cardinalate, the venerable prelate not only continued his yearly practise of repairing to the College church of the Company to venerate the tomb of Aloysius on his anniversary, but used to make a devout visit to the room whence he had taken his flight to Heaven, and there would shed tears of tenderness in memory of their last parting. Viewing this apartment as a hallowed spot, he did not think it ought to be used any longer as a common infirmary, and the superiors readily acquiesced in his desire. Heaven itself seemed to signify its approval, for many times was sweetest music heard to issue from it. No research could ascertain the source of these melodious strains; whence it was piously inferred that they proceeded from choirs of angels who descended to consecrate with their songs the spot from which their loved companion had left the earth to take his place in their glorious ranks. When the Holy See had declared Aloysius to be in the possession of eternal glory, the cardinal had this room converted into a chapel at his own expense.* He rendered his crowning testimony by desiring to be laid after death at the feet of "the blessed Aloysius," once his spiritual son, but, in the spirit of obedience left the disposition of his body to the will of his supe-

* When the new church of St. Ignatius was erected, this part of the college was pulled down, and the area of the apartment in which Aloysius died was included in the sacred edifice. In the side chapel, occupying a portion of its site, an altar was dedicated to the saint, where his relics reposed for fifty years, as hereafter to be noticed

riors; and they, to confer upon him the greatest honour within their power, deposited him in the same tomb where up to that time had reposed the venerated remains of their great patriarch, St. Ignatius

We must not leave this subject without recording one further testimony, and that of more than common interest. In the year 1599, P. Cepari, being rector of the College of the Company in Florence and confessor extraordinary to the convent of Santa Maria degli Angeli, whose superioress was that marvellous and glorious virgin, St. Mary Magdalen of Pazzi, lent her in manuscript the account he had compiled of the acts and virtues of Aloysius, and presented her at the same time with a portion of the bone of his little finger. Great fervour of spirit was kindled in the community by the perusal of the life, and each of the nuns desired to possess a portion of the precious relic. On the 4th of April in the ensuing year, while the blessed mother, surrounded by ten of the sisters, was engaged in satisfying their pious wish by dividing the relic into fragments, she was seized with one of her raptures and, beholding the glory of Aloysius in Heaven, began, as she was wont in her other visions, to describe what she saw. The nuns had for some time given up registering her utterances on these occasions, so frequent had her raptures become, but the mother prioress, Sister Vangelista, instinctively feeling that her words might one day help to swell the testimony to Aloysius's sanctity, ordered them to be taken down in writing. We will give them here, indicating also the pauses which she made during the progress of the vision she was contemplating.

"O how great," she exclaimed, "is the glory of

Luigi, son of Ignazio! Never could I have believed it, if Thou, my Jesus, hadst not shown it to me!—It would almost seem to me as if there could not in Heaven be any glory equal to that which I see Luigi to possess.—I tell you, the little Luigi [Luigino] is a great saint. We have saints in our church [alluding to the relics of saints in their own convent church] who, I believe, do not possess such great glory.—Would that I could go through the whole world proclaiming that Luigi, the son of Ignazio, is a great saint; and that I could show his glory to all, that God might be glorified.—He has such great glory because his work was interior.—Who can tell the value and virtue of interior works!—There is no comparison between the interior and exterior.—Luigi, while he abode on earth, kept his mouth ever open before the regards of the Word, and therefore he has such great glory. [The saint, as she afterwards herself explained, alluded to Aloysius's attention to the inspirations which the Eternal Word was ever sending to his heart, and his continual co-operation therewith.]—Luigi was an unknown martyr. For he who loves Thee, my God, knows Thee to be so great and so infinitely worthy of love, that it is a great martyrdom to him not to love Thee as he aspires and desires to love Thee, and to see Thee, not only not known and not loved by creatures but even offended by them.—Moreover, he made himself a martyr.—O how he loved while on earth! Wherefore now in Heaven he enjoys God in the fulness of love. He shot arrows into the Heart of the Word, whilst he was mortal, and now in Heaven these arrows rest in his own heart, for the communications he merited by the acts of love and union he made (for these were the arrows), he now comprehends and enjoys."—Then, observing the saint praying for those who on earth had given him spiritual aid, she said, "And I also will strive to help souls, that if any of them go to Heaven, they may pray for me, as Luigi does for those who helped him while on earth. Amen."

Such were the words uttered by this holy nun while in extasy, but this was not the only time that she had the vision of Aloysius's glory, and declared that he was exceedingly pleasing to God. On this occasion, so overflowing was her jubilation of spirit that when she came to herself she exclaimed, "Ah! my God, why dost Thou break the pact I have made with Thee, having for the love of Thee given up all contentment?" and so possessed were her mind and imagination with the memory of this vision, that she drew a portrait of Aloysius, representing him, although not yet beatified, with rays of glory round his head. A copy of the words she had spoken were sent to P. Cepari.* When it was shown six years afterwards to the saint, she attested its correctnesss, declaring on oath that she had this vision as therein narrated. But, like him whom her words had honoured, her humility so abashed her, that her confessor had to console her by saying that God had permitted this manifestation for the greater glory of the blessed Aloysius. Four days after the

* It is worthy of notice, as conferring peculiar value on whatever proceeds from the pen of P. Cepari, that St. Mary Magdalen of Pazzi one day called to her one of her novices, while that father was engaged in discoursing in the college of spiritual things, and said, "Sister, the Father Rector of the Company of Jesus is speaking to his fathers: he is saying such and such things to them" [her statement proved to be perfectly accurate], "and I see that the Holy Spirit forms all the words he utters."

vision, occurred the miracle in Florence which was placed first on the list of the fifteen recorded in the process of the saint's canonization; a nun in this same convent of S. Maria degli Angeli being cured of a malignant cancer after fervent supplication to the saint and application of his relic. It may be remarked that this nun had long concealed her painful malady, partly from love of suffering, and partly from a sentiment of modesty, which made her shrink from subjecting herself to surgical treatment.

But we must not forget the pious mother of our saint. Great troubles came upon her soon after the loss of her angelic son. Alfonso Gonzaga did not survive his nephew above a year. At his death, it will be remembered, the fief was to revert to the marquisate of Castiglione; but when Ridolfo prepared to take possession, he found his rights disputed by his cousin, Donna Caterina, Alfonso's only child. The destined spouse of the head of the house of Castiglione, she had twice been rejected; first for One infinitely her superior, next for one whom she must have held to be far below her; but, what was more serious, she was thereby deprived of her inheritance. This was not to be given up without a struggle. The lawful heir, accordingly, had to make good his claim by force of arms. It was now just two years since Aloysius's blessed death when Ridolfo, full of youth, but with his cup of life embittered by the disgusts and anxieties which worldly honours and worldly affairs bring to those who are attached to them, received his mortal blow at Castel Goffredo. The strength of that fortress had seemed to render it a secure residence for his family during the troubled state of his dominions; hither, accordingly, he had removed them, and was himself with them when he received private intimations that his life was in danger. Naturally bold, he disregarded these warnings, and left the castle with his wife and child to hear mass at a neighbouring church. As he was on the point of entering the sacred building he was fired upon by assassins placed in ambush, and a ball from an arquebuse laid him dead on the threshold. The details and attending circumstances of this fearful tragedy do not belong to our immediate topic;* suffice it to say that so overwhelmed was the bereaved mother by the fatal news, that she fell sick unto death. She had received the Viaticum and Extreme Unction, and her attendants were standing round her expecting her speedy departure: suddenly a ray of joy passes over her pallid countenance. What is it she beholds? Whence this light that beams amidst the shades of death? She sees before her eyes a globe of intense brilliancy, and in the midst of it is her Aluigi. He speaks not a word, but he gazes at his mother with a smile of ineffable sweetness and consolation. After awhile he vanished, but with him were gone sickness, and care, and sorrow. Donna Marta shed some tender and refreshing tears after the vision had departed, and in a very few days she had risen from her bed in perfect health, which she was to preserve for yet many years. But more than this: Aloysius's loving smile had restored hope and confidence to her amidst her complicated troubles and perplexities. By the death

* Castel Goffredo was afterwards, with the Imperial consent, exchanged by Francesco with the Duke of Mantua for Medola, which was erected into a marquisate, Castiglione being raised to the rank of a principality; Solferino was at the same time bestowed on Cristiano, Francesco's brother.

of Ridolfo, who left four daughters but no son, the weighty cares of his estate had devolved on an inexperienced youth of sixteen. Of her flourishing family of eight children, three sons* alone remained to Marta, the eldest of whom was apparently incapable by his tender age of coping with the difficulties which beset his house. Possibly she may now have recalled to mind her angel's prophecy, that Francesco would sustain the honour of his family. The prediction was, indeed, strikingly fulfilled; for young as he was, the boy on whom the cares of government had fallen so early, acquitted himself of his charge in a manner which won universal respect and esteem. True, he enjoyed through life the special patronage of his sainted brother, exhibited, we are told, on many striking occasions; and it may be said that they vied with each other in an interchange of mutual love, for we shall find Francesco exerting himself strenuously to obtain Aloysius's beatification from the Holy See.

In the year 1598, in consequence of an inundation of the Tiber, the vaults of the Annunziata were flooded; whereupon, the Father General gave orders for moving the relics of Aloysius from the low situation which they had hitherto accupied. Occasion was taken to open the coffin and examine the state of the body; it was found with the head gently inclined on one side, Aloysius's habitual attitude in life. Portions were now abstracted in order to satisfy the desires of the faithful. P. Lancicius requested relics for Poland;

* Francesco, Cristiano, and Diego. The last was, three years later, to expire mortally wounded in his mother's arms. As it is purposed to give, in a separate volume, Lives of the three venerable nieces of St. Aloysius, these and other particulars will there find a more appropriate place.

P. Corso for the Indies; besides which, every one wanted some for himself. After reverently kissing the precious deposit, the fathers re-enclosed it in a smaller case, and it was then placed in a higher part of the wall. The fruits of the holy youth's intercession multiplying every day, it became very difficult to restrain the ardent devotion of the faithful, who, especially after the signal miracle at Florence in the year 1600, became very importunate, complaining of the fathers for taking away and hiding the ex-votos and tablets which they brought to suspend before the tomb, a public manifestation of devotion not being permitted by the Church before she has herself made any authoritative declaration. In 1602, it was judged fitting, considering the miracles by which God was attesting the sanctity of Aloysius, to give his relics a separate and more honourable position. Accordingly, the body was placed in a coffin of lead, inclosed in one of wood, and then laid under the step of the altar of St. Sebastian in the same church. Although the translation was performed with the utmost secrecy, yet the faithful contrived to become acquainted with the spot where the relics were deposited. Their devotion had now waxed the more clamorous that a report had spread that a large amount of documents was already in the hands of the Ordinaries, testifying to the wonders everywhere wrought by the intercession of Aloysius. The time seemed come for the Fathers of the Company to take some active step towards obtaining public honours for one who had shed so much lustre on their order. Accordingly, on the 22nd of September, in the year 1603, P. Cepari laid before a provincial congregation assembled in

Piacenza the numerous processes and authentic documents which he had himself collected; with a view to the compilation of a life of their dear and venerated brother. Most of the fathers present had known and conversed with Aloysius, and not one of them but judged that there were abundant grounds for his canonization. They presented therefore a united supplication to the Father General to lay before the Pope a petition expressive of the earnest desire of their province (Venetia) that the cause might be taken in hand by the Holy See.

In the May following, a still more solemn application was made. The former general of the Franciscan order, the venerable Francesco Gonzaga, whom the reader will remember as having, by desire of the Marquis of Castiglione, examined the vocation of the young Aloysius when at the court of Madrid, occupied at this time the Episcopal See of Mantua. He warmly took up the affair, and caused a summary to be compiled of the contents of the processes; he communicated on the subject with the Duke Vincenzo, who was animated by a like eager desire to forward the cause; he convoked a diocesan synod in the cathedral, and, laying the matter before it, proposed to present a formal request to the Holy See in the name of the whole clergy of Mantua, secular and regular, for the canonization of this holy youth, who was sprung from the race of their own princes and whose exaltation to the altars of the Church was ardently desired by both sovereign and people, as the patron and protector of their state. The proposal was joyfully received by the assembly, and when Mgr. Matteo Arigoni, canon of the cathedral, vested in his dalmatic, ascended the pulpit and delivered to his audience a compendium of Aloysius's holy actions and virtues, extracted from the processes, the enthusiasm excited was intense; and not only did all sign the address, but many declared that they had no greater desire than to be able to celebrate the Mass of the Blessed Aloysius. News of these proceedings spreading throughout Lombardy, coupled with the assertion that the synod had given to Aloysius the title of "Blessed," no one now named him without this appellation; nor did the ordinaries raise any objection. In those times the rule was not so strict in these matters, and they easily allowed portraits of the saint to be distributed, with the aureole of glory round his head. The first thus painted was for the dowager duchess of Ferrara, Margaret of Gonzaga, Duke Vincenzo's sister, and copies were executed for all the princes of that noble house.

People would no longer rest satisfied without some public manifestation of their devotion; and here again, the bishops offered no opposition. In the year 1604, Aloysius's anniversary began first to be observed, and his picture suspended in the churches. The students at Brescia took the lead in paying him public homage. On the 21st of June, the church of the Company was adorned as for some great festal solemnity; high mass was sung in thanksgiving for the exaltation of Aloysius, and an eloquent panegyric pronounced in his honour. So great was the enthusiasm which prevailed that the eighty cantors were about to intone in full choir, "*Gaudeamus omnes in Domino, diem festum* *celebrantes sub honore beati Aloysii,*"* had not the fathers, who perceived their preparations, interfered to check this premature demonstration. The fervour of the students was shared by the whole city, lay and clerical. Tears of joy or of contrition fell abundantly from many eyes. Not a few passed immediately to the long neglected confessional, and others, moved to more exalted aims by the example of this glorious youth, conceived such contempt of the world that they resolved to give themselves to God in religion. Castiglione, the native place of the saint, could not remain behind in doing him honour. Leave was asked of the bishop, in the name of the whole people, and, in particular, of the venerable marchesa and of the archpriest, to enjoy the same consolation which had been accorded to Brescia. This favour was granted, and on the 28th of July, being the feast of SS. Nazarius and Celsus, and consequently the festal day of the collegiate church, the picture of Aloysius was exposed to the veneration of his loving people, who had continued affectionately to call him their holy marquis, their beloved lord, and now hailed in him the tutelary angel of Castiglione. Suspended over the altar amidst a blaze of lights, it their received the homage of a whole prostrate population; and the first to come and kneel before it was she, the happy mother of this blessed youth, followed by Francesco's young Bohemian bride, Donna Bibiana.†. The Dominican father, Silvestro

* "Let us all rejoice in the Lord, celebrating a festival-day in honour of the blessed Aloysius."

† This lady's name, Italianized by Cepari into Perneste, was Pernstein. She was of very noble descent. Her family was originally Moravian; her father held a high position, as privy councillor to the Emperor and chancellor of Bohemia. Her

Ugoletti, preached the panegyric of his late brother in religion and former lord in the world, for his family were vassals of the house of Gonzaga; all circumstances therefore combined to animate his tongue, and make it eloquent upon a theme so interesting to his hearers. He preached from the Apocalypse: "*Qui vicerit, faciam illum columnam in templo Dei mei; et foras non egredietur amplius: et scribam super eum Nomen Dei mei;*"* descanting upon the heroic victories achieved by Aloysius in his flight from the world, and showing how God had stamped the Most Holy Name of His Son on his forehead by calling him to the Company of Jesus. But how must every heart have been electrified when, turning towards Donna Marta, and calling her a thousand times more fortunate than queen or empress who had shared the earthly triumphs of her sons, he exclaimed, "O most happy mother! who beholdest him whom living thou wert wont to call thy angel, now crowned with glory upon the altar!" Then, addressing the Princess Bibiana, who was about to join her husband, at that time Imperial ambassador at the court of Rome, "Go, lady," he said, "and may your journey be as prosperous as we all beseech Heaven to grant you,—go, and so plead our cause before the Sovereign Pontiff that he may accord with-

maternal grandfather is stated confidently by a respectable authority (Balbinus in his *Nobilitatis Bohemicæ Tabula*) to have intermarried with the Kostkas; an interesting circumstance, if true, as connecting in life the two who, as in glory they are eternally united, so in the devotional remembrance of the faithful are ever conjoined—St. Aloysius Gonzaga and St. Stanislas Kostka.

* "He that shall overcome, I will make him a pillar in the temple of my God; and he shall go out no more: and I will write upon him the Name of my God."—Apoc. iii. 12.

out delay to your faithful vassals the favour they so earnestly long for, to see our prince inscribed in the catalogue of the saints." The festival lasted three days, during which Castiglione gave itself up to an exuberant joy surpassing all that the greatest patriotic triumph could have called forth.

It was but a few days later, on the 5th of August in this same year, when the Prince Francesco Gonzaga, being admitted to audience by Pope Clememt VIII., at whose court we have seen he was the Emperor's accredited ambassador, was asked by his Holiness whether he was related to a Gonzaga who had studied in the Roman College of the Jesuit Fathers, and had died with the reputation of great sanctity. "I remember," he continued, "hearing Cardinal Scipione Gonzaga relate wonderful things concerning that youth before I was Pope; and, in particular, that he never went to converse with him at the college without returning with his handkerchief steeped in tears." "He was my brother," replied Francesco. "Now," rejoined the Holy Father, "I have the explanation of what has often caused me to marvel, how you have safely passed through so many perils;* this you undoubtedly owe to his intercession." Then, gazing on a holy image which was before him, his eyes gently filling with tears, he exclaimed, "Blessed he who is in the enjoyment of eternal glory, and blessed you also, who have such an intercessor in Heaven." He then asked the prince if his brother's life had been printed, and when Francesco answered in the negative, he reproved him for his neglect, and exhorted him to

* P. Cepari does not explain what these perils were; probably they were too notorious at the time to need more than a reference.

procure its publication for the general good. Francesco, whose heart was already full of zeal for the honour of Aloysius, so dear to his youthful memory, and whom he now esteemed to be the glory of his house, did not fail to press forward the completion of P. Cepari's biography; and while the father was finishing the work, emboldened by the devotion which Clement had manifested towards his brother, he solicited and obtained, a few months later, leave to have Aloysius's body transferred from the altar step of St. Sebastian, where it lay concealed, to a more honourable position. But Clement died soon after the accorded permission; his successor on the Papal chair followed him a month after his election; and Francesco had to wait his opportunity to obtain the sanction of Paul V. for the ceremony of the removal of the holy body. On the 13th of May, 1605, it was borne by the fathers of the Company in procession, with solemn pomp of lights and music, to the place destined for its reception in the chapel of the Madonna in the same church of the Annunziata. The relics had been previously again examined, and a portion of them given to Francesco di Gonzaga for himself and for the Duke of Mantua, the head being reserved in the church of the Gesu at Rome; but afterwards, at the request of the same prince, it was bestowed on the church of the Company in Castiglione. Although it was attempted to keep this translation as private as possible, and to conduct it with closed doors, this was found to be impossible. In the first place, the Imperial ambassador must needs be present—he had an irrefragable claim; and then the ambassadress, his consort could not be excluded; the duke of Poli and other lords followed in their train: the door could not be shut in their face; but then the devout crowd pushed in after the nobility, and the fathers were obliged to be content to regulate what they could not prevent. After all, perchance, they were little to be pitied if they had to be long engaged in marshalling the pious throng come to present their loving homage to him whom they themselves so cordially delighted to honour, admitting them one by one to venerate and kiss the sacred relics, and touch them with their beads, before consigning them to their new resting-place. Here they no longer remained underground, occupying an obscure position, but were lodged aloft in the wall, with this conspicuous inscription: "*Beatus Aloysius Gonzaga a Societate Jesu.*"*

Nothing was now wanting to complete the satisfaction of the people but the permission for the public exposure of Aloysius's picture with the rays of glory encircling his head, a lamp burning before it, and the *ex-voto* offerings hanging around. This favour had been already requested by Francesco when, on the first visit he had made to the new Pope, he had preferred his petition for his brother's canonization. Paul V. allowed him to hope, but to a former co-disciple of the saint was reserved the honour of obtaining this exceptional grace. On the 21st of this same month of May, Cardinal Dietrichstein went to take leave of his Holiness, preparatory to his return to Germany. He had already left the Papal presence, when, as he was descending the stairs, the remembrance of Aloysius rose before his mind. Forthwith he returned, and besought the Pope most earnestly to allow

* "Blessed Aloysius Gonzaga of the Society of Jesus."

proceedings to be commenced for his beatification. He urged the many processes which had been drawn up and attested by the bishops who had given licence for the exposure of pictures of Aloysius in churches, and reminded his Holiness that Pope Clement had urged the publication of his life and permitted his relics to be venerated; in conclusion, he solicited leave, while the cause was in progress, to have Aloysius's picture suspended at his tomb. The Pontiff benignantly acceded, and the delighted cardinal went straight to the church of the Roman College. He kept his secret, enjoying, no doubt, not a little the sweet surprise he was about to cause the good fathers of the Company. The Imperial ambassador was in the chapel waiting for him. They repeated the canonical hours together on their knees; the cardinal then rising, asked for Aloysius's picture. The fathers listened in silent wonder to the unexpected request; but Francesco di Gonzaga—to whom his Eminence had whispered his success—unable to restrain his own eager impatience, went himself at once into the sacristy, where the portrait with the aureole of glory was kept; mounting on a chair, he took it down and bore it to the tomb, where he with one hand and the cardinal with the other gave it to the accompanying priest, the Abbate Paolo de Angelis, that he might raise it to its appointed place. Then all the tablets and votive offerings which had been laid by were produced and suspended around, the ambassador himself fixing the first, while his major-domo, the good Clemente Ghisoni, had the welcome office of hanging up the lamp before his young lord's glorious tomb. The cardinal immediately offered in thanksgiving a votive mass of the Holy Spirit in the chapel, and was observed, both before and frequently during the celebration, to turn to do reverence to the blessed Aloysius.

The delight of all the devout clients of our saint may well be imagined at this first public cultus in his honour conceceded by the Holy See. The news soon spread throughout the Catholic world, and was received with universal applause. The next 21st of June was solemnized with festal joy, by many Italian cities. Castiglione, Brescia, Parma, Florence vied with each other in the pomp of their celebrations; but it was in Rome especially that the demonstration was the most remarkable, for Francesco Gonzaga, after obtaining the Pope's sanction for keeping, not one day only, but an octave in honour of Aloysius in the church of the Roman College undertook the expense of the festival at his own entire charge, with a magnificence worthy of a canonization. Besides the splendid ornaments with which the sacred deposit was surrounded, he presented to the Chapel of the Madonna the most costly altar furniture, including a splendid set of vestments blazing with gold embroidery, in order, as he said, to testify his gratitude to the Blessed Mother of God for having received his sainted brother into her sanctuary.

It would be vain, however, to attempt to narrate in detail all the honours which were paid to Aloysius even before his solemn enrolment amongst the saints. His beatification, indeed could not now be far distant; it required but the final seal to be affixed by the Vicar of Christ to what he had already orally conceded, and the faithful throughout the world were irresistably proclaiming with one united voice. On the 29th of

July, Francesco was again at the Pontiff's feet to renew his supplication, with eighteen processes of bishops in his hand. In August his holiness was besieged with fresh petitions. The grand dukes of Tuscany and Parma sent in pressing memorials to the same effect, and the venerable bishop of Mantua, P Francesco Gonzaga, came in person to express the eager solicitude of both himself and his clergy. The following day brought Duke Vincenzo of Mantua to urge his suit for the beatification of his relative, so earnestly desired by the whole Gonzaga family as well as by his subjects. The Pontiff gave a favourable reply, and as the cause of St. Frances of Rome was then pending, he appointed a special Congregation of three cardinals, one of whom was Aloysius's old confessor, Bellarmine, to examine the processes, causing also the written life of P. Cepari to be compared therewith, and to report their opinion whether the title of *Beato* could be in the meantime accorded to Aloysius, according to the earnest request of the Prince Gonzaga. Their judgment was to this effect: that, considering his high sanctity, and the thirty-one instantaneous miracles extracted from the hundred contained in these processes, Aloysius Gonzaga was worthy not only of beatification, but of canonization. His Holiness accordingly at once decreed him the title of "blessed," and ordered his life to be printed with the same appellation. The brief addressed to Francesco Gonzaga was dated the 10th of October of this year, 1605; and Heaven itself appeared to add its own approving seal to this solemn document, by a striking miracle worked in the person of the Doctor Flaminio Bacci, the substitute of the Secretary of Rites, who specially invoked the saint that he might not be hindered by illness from labouring in promoting his canonization.

It was not until the time of Pope Alexander VII., that the practice was adopted of solemnizing the beatification of a servant of God in the Vatican; although therefore this ceremony did not take place in the case of our saint, nevertheless his exaltation was honoured with great pomp and festal rejoicing both at Rome and in other Italian cities. The princes of the house of Gonzaga, as participating most largely in the joy and glory of the occasion, were foremost in magnificent and costly display. The feast of St. Thomas the Apostle was selected for the celebration in Mantua. By order of the bishop, the Advent preaching was that day suspended at the Duomo; and on the very threshold of the great feast of the Nativity the Church paused, as it were, to turn herself with loving reverence to one whose innocence, meekness, and sweet humility must have made him specially dear to the heart of the Babe of Bethlehem.

A new chapel had been constructed in the cathedral by the bishop; it was splendidly adorned, and enriched with a relic of the saint, which the venerable prelate had received from Rome. On the vigil, this chapel was opened to public view; and on the following day a gorgeous procession bearing the picture of the saint, with the bishop clothed pontifically and accompanied by all his clergy, advanced through the streets, with pomp of music and choral voices, to the Duomo. Vincenzo, his family and court, and all the nobility of the land followed in their train. A Pontifical Mass of the Holy Trinity was celebrated with all the accompanying magnificence with which the pious love of the house of Gonzaga could adorn it; and a sermon, which lasted nearly two hours, was delivered in praise of the saint. Attention and interest never flagged on the part of the audience, and the Capuchin preacher concluded by protesting that he had *said* nothing, but had only *wished* to say; nay, so inexhaustible was the theme, that at vespers, when the relic was exposed in the chapel, there was a second panegyric of the Blessed Aloysius pronounced by a father of the Company. But that which did most honour to the saint, and is the most worthy of remembrance, was the fervent devotion manifested in the multitude of communions which were made on this day. The spectacle which was presented on this occasion is one which must have stirred every Christian heart to its lowest depths; but when we remember that the crowd which knelt before the holy relic, and which included some of the highest nobility of the land, numbered in its ranks hundreds who had seen and known that modest, humble, silent boy whom now they were venerating as a saint in glory,—that not a few among them were connected with him by ties of blood,—and that the bishop who offered mass in his honour was the very person who had been called to examine the vocation and try the spirit of the youth who was now exalted to a throne in Heaven, the very same who had held sweet familiar converse with him, as day after day they paced together the deck of the vessel which bore them over the Mediterranean waters,—the scene acquires a touching interest, which must have enhanced even the joys of one of the greatest triumphs which the Church can celebrate on earth—the first public manifestation of homage to a beatified servant of God.

CHAPTER II.

The Saint's Canonization.

It seems at first sight matter of no little surprise that a saint so universally honoured, whose exaltation was desired and promoted by kings and nobles, and who was beatified but fourteen years after his death, should not have been canonized before more than a century had elapsed. Some apparently accidental reasons may be assigned, but it would seem as if God had designed this delay for the purpose of conferring the greater honour on His servant. During this interval no less than eighty supplications from emperors, kings, nobles, and communities, religious and secular, were presented to the Holy See, and no canonized saint perhaps ever received more affectionate and ardent homage, or had his name illustrated by more numerous miracles.

We cannot pass without notice what may be considered as one of the blessed fruits of the intercession of our saint, the sanctification of the children of his brother, the turbulent and unspiritual Ridolfo. The reader will remember that the murdered prince left four daughters; of these the second, Elena, died in infancy, but the other three, Cinzia, Olimpia, and Gridonia, survived to become distinguished in the annals of the Church. Their mother, Elena Aliprandi, after undergoing with her children many troubles and vicissitudes, contracted a second marriage with another member of the Gonzaga family, Claudio, lord of Borgo-Forte. The tutelage of her daughters was now conferred by the Emperor on their uncle Francesco. These girls from their earliest childhood had been remarkable for their piety and love of mortification. Cinzia and Olimpia, as they advanced in years, had been also peculiarly drawn to tread in the steps of their saintly uncle; but Gridonia was for a while seduced by the flattering visions of earthly felicity. Cinzia was the first to vow her virginity to God, in which she was followed by Olimpia; and by their united prayers they won from Heaven Gridonia's conversion. With the consent of her uncle, the Prince Francesco, Cinzia founded a religious house at Castiglione; he resigning to her and her companions, who took the name of the Virgins of Jesus, the palace which his mother used formerly to occupy, and founding a house of the Company in that city, in order that his nieces might continue to enjoy the direction of the Jesuit Fathers. In the year 1608, on the 21st of June, the anniversary of the Blessed Aloysius, the sisters passed from the Rock castle to their house of retirement, followed by ten other ladies, their associates; and in the same year Paul V. allowed this house of holy virgins to take the Blessed Aloysius as their protector and patron. So manifest had been the intervention of the saint in the whole affair, that Francesco, desirous of perpetuating its remembrance, after converting the room in which Aloysius was born into a chapel, had a picture hung over the altar representing him standing crowned with glory before the Queen of Virgins, in the act of drawing his nieces Cinzia and Olimpia by two golden chains and presenting them to Mary. The absence of Gridonia from the picture marks that the vocation of Cinzia and Olimpia was more immediately referred to Aloysius ; Gridonia's conversion, if it had taken place, was quite recent.

The mother of the three foundresses also experienced the benefit of the saint's patronage. She fell ill in the commencement of the same year, but she was still in the flower of her days, and might well hope for many years of life, and that youth and strength might yet avail her to battle with her malady. But the hand of death was on her ; and Aloysius, for whom she entertained both a warm gratitude and an ardent devotion, would obtain for her the grace to make a truly devout and Christian end ; he appeared to her, and told her she was to die in eight days ; he fortified and consoled her, and his words brought peace to her troubled soul : from that instant she calmly prepared for her departure.

Her three daughters lived like angels, and died the death of saints. To their heroic virtues God bore witness by the preservation of their mortal remains from corruption. In the year 1679, and again in 1720, their tombs were opened, and though their clothes were found crumbled to dust, yet their bodies had remained intact : their limbs were quite flexible, and the resemblance to their portraits was clearly perceptible. Each time they were clothed anew ; and on the last occasion it was necessary, in order to satisfy the popular devotion, to leave them with their faces exposed to view for three days. The tombs were again opened in 1815, and again no change had taken place. The last examination was made as late as the year 1838, when the bodies were found still uncorrupted, and were once more exposed to public veneration.

To return to our main subject from what, however can scarcely be considered a digression, so nearly concerning as it does the honour of our saint: from all parts of Europe the richest presents were continually arriving at his tomb, and the concourse of devout worshippers was ever on the increase. Amongst them are reckoned names high in honour in the Church. Cardinal Baronious, we are told, used to kneel and kiss the pavement, and he had himself carried thither to invoke the saint two days before his death. Sometimes no less than twelve masses would be said in the little chapel in the course of a single morning. The desire for his canonization increased proportionately with the increasing devotion. Already Paul V., in the year 1607, having regard to the twenty-two processes presented by the bishops and to the urgent petitions, not only of the Prince Francesco Gonzaga, but of several crowned heads—not to speak of the great number of distinguished persons, religious and secular, whose requests had poured in upon him—had referred the cause for examination to the Sacred Congregation of Rites, which gave its favourable judgment on the 19th of January, 1608, deciding that the mass and office in his honour might be conceded, if so it pleased the Sovereign Pontiff. It was on this occasion that Cardinal Bellarmine declared that, there being two roads to the highest honours of the Church, innocence and penitence, Aloysius had trod them both. So great was the joy of the assembled prelates, when the decree was given, that at the close of the congregation they sent for the postulator, P. Cepari, to congratulate him, and the Cardinal Ferdinando Gonzaga, in a transport of joy, threw his arms round the father's neck, whom, as belonging to Aloysius's spiritual family, he regarded as having an equal share in the exultation of the saint's natural relatives. Five years more elapsed while the Rota, according to the then practice, was examining the processes. Of the three auditors appointed, one, Giovanni Battista Panfilio, subsequently occupied the Papal throne as Innocent X. After twenty-three sessions, in which the virtues and twelve miracles of the saint were examined and approved, the Sacred Tribunal, on the 1st of February, 1617, gave its final decision that, for his eminent sanctity and signal miracles, Aloysius was worthy of canonization.

It may be worth observing here that the Sacred Tribunal of the Rota, in the relation which it presented to the Pope, from first to last gives Aloysius that name of "angelic" so specially attributed to him by the devotion of the Church; "*De sanctitate et miraculis angelici Aloysii Gonzagæ virginis*," being the very title which heads the report. His mother, it will be remembered, as by a kind of supernatural presentiment, called him by this name from his very infancy and now in heaven, it forms one of the radiant gems of his crown, as on earth, it has added lustre to the Society of Jesus; for the Blessed John Berchmans, himself so close an imitator of the angelic virtues of Aloysius, remarked that as St. Francis Xavier was the first to introduce into the Company the title of *Apostle*, so did Aloysius, with exceeding glory, bring into it that of *Angel.* The Congregation of Rites having, on the 31st of March, 1618, approved the report of the Rota, and confirmed its own original decision, given six years before, it was judged that the mass and office of the "Beato" might be granted for all the states belonging to the different branches of the Gonzaga family in Italy, and for the churches of the Company of Jesus in Rome. Paul V. ratified this judgment, and benignantly made the concession which filled with joy the numerous princely families which claimed kindred with the saint, and that family of his adoption which was bound to him by the far closer tie of spiritual relationship. Nothing could surpass the enthusiasm and splendour with which the festival of Aloysius was celebrated that year by the Gonzaga princes, but nowhere with such touching affection as at Castiglione, where the warm attachment of his vassals had never cooled. In throngs they went in procession with their princes* to honour his sacred head at the Company's church, and then poured back to the collegiate church of SS. Nazarius and Celsus, where high festal pomp in honour of the saint was also being kept; while in the streets, resounding with music and the martial din of the Rock artillery, the shout perpetually rent the sky,—a shout like to that which greets some living conqueror returning with the spoils of victory—" Viva, viva in eterno, il nostro principe Aluigi (Live, live for ever, our prince Aluigi)!"

Whether or not it were because he had already canonized St. Frances of Rome and St. Charles Borromeo, and that he therefore judged it more convenient to defer that of Aloysius Gonzaga, Paul V.

* Francesco Gonzago died in the year 1616, and was succeeded by his son Lewis.

contented himself with the above concession. Certain expressions in the brief which he addressed in reply to an application from the duke of Mantua would lead to this conclusion. These causes besides, as is well known, meet with many delays, and always advance at that thoughtful and deliberate pace which characterizes all the proceedings of the Roman See ; add to which, desirous as was the Company to see its dear son Aloysius raised to the altars of the Universal Church, it had other objects of a similar character in view, which possessed a previous claim. The great founder Ignatius was himself not yet canonized, and then there were St. Francis Xavier and the General St. Francis Borgia, to both of whom, it might be well presumed, the younger children would willingly yield precedence.* Supplications, however, continued to be presented by the Gonzaga family, and Urban VIII. having, in the year 1630, published a jubilee to obtain peace for Europe, disturbed by the war of Mantua, the Emperor Ferdinand II. and his consort, Eleanora Gonzaga, having great confidence in the intercession of their holy kinsman to restore the blessings of concord, earnestly entreated for his canonization. But Urban had already canonized St. Elisabeth of Portugal, and in the previous year, St. Andrew Corsini; he had also just given to the Company St. Francis Borgia and the Japanese martyrs, all of whom he had beatified : while commending therefore the piety of the Imperial sovereigns, he declined at present awarding the highest honours of the Church to Aloysius. Nevertheless from time to time the

* St. Ignatius was canonized in 1622 ; St. Francis Xavier in 1662 ; and St. Francis Borgia in 1671.

original concession was greatly extended; so that at last, not only did all the houses of the Company enjoy the privilege of his mass and office, but many other churches besides. Indeed, it would be difficult to enumerate the various altars at which the saint was venerated previously to his final exaltation; not a few of them, from the number and richness of their votive offerings, rivalling the most celebrated sanctuaries of Christendom. The rooms which he had inhabited, both in the secular and in the religious state, had been converted into chapels, while his sepulchre every day increased in glory. A splendid church had been built and dedicated to St. Ignatius; begun by the Cardinal Ludovisi in 1626, but interrupted in the course of construction by that prelate's death, it was completed in the year 1649. The translation of our saint's relics to a side chapel in the new edifice, where now stands the altar of St. Joseph, occupying the site of the apartment hallowed by his precious death, has been already mentioned; but this was not to be their final resting-place. In order, however, that with the lapse of time the memory of this circumstance might not perish, a picture representing the dying saint was suspended at the spot, with this inscription: "*Hic olim Beati Aloysii cubiculum fuit et sepulchrum* (Here formerly was the chamber of the Blessed Aloysius, and his tomb)." In the year 1699 his holy body was once more removed, and placed in the sumptuous chapel which the family of Lancellotti had constructed in gratitude for the numerous benefits conferred upon them for a century past through the saint's intercession. Meanwhile he had received in the year 1672, fresh honour from the reigning Pontiff, Clement X., who caused his name to be inscribed in the Roman martyrology, with the eulogium bestowed on him by the Rota: "Famous for the innocence of his life and the contempt of his principality."

During the Pontificate of Clement XI. many requests were again presented by crowned heads and other conspicuous persons to the Holy See, but Clement died before being able to more than approve some of the saint's writings and give permission to proceed with the cause. By his successor, Innocent XIII., it was resumed at the stage it had previously reached; but to Benedict XIII., who from his earliest years had cherished the tenderest devotion for Aloysius, which he had manifested by many acts during his episcopal career, was reserved the glory of terminating it. This great pontiff was no sooner seated on the chair of Peter, than one of his first cares was to hasten forward the canonization of the saint whom he so deeply venerated. The decree and bull were promulgated on the 26th of April, in the year 1726, and on the 31st of December of the same year, Aloysius Gonzaga was raised to the highest honours of the Church along with the Blessed Stanislas Kostka, the twin-glory of youth and the Company which had possessed them. His canonization seemed to be the signal for the pouring forth of fresh graces and mercies through his pure hands. Countless as were the miracles of healing and the other temporal blessings thus obtained, they were surpassed by those which had reference to the spiritual order; it seemed one and the same thing to be devout to this saint and to have an ardent love of purity, the spirit of contrition, and a desire to please

God in all things. On the 22nd of November, 1729, Benedict XIII. gave St. Aloysius to the young students of the Company as their special protector; and, not contented with this, he extended his patronage to youth generally, whereever they might be receiving their education. Clement XIII. conceded a plenary indulgence to the faithful who should communicate in his honour on the six Sundays preceding his festival, or any other six consecutive Sundays in the year.* All the Popes, indeed seem to have emulated each other in the zeal with which they encourage devotion to the angelic Aloysius. It is not purposed here to attempt any enumeration of the privileges accorded with this view; suffice it to say that our revered Father, the present reigning Pontiff has trod in the steps of his predecessors by adding to them, while he has signally marked his desire to honour St. Aloysius in his own person, as well as to promote the love and veneration of him in the hearts of all his children.

CHAPTER III.

THE SAINT'S MIRACLES.

THE lives of saints are set before us, not only to excite our admiration and veneration and thereby move us to imitate them according to our individual measure and capacity, but also to inspire us with confidence in their aid and protection. It is the lively conviction

* This indulgence can be obtained on each of the Sundays the question having been mooted and decided affirmatively.

of their intercessory power with God which creates this feeling in us, and if we fail to pay them this tribute of holy trust, we so far withold from these favourites of Heaven the honour which is their due, not to speak of the loss which such defect entails upon ourselves. For this end the Lord has been pleased to set the seal of miracles on their sanctity; and the biographies of saints commonly conclude with a detailed account of favours and cures obtained through their means. Writers feel that their work is incomplete without such addition; and yet in the case of one like Aloysius, who has been glorified by countless attestations of his power with God, it seems utterly hopeless to do any justice to the subject without appending such a voluminous catalogue of prodigies as most readers would consider tedious. Well indeed, when we reflect on the prodigality of wonders with which God has honoured this great saint, can we realize the truth of what the holy widow Arsilia in a vision heard the Lord say to him: "Ask and grant." The truly gracious Aloysius is never weary of asking favours for his devout clients, and is ever faithfully granting what God never refuses to pour into his beneficent hands. The promoter of his canonization, P. Budrioli, alone noted as many as 2,345 acknowledged miracles, and this number of course very imperfectly represented the real untold amount of the favours, spiritual and temporal, which, even a hundred years ago, had been accorded to his intercession: and who can reckon the number of those which have since been added to the list! The plan which we therefore propose to follow is to limit ourselves to recounting a few instances of Aloysius's miraculous intervention selecting such as may prove interesting from their circumstances, without any regard to chronological order, and interspersing occasional remarks on some of the characteristics by which they are often distinguished.*

We have seen the complete disengagement of the saint. while on earth, from all domestic ties and affections; some might even think that he pushed this renunciation to the verge of a cold indifference; but this would be an illusion. When creatures are no longer loved for their own sakes, they are really loved with a deeper and a truer love. The ingredient of self-love is commonly very strong, and is never entirely wanting in natural affection; this self-love goes to increase the seeming vivacity and to swell the apparent amount of the love we bear to others. while it detracts from its sterling value. But when the love of our neighbour has become merged in the love of God, then it begins to partake of the qualities of perfect love; then for the first time do relatives and friends become the objects of a pure and disinterested affection; for it is truly *they* who are now loved, not *theirs*. When Aloysius had passed into Heaven the many favours and graces obtained by him for his kindred are proof sufficient that their claim on his affection was not disavowed by the glorified saint. Mention has already been made of his apparition to his mother, and her instantaneous recall from the gates of death and from the depths of mental despondency; she herself re-

* The miracles related in this chapter have all been extracted from the authentic processes which, contain the original depositions of the witnesses, taken down before judges specially delegated by the Apostolic See or appointed by the ordinaries of the places where they occured.

lated the vision to Cepari. We have heard how he was the defence of his brother Francesco in many unrecorded perils and troubles; we have seen the fruits of his intercession in the vocation of his nieces; Cinzia, the eldest, was miraculously raised from a bed of suffering, while their mother, Elena Aliprandi, was comforted and strengthened by him in her dying hours. A like favour was in later years accorded to Prince Luigi, the son of Francesco, who ruled Castiglione after his father's death. He fell a victim to the plague at twenty-six years of age; the terrors of death assailed him, but Aloysius appeared to him, and so fortified and consoled him, that he resigned himself with perfect submission to the Divine will and mercy. Another child of his loved Francesco also experienced the saint's protection. Giovanna Gonzaga having gone, in the year 1674, to visit the blessed Aloysius's sanctuary in Sasso, which will be noticed bye and bye, was thrown in her carriage over a precipice. As she was falling, she invoked her sainted uncle, and felt the vehicle sustained in its decent, till it gently rested at the foot of the cliff, where the princess was found by her servants sitting uninjured with her little dog still in her lap. Aloysius's powerful patronage was also experienced by the collateral members of his family, as well as by others more remotely connected. Vincenzo Gonzaga. the duke of Mantua, loudly proclaimed his deliverance from an excruciating malady by the application of a relic of the saint; and a splendid lamp which was sent from distant Poland and suspended at his sepulchre, bore testimony to the gratitude of the grand marshal of that country, the Marquis Sigismond Mikouski Gonzaga, for instantaneous freedom from indescribable torture by pressing to his bosom a picture of Aloysius and a manuscript compendium of his life which he had in his possession. His old servants and dependants alike experienced Aloysius's protection. Camilla Ferrari, who had borne him as an infant in her arms, was miraculously cured by the saint when at the point of death, and received a like favour in the case of two of her children. His faithful cameriere, Clemente Ghisoni, who had been promoted to the office of majordomo, dismayed and confounded at a large discrepancy in the balance of his accounts, knelt down and invoked his blessed master Aloysius, reminding him of the fidelity and devotion with which he had served him on earth; then full of trust he lay down to rest. When morning dawned, he heard the loved familiar voice calling to him and telling him where to look for the entry of the disbursed sum for which he had been unable to account.

If generous to the family connected with him by blood or service, we may well expect that he was not niggardly of his favours to the spiritual family of his adoption, of which he had been in life so loving a member. From amongst the many on record we will select two.

In the year 1634 Giuseppe Spinelli was seized, at the age of twenty-two years, with a kind of fit or swoon, followed by delirium, which left him in a state of total bodily prostration. He was paralyzed in his limbs, had lost his speech, and seemed in hourly danger of suffocation. The last sacraments were administered to him, and no hope was entertained of his recovery, nor, indeed, was it supposed to be possible. His mental faculties, however, were unimpaired, and he occupied himself in fervent prayer, especially begging the intercession of St. Aloysius, for whom he had a great devotion. The relic of the saint was brought into his room, and he promised him to fast upon his vigil every year if he would restore him to health. The first effect of his patron's intercession was a great accession of ardour to devote himself to God's service: this was an earnest of what was to follow. The sick youth now redoubled his supplications, and fell asleep praying so that he seemed in his dream to continue still to pray, when suddenly he heard a clear, sonorous voice calling him by his name,—"Giuseppe, Giuseppe;" and he, still asleep, replied, "Who is it that calls me! So loud was his cry that it roused the infirmarian in the adjoining room, who hoped that his patient had recovered his speech, and hurried in to know what he wanted. But Spinelli, when awakened, could no longer utter a word. To his confessor alone did he impart (and that, of course, in writing) what had happened, in order that he might assist him by his prayers in obtaining the boon he sought from Aloysius.

Four days later, he had another dream. He felt his right hand taken by some one, and, looking round, beheld two youths of the Company, habited in cottas, at his bedside. He at once recognized them as St. Aloysius and the Blessed John Berchmans. Aloysius lovingly addressed him; "What do you desire, Giuseppe?" "To recover my speech," Spinelli replied, "and to be able to walk." And Aloysius, "Why not rather die?" To which Giuseppe simply rejoined, "*Dominus est: quod bonum est in oculis suis faciat* —(It is the Lord: let Him do what is good in His eyes)." "Be of good cheer," said the amiable saint; "you shall recover your speech, but God does not will that you should as yet have the use of your feet:" then he added, "nevertheless *confortare et esto robustus; grandis enim tibi restat via*—(Take comfort and be strong; for thou hast yet a great way to go)." This said, he and his companion disappeard, but Spinelli went on dreaming, and seemed to see the image of the saint, with his relic, before the bed, and around it some of the brethren of the house praying for his recovery. He thought that the use of his tongue was restored, and that he intoned the *Te Deum*, in which the others joined. But, awaking soon after, he found his tongue still tied. Interpreting the dream to signify what he was to do in order to obtain the favour he desired, he begged his confessor, in writing, to have the image of Aloysius, which contained the relic of the saint, brought to him. It was accordingly carried into his room by the rector, some of the lay brothers accompanying it with lighted candles. Giuseppe was now filled with joyful confidence. Left alone with the image he fell asleep, when behold! again the two spotless youths, Aloysius and John, stood before him. Aloysius said, "God has vouchsafed you the restoration of your speech Know, however, that by His just judgment you would have remained dumb all your life; but for my merits this boon has been accorded to you. Now it is God's will that you should consecrate your tongue to His honour, by praising and blessing Him; beware of ever abusing it to His offence. Know that this is to be the principle of your salvation and religious perfection, and that you must daily renew the determination you have made, to give yourself henceforth with more fervour to perfection; and thank God for having, for my merits restored to you your speech. Let not hard trials and adversities—for you will encounter many—terrify you; I will be your guide; of this be well assured. As for the power of walking, the time is not yet mature for your recovery. But do you not remember your vow to fast every year on my vigil?" Spinelli replied in the affirmative. Aloysius continued, "And will you not also make a vow to add a quater of an hour to your morning prayer, and another half-hour when you receive communion?" Giuseppe agreed, and made the vow. Then the saint opened a silver vessel which he had in his hand, dipped his finger in it, and made the sign of the cross on the sick youth's tongue, who awoke exclaiming, "O blessed Luigi! O blessed Luigi!" His speech was perfectly restored.

Four more days now elapsed, when one afternoon, while Spinelli was discoursing with some of the brethren about his beloved saint, he fell into a light sleep, and seemed to say to himself, "When shall I at last be able to say, '*Lauda, anima mea, Dominum; quoniam non deserit sperantem in se et in beato Aloysio* (Praise the Lord, O my soul; for he forsaketh not him that hopeth in Him and in the blessed Aloysius)'? Nevertheless I resign myself entirely to the good pleasure of God, and desire that His holy will may be accomplished in me." While he was thus speaking to himself, the Blessed Berchmans appeared and said, "Do you sleep, Giuseppe? Know you not that the time for your cure is come? Pray earnestly with others before the relic of the Blessed Aloysius, that he may finish the work that is begun." Spinelli awoke, and confided all to the rector and to his confessor, begging them to keep it secret, but to ask the prayers of all the fathers and brothers. That evening the image was again brought and left in his room. Spinelli gave himself with redoubled confidence to prayer; at last he fell into a sweet sleep, and heard the words, "The time of your cure is come," again repeated. At the same moment he beheld the two heavenly companions enter the room. Aloysius bore his silver vessel, and Berchmans on this occasion had a napkin hanging on his arm. "Courage, Giuseppe," said Aloysius drawing near, "and be joyful." To which Giuseppe replied, "What greater joy can I have than your presence? What return can I make for such a favour?" "I desire nothing but your sanctification," said Aloysius: "labour to become a saint. God requires many and great things of you. Do you wish to have me for your guide?" "What dearer wish can I have?" answered the sick man; "with you as my leader, if hosts should encamp against me my heart will not fear." "Be of good courage, then," replied Aloysius; "for I will direct you in the way; and I desire that henceforth your name should be Luigi, in remembrance of so many benefits, and to serve you as a stimulus to follow diligently after perfection." "I am not worthy," said Giuseppe, "of such a name or of such favour; nevertheless I willingly accept it." "It is time now," said the saint, "for you to walk. But first I wish you to bind yourself by vow to make the Spiritual Exercises of our holy father St. Ignatius for a month." To this Giuseppe at once consented. The Blessed John Berchmans now approached the bed of the paralytic man, and removed the bandages from his leg; Aloysius dipped his finger into the vase and signed the limb with the ointment. saying, *Deus omnipotens det tibi, per merita sancti Patris nostri Ignatii et Aloysii, ut possis ambulare, et faciat ut ambulatio ista sit ad vitam eternam* (May Almighty God grant thee, by the merits of our holy father Ignatius and of Aloysius, that thou mayest be able to walk, and that thy walking may be to life eternal)." John Berchmans then wiped off the ointment with the napkin which he carried. The saint next signed the thigh with the same prayer, and then the arm in like manner, varying only a few of the words. This done, he again addressed the sick man: "Now, my Luigi, you are cured, and nothing remains for you to do but to strive after the acquisition of virtue." He then graciously added, "Do you desire anything more?" Spinelli answered "The spiritual health of my companion and the fulfilment of his desires" (he meant the novice who habitually shared his room), "as also those of the infirmarian, and of all who have recommended themselves to my prayers." "You have made a good request," said Aloysius: "you shall obtain spiritual health; but remember—and lay this up in your heart—sedulously to preserve it." So saying he gave his hand to the youth to kiss, blessed him, and disappeared with his heavenly associate. At the same moment Spinelli awoke, exclaiming, "O my Luigi! O my Luigi! I am cured, I am cured," and, springing from his bed, he threw himself at the feet of the image of his deliverer, where he remained an hour in fervent thanksgiving. The morning saw the new Luigi in the church, serving mass at the altar of his holy benefactor. Spinelli was afterwards ordained priest, and at his own earnest desire was sent on the Indian missions. In the Philippine Islands, he consumed his life in Apostolic labours, and died the death of a saint.

About a century ago, Nicolo Luigi Celestini, a Jesuit novice, who like Spinelli, was twenty-two years of age, lay sick unto death. A violent pleurisy, combined with a pulmonary affection, having reduced him to a very suffering and debilitated condition, he had been bled, and instead of becoming better, grew much worse. His pains increased in intensity, and he was now seized with convulsions, which attacked every part of his body and specially his throat, so that he could not swallow even a drop of water. Sometimes his body became as rigid as a corpse, then he would be agitated with all the violence of one possessed, and it required two persons to hold him. For nine days he continued in a state of fearful delirium; on the ninth day the convulsions left him, but on the tenth returned with aggravation. Then the physicians gave him up. Already his face had assumed a cadaverous hue, the power of speech was gone, and he seemed to be unconscious of all around him. It was the prelude of dissolution. Suddenly his colour returned, a smile beamed on his face, he moved, he spoke, not in the faint tones of the dying, but with the clear and strong voice of health. "I am cured!" he joyfully exclaimed, "St. Aloysius has cured me. My head, my throat, my chest pain me no longer. I have no pain anywhere; my convulsions are gone. I can see everything distinctly. Look at me: I am quite cured. Give me my clothes, give me something to eat." Questioned as to how all had come to pass, he said that when the relapse occurred, he began to observe the portrait of St. Aloysius which hung on the wall facing his bed, but which during his illness he had hitherto never noticed. For that whole day his attention continued to be directed to it; at last the picture became illuminated, and from the midst of the light the saint appeared to come forth, no longer seen in profile, as there depicted, but confronting him, and with a most gracious countenance, lovely to behold.* In his left hand he held a crucifix, and with his right he made a sign for the sick youth to draw nigh; whereupon he made an effort to spring out of bed—as he had in fact been observed to do by his attendants—but from weakness fell back. He still kept his eyes fixed on the saint, and seemed to himself to exclaim, "*Quanto siete mai bello, Luigi mio! Quanto siete bello!* (O my Luigi, how beautiful you are! How beautiful you are!)" Aloysius having again beckoned to him, he once more rose, when the saint said, "What would you have, health or death?" "*Fiat voluntas Dei* (God's will be done)," was Nicolo's reply. Then said Aloysius, "Since through the whole course of your illness, you have had no other desire but to receive the Holy Viaticum, and in everything have conformed yourself to the will of God, the Lord grants you life through my intercession, that you may attend to your perfection, and during the remainder of your days labour to propagate devotion to the Sacred Heart of Jesus; for it is a devotion most pleasing to Heaven." Various other things did the saint say, partly consolatory, partly instructive. He assured Nicolo that

* In memory of this miracle the picture has been preserved in the little chapel of St. Stanislas, with a commemorative inscription.

he would never again suffer from his present malady and bade him practice the devotion of the six Sundays.* to honour the six years he himself spent in religion. Nicolo, emboldened by the saints graciousness, begged for relief from the acute head-ache to which he was subject at all times. But Aloysius told him that it was not God's will that he should be entirely freed from this affliction. "I wish you," he said, "to continue to feel it a little in memory of the Passion of Jesus, and to imitate me, who desired always to keep a similar pain, that I might be conformed to my Lord, who suffered so much for me." Having thus spoken he blessed the sick man and disappeared. Nicolo rose and, prostrate before the portrait of his deliverer, returned him humble thanks; and soon he was in the church, vested in his cotta, and with a wax light in his hand, assisting at a *Te Deum* for his miraculous recovery.

Aloysius also manifested the love he bore to other religious orders, as well as to the priesthood in particular by the numerous prodigies he worked in behalf of so many of their members, not only by healing bodily infirmities, but by inspiring youths with the desire to enter their ranks or wonderfully removing obstacles to the fulfilment of their vocations.

We have seen our saint in the world, shunning society and keeping almost perpetual silence, while, even in religion, dear as were to him his brethren and fathers in the bonds of spiritual love, he sat loose from all his affections and had his conversation more in heaven than on earth. That no unsociable temper

* See page 332

had anv share in causing this habitual estrangement from human intercourse, his singular loving amiability would have been sufficient to prove; and after he had broken the bonds of the flesh, his frequent apparitions in company with other saints would seem, as it were to furnish fresh evidence of the same character. Amongst his companions, St. Stanislas Kostka and the B. John Berchman's stand conspicuous. There is something peculiarly interesting in this exhibition of heavenly friendship, indicating as it does that the glorified state does not exclude those sweet affinities and sympathies which spring from congruity and similarity of disposition; but these two have by no means been the saint's only associates. He has appeared also with S. Francis of Geronimo, the V. Antonio Baldanucci, and the V. Francesco Maria Galluzzi, all members of the Company, and has shown his love for other orders by working miracles in concert with St. Francis of Paula, St. Dominic, and S. Anthony of Padua. Within the course of a very few years he appeared no less than six times to different persons accompanied by St. Vincent Ferrer. Again, later he appeared. with the same saint, to Teresa Pongelli, niece to the Bishop of Terni, who was receiving her education in the Franciscan convent of S. Margarita in Fabriano, and lay at the point of death, telling her that he had obtained her recovery through the intercession of the Blessed Virgin. The two saints laid their hands on the girl's head and blessed her. She described their appearance accurately and spoke in raptures of their surpassing beauty. "Poor painters and sculptors!" she used to exclaim when she saw the pictures and images of her two benefactors; you have been utterly unable to catch that air of Paradise which renders them so lovely!" In like manner Aloysius worked miracles in company with St. Nicholas of Bari, St. John of Matha, St Philip Neri, St. Catherine of Siena, St. Mary Magdalen of Pazzi, and the Apostle of Ireland, our own St. Patrick.

No saint, moreover, has perhaps either appeared more frequently, or conversed more familiarly with those whom he has favoured with his visits. He may be said to be a saint not only most gracious, but accessible beyond what could be imagined, to such as cultivate an intimacy with him. To Arsilia degli Altissimi, a holy widow of Tivoli already mentioned, who died in 1644, he visibly appeared no less than sixteen times. She had caused an image to be made of him, which became the source of countless benefits, spiritual and temporal, to herself and to her neighbours. It often went the tour of the place on missions of mercy, and never returned without having healed bodies or converted hearts.* The confidence which this devout women placed in her patron was well expressed

* This image, bearing in its hand a lily and a cross, was vested in the habit of the Company, with the cotta over it, as we so often see St. Aloysius represented. After Arsilia's death it passed into the possession of the Lancelloti, so noted for their devotion to the saint, where it remained until it was taken to the convent of Torre de' Specchi by one of the family who became a religious inmate of that house. In 1714, it was given by the superioress of this same house, Maria Francesca Lancellotti, to the Discalced Carmelites of San Guiseppe, at that time much reduced in numbers, and distressed for want of novices; no one having requested the habit for six years. Aloysius soon brought postulants in abundance, and ministered also miraculously to the temporal needs of the convent on many occasions. The image was held in high veneration in this house, where, to the best of the writer's knowledge it still remains.

upon one occasion when, having carried his image to the palace of the Cardinal Altieri, brother of Pope Clement X., who was dangerously ill, and hearing those about him talk of calling in a physician to be in constant attendance, she said, "You will do well; but let me provide you with one. Take my Luigi, and do not change him for any doctor in the world." Her recommendation was followed, and with full success. This same Arsilia once asked Aloysius, when communicating at his tomb, to give her a share of the contrition he felt at his own first communion. She immediately felt so piercing a grief that she thought her heart would break, and exclaimed, "*Basta, basta,* (It is enough; it is enough)!" but the saint replied that it was not enough. At last she fainted from excess of feeling, when Aloysius himself came to comfort and restore her, anointing her with some of the miraculous oil of his lamp.

Of another devout client of Aloysius, Giovanna Paolesi, a Florentine woman, who lived about a century later, it is related that her confessor having given her a picture of the saint, she used to place herself before it and address her patron with the most perfect confidence,—a confidence so abundantly warranted by the results that she might be said rather to give commands to Aloysius than offer petitions. He often appeared to her, showing her on one occasion the rich crown prepared for her in Heaven. By his intercession she was more than once raised from the bed of death; so well, indeed, did her confessor know her power with the saint, that in her many bodily sufferings he used often to bid her apply to her patron for relief. Once, when at the utmost extremity she received a similar injunction, Aloysius appeared, all resplendent with glory and with his hands full of lilies, and assured her she would get well without the help of either doctors or medicine. "But my confessor," she said, "desires you to free me from my inveterate bad cough." The saint, however, was not entirely at the confessor's bidding, for he replied with a heavenly smile, "Oh, no, not that (*O questo poi no*)!"

About the same time there lived in Florence another devout worshipper of Aloysius, Gaetano Pratesi, equally enamoured of his virtues, and in the habit of receiving similar favours. He was a farrier, and had been presented by a painter, a friend of his, with a portrait of his favourite saint. It became as famous for the wonders which it worked as Arsilia's image. Gaetano at last spent nearly his whole time in going round with his miraculous treasure to every house into which suffering and affliction had entered. He was ever holding colloquies with his patron, and interceding with him in behalf of his neighbor, as the saint, on his part, was meanwhile efficaciously presenting his client's petitions at the throne of grace. From this continual intercourse with the angelic Aloysius he had grown into his likeness, and offered to the eyes of all a lively and faithful reflection of his virtues. The love begun on earth was, doubtless, perfected in the true and everlasting home of love. He had not long departed this life, when a pious woman, Maria Caterina Magnolfi by name, a warm friend of the deceased and sharing his devotion to Aloysius, dragging herself one day, in spite of grievous infirmities, to church through the great desire she had to partake of the Bread of Life, encountered, as she left her door,

Gaetano himself, in company with his heavenly patron. They separated a little to admit her between them, Aloysius taking the right hand, Gaetano the left, and accompanied her on the way, encouraging her in the love of every virtue, and specially of suffering. As she was returning after mass, they were again at her side to escort her home, teaching her maxims of perfection and leaving her filled with joy unutterable. But perhaps the saint's kindness, and what might be called his courteous charity, was never more exuberantly displayed than in the series of miracles he worked in favour of a noble Bavarian, Wolfgang of Asch, crowning all his favours by accompanying him on a long and perilous journey, throughout which he acted as his loving guide and protector; reminding us in this character of the glorious St. Raphael, Tobias's celestial guardian, whom Milton by a happy thought calls the "sociable spirit."*

After Castiglione, his own native place, and Florence where he had been so well known, there was no spot—always excepting his tomb at Rome—in which Aloysius was more highly venerated than in the Valtelline, and nowhere was his power with God more splendidly illustrated. This devotion took its rise from a very simple, and as we should say, casual circumstance. In the September of the year 1607, Monsignor Peranda, the arch-priest of Bormio, being on his way to Tirano to keep one of our Lady's festivals in her sanctuary at that place, happened to travel in company with the rector of the Jesuit college at Como, P. Carrara. The conversation fell on the

* "Raphael, the sociable spirit, that deign'd
To travel with Tobias."—*Paradise Lost*, v. 221-2.

eminent sanctity of Aloysius, who had been beatified by Paul V. the previous year. Peranda's interest was awakened, and on parting with his companion, gladly accepted a copy of the Life of the saint which the father gave him. On his return to Bormio he stopped at Ponte, at the priest's house who so earnestly pressed him to lend him the book, that he was prevailed upon to leave it in his hands. Sasso, a little village, at that time forming part of the parish of Ponte, lay about two miles distant. The assistant priest, Nicolo Longhi, got a sight of the first few chapters at the house of the *curato*. Immediately he was all on fire with devotion: with his own hand he wrote out a short compendium of the work, and returned to his parishioners as joyful as if he had found a treasure; and a treasure it did indeed prove, such as money could not purchase. The good priest was now always talking of the saint in public and in private, of the graces he had exhibited in life, and the glory with which God had crowned him in Heaven; and besides, he lent the book. It passed from hand to hand, till bye and bye the parishioners were as full of love and veneration for the saint as was their pastor. The devotion spread through the neighbourhood till it had gained the whole of the Valtelline. The first miracle occurred in the December of the same year, and was followed by more. But the prodigies of healing multiplied exceedingly after Longhi had obtained from the Jesuit house at Como the donation of a picture of Aloysius. Miracles attended it from the moment of its arrival, even before it had been installed in the church, as was done with much pomp on the 24th of June, 1608, St. John the Baptist's day;

and, in the fourth year after its exposition, the processes contained 132 well attested miraculous cures. It will be remembered that all such cases are supported by evidence prepared to encounter the strictest scrutiny.* Neither does this number include the many spiritual graces and conversions obtained through the saint's intercession, which were more abundant even than the bodily cures, numerous as these were. †From the lamp kept burning before this

* How strict a scrutiny these cases have to undergo, the following remarks from the pen of F. Faber may serve to indicate:—"The number of witnesses, the classification of their testimony, and the ingenious interrogatoria sent from Rome into the country at the formation of the processes, all increase the difficulty of getting a cause through the different stages, and add proportionably to the weight of the judgment when given. . . . . Putting out of view all idea of divine assistance, and looking at the matter simply as a question of evidence, it is hardly possible to conceive any process for sifting human testimoy more complete, more ingenious, or more rigid than the one scrupulously adhered to by the Congregation of Rites in this respect. . . . . A fact only requires the appearance of being supernatural to awaken against it every suspicion; every method of surprise and detection is at once in array against it; it is allowed no mercy, no advantage of a doubt, and anything rather than the benefit of clergy. All this really gives to Lives of Saints drawn from the processes a trustworthiness which scarcely any other historical or biographical works can possess. . . . . Let any one look at the way in which miracles are dealt with in the Congregation, their accurate division into three classes, the necessity of what is called *instantaneity* in order to distinguish a miracle from a *gratia*, the length of time required to prove the absence of a relapse the interrogatories, the requisites in witnesses, the presence of the first physicians of Italy and their opinions in writing, and sundry other precautions. Many a candid Protestant would be surprised, if he only took the trouble to peruse a few of the processes of the Congregation in matters of beatification and canonization."—*Essay on Beatification and Canonization*, pp. 58, 63, 64.

† The lamp burning before the saint's tomb in Rome obtained a like or even still greater virtue, since even the dead were raised to life by application of the oil taken from it.—*Acta Sanctorum: Miracula B Aloysii Gonzagæ*, cap. xi.

picture the miraculous oil was taken, so famous in those parts as the oil of St. Aloysius, which worked prodigies of healing far and near. It was the priest Longhi who had first the inspiration to prove its supernatural powers, and employ it in the cure of a sick girl. The little church of Sasso was soon found too small to contain the crowd of pilgrims who flocked to it. The project of constructing a larger one was formed as early as the year 1608, but it was not until 1664 that the new and sumptuous edifice was consecrated. Like its modest predecessor, it was dedicated to the Archangel St. Michael, yet owing to the circumstances which led to its erection, and the concourse of devout worshippers who came to visit the saint's chapel, full of votive tablets and inscriptions recording the favours received by his means the familiar name by which it was known was the Church of Il Beato. Nay, the little village itself exchanged its name in common parlance for that of its patron, and its natives, when asked whence they came, would say, "We belong to the Beato." Sasso, in fact, became as famous as its neighbour Tirano, and drew as many pilgrims as that venerated sanctuary of Mary. The Mother of God and Aloysius seemed to emulate each other in conferring favours; and miracles were not wanting which marked her gracious pleasure in this association with her dear son. One in particular is recorded of a deaf cripple: Mary opened the sufferer's ears, but left the rest of the cure to be completed by Aloysius.

Having spoken of the miraculous oil, we must not omit some notice of the no less wonderful series of miarcles wrought by water blessed with the saint's relics, the multiplication of flour, oil, and many other things, which again in their turn became the instruments of almost countless prodigies. At a Carmelite convent at vetralla, a father of the Company being appointed confessor extraordinary, in the year 1728, the prioress begged of him a relic of St. Aloysius, to whom she was very devout, and who had been so magnificently extolled by their holy mother St. Mary Magdalen of Pazzi. He gave her some small chips of stone broken off the sepulchral arch under which the body of the saint had reposed for fifty years. In the month of March in the ensuing year, the prioress begged another father to bless some water with one of these fragments, invoking the saint at the same time. He complied with her request, and from that moment this water became the instrument of miraculous cures in the convent. Its virtue becoming thus known, it occurred to the prioress to apply it in other cases. There was not flour enough in the house to last beyond the coming month of April, and money there was none to purchase any. A novena to St. Aloysius was begun. At its close, the whole community proceeded to the room at which the flour was kept; having recited some prayers, the prioress opened the chest which contained their poor remaining stock, and sprinkled it with a few drops of the blessed water. Shortly after, Sister Agnese Teresa, a lay sister, went to fetch some flour for baking, and took out six bushels, but upon re-examination she found the quantity she had brought away much increased, while the quality was of the finest description. However, she held her peace. Bye and bye Sister Maddalena Rosa, the cook, came in, and no sooner had she looked into the tub than she exclaimed, "O what beautiful flour! Just look, sister; and such a lot of it!" "I am quite aware of that," replied the discreet sister Agnese, "but we nuns, and particularly lay sisters must not be in a hurry to talk." Others, however, soon became cognisant of the prodigy, and the cry of "Miracolo! miracolo!" ran round the house. But this was not the end of the marvels wrought by the saint. The six bushels in Sister Agnese's tub proved to be seven bushels, and when they were taken out the tub filled again. The details of the process would be too long to follow; suffice it to say that the flour grew and multiplied everywhere, in tub, in sifter, and in kneading-trough, as well as in the chest, into which the nuns made the pious experiment of lowering a picture of Aloysius. Wonderful to tell, wherever the portrait rested a little white hillock was seen to form itself. The increase continued until the end of July, by which time their kind patron had supplied them with 149 bushels of purest wheaten flour. But his condescension was not limited to providing for the sisters' immediate wants. The flour containing no bran, it was not suitable for their poultry. Having begged the saint to take pity on these poor creatures also, he sent them at the next increase a portion of coarser flour. These benefits were not confined to the convent, for this flour possessed miraculous virtues for the cure of the sick, as was proved in countless instances. We must add that the most minute and rigorous inquest was made into all these particulars by the direction of the Cardinal Bishop of Viterbo, and the process published in 1752, only twenty-four years after the events.

The miraculous multiplication of oil took place at Sezze, in July, 1731. It will be noted how many special manifestations of the saint's power occurred about this date, which is not surprising when we recall the fact that he was canonized in 1726;* it may serve to remind us how confidently faith may reckon upon the favours of those great servants of God to whom Christ's Vicar on earth has recently decreed the highest honours of the Church. The Count Francesco de Ovis had sold all the produce of his oliveyards, and reserved but a single barrel of oil for domestic uses. His wife did not expect that this small stock would prove sufficient, but, fearing either to annoy or to displease her husband by such an anticipation, and having heard of the miraculous multiplications wrought Aloysius, she had recourse to him in simple faith, begging him to increase their supply of oil. She preserved in her petition until the 19th of December, on which day the servants went down to get ready the barrels for the reception of the year's oil, when, to their surprise, they found one of the barrels, which had all been emptied and cleaned in the summer, so heavy that they could not move it. It was, in fact, full of oil, and that of a kind unknown in all that part of the country. The countess now explained the mystery. Her husband prohibited the use of this oil in his house, but desired it to be kept for distribution among those devout clients of Aloysius in the neighbourhood who should ask for any, in the confident hope that oil of so miraculous an origin would prove to be itself endowed

* A parallel shower of graces may be noticed just after his beatification.

with miraculous virtue; and so the event abundantly demonstrated.

A parallel miraculous supply of nuts occurred in the convent of S. Giovanni Battista at Todi, in the same year, when there was a failure in the gathering of that fruit, which formed an essential article of diet to these poor religious, particularly during Lent. No doubt could exist in the minds of the pious sisters as to who was their secret benefactor, and, if incredulity might have raised any question, the miraculous virtue of these nuts would have proved whence they came. Miracles were wrought by them both within and without the convent, and six months had not elapsed before the number in Todi alone rose to 150, and these all authenticated.

The miraculous multiplications due to St. Aloysius were by no means confined to flour, oil, and nuts; these three articles have been singled out for notice because so considerable a number of his miracles was worked through their means. Neither must it be supposed that the multiplication of flour which took place in the Carmelite convent was a solitary instance of the kind. Similar cases were very numerous, particularly in religious houses. In some it would seem as if, when they were in any strait or want, whether of oil, fruit, wine, or whatever it might be, the nuns had only to ask Aloysius with confidence in order to obtain immediate relief; their very animals were taken under his protection, and were the objects of his provident care. Amongst these convents that of Todi already mentioned, is remarkable in all respects. For instance, in the same year in which the supernatural supply just related took place, we find several other similar prodigies occurring. But space would fail us to attempt to recount even a small portion of the miracles of this special class alone, of which this one house was the theatre. Well might the good sisters call Aloysius "provider" of their convent, as they styled him in the inscription placed at the foot of his image in their private chapel. This image was also miraculous, and it was with great reluctance that the nuns were subsequently induced to yield to the devotion of the people, and allow it to be removed from the interior of their convent to the Church of S. Giovanni. While preparing it for the transfer, they observed the glowing hues of youth and health come over its pale features; "No, no," they said one to the other, "we will not keep him any longer; he wishes to go into the church." Here, exposed to public veneration, this appearance was often renewed, and used to be regarded as a sign that the petition preferred would be granted.

Aloysius was also extremely liberal of his favours to those charitable institutions and asylums for the education of girls called *conservatorii*, which in many cases were attached to convents or managed by religious. His graciousness to these children was so extreme, that it was a question which was the most wonderful, his liberality in rewarding them for the homage they paid him, or his patience in bearing with their strange tempers and ways. We have often heard of the freedom with which Southern Catholics will at times permit themselves to treat the saints they most honour. It has been a fruitful topic for the scorn of the unbeliever and the contempt of the alien. We have here a story to the purpose, which at the same time illustrates the saint's forbearance. Domenica

Negrone, a girl brought up in one of these asylums dedicated to SS. Clemente and Crescentino at Ponte Sisto, who had been, not once only but many times, miraculously cured by St. Aloysius, was in 1733 entrusted with the baking department. Having experienced the great power of the saint, she hung up his picture over some flour, in the hopes that he would multiply it. That great pattern of exactness and the perfect accomplishment of every minute duty belonging to our state had not, now that he was exalted to Heaven, become the patron of carelessness and sloth. Domenica neglected the flour, she did not give it any air, she allowed it to contract damp; in fine, instead of being multiplied it was spoilt. Domenica now flew into a passion with her saint · "What," she said, addressing his picture, "have you been here all this time for? I put you here to increase my flour, and, instead of that, you have let it spoil. Go along, then, with you." Saying those words. she handed it over to one of her companions to take away. When her confessor reproved her for her irreverence, she, still out of temper, pettishly said, "And hadn't I good cause? From morning to night we are offering prayers to this saint, and then he goes and lets ten *rubbia* of our flour spoil." However, Domenica bye and bye came to herself, and was truly sorry both for her own neglect and for her irreverent behaviour. She carried back Aloysius's picture to its former place, and the forgiving saint restored the musty flour to freshness. We need scarcely observe that such behaviour as the foregoing was well worthy of the reprehension it met with, but we cannot see why such cases should excite the peculiar species of contempt of which they have been so frequently the object; a contempt, moreover, which is reflected from the perpetrator of the offence upon the devotion which is viewed as the occasion of so lamentable an exhibition. These acts, after all, admit of very easy explanation, albeit the result of a combination fully intelligible only to Catholics. Proofs they undeniably are of the lively faith and vivid realization of the supernatural possessed by the otherwise imperfect creatures who are guilty of them. To them the saints are living and present persons. It is only with the living that we get out of temper; we are not angry with the dead, still less with abstractions or phantoms of the imagination. They are equally clear indications of a deficiency in self-control as well as in due reflection and a reverential spirit. When these defects are conjoined in the same individual with a strong and lively faith, the results, however unpleasing, can hardly be regarded as unnatural, especially among a people of ardent temperament and impulsive nature, as are the races of Southern Europe.* We

* The following passage from F. Newman's "Lectures on Anglican Difficulties" so powerfully enforces the writer's meaning, that the Editor is induced to place it before the reader:—

"Just as in England, the whole community, whatever the moral state of the individuals, *knows* about railroads and electric telegraphs; and about the Court, and men in power, and proceedings in Parliament; and about religious controversies, and about foreign affairs, and about all that is going on around and beyond them; so, in a Catholic country, the ideas of heaven and hell, Christ and the evil spirit, saints, angels, souls in purgatory, grace, the Blessed Sacrament, the Sacrifice of the Mass, absolution, indulgences, the virtue of relics, of holy images, of holy water, and of other holy things, are *facts*, which all men, good and bad, young and old, rich and poor, take for granted. They are *facts* brought home to them by faith; substantially the same to all, though coloured by their respective minds, according as they are religious or not, and according to the degree of their religion. Religious men use them well, the irre-

omit many other instances of the saint's sweet and gentle patience with these often wayward children. He could, however, on occasions reprove as well as forbear. This same girl, Domenica, was one day carelessly and sleepily repeating five Paters and Aves to Aloysius as she was dressing, when he appeared to her and said, "Domenica, I have cured you several times, but you do not perform what you promised me." "I do it," said Domenica, "but not well." "True," replied Aloysius; "*ma il bene s' ha da far bene* (but the good we do ought to be well done)."

Youth, as may be supposed, has always enjoyed the peculiar protection of Aloysius, and in particular studious youth, to whom Benedict XIII. accorded him as their special patron. The miraculous cures recorded amongst this class alone are exceedingly numerous. We must, as usual, refrain from details, on account of their very abundance, but it will be matter of interest to note in passing the case of John Doyle, a

ligious use them ill, the inconsistent vary in their use of them, but all use them. As the idea of God is before the minds of all men in a community not Catholic, so, but more vividly, these revealed ideas confront the minds of a Catholic people, whatever be the moral state of that people, taken one by one. They are facts attested by each to all, common property, primary points of thought, and landmarks, as it were, upon the territory of knowledge. Now, it being considered that a vast number of sacred truths are taken for granted as *facts*, by a Catholic nation, in the same sense as the sun in the heavens is a fact, you will see how many things take place of necessity, which to Protestants seem shocking, and which could not be avoided, unless it had been promised that the Church should consist of none but the predestinate; nay, unless it consisted of none but the educated and refined. It is the spectacle of supernatural faith acting upon the multitudinous mind of a people; of a divine principle dwelling in the myriad of characters, good, bad, and intermediate, into which the old stock of Adam grafted into Christ has developed."—Pp. 217, 218.

student at the Irish College in Rome in the year 1736. An incurable disorder had brought him to the point of death. The doctors had given him up, and resigned their place to the physicians of the soul. Doyle had received the last sacraments, and the priest was making the recommendation of the departing soul, when the dying man inwardly called upon Aloysius, and upon St. Patrick, the patron saint of his own land, beseeching them to cure him, if it would be for the glory of God and for the good of his neighbours, for whose salvation he desired to labour. Moreover, he promised St. Aloysius that when he returned home, he would do his utmost to introduce and propagate devotion to him in Ireland. Having made a vow to that effect, he fell asleep, and awoke half an hour later perfectly recovered.

But it was not only regard to the bodily health of the youths for whom his intercession was invoked that Aloysius showed himself most bountiful; he was as ready to help the feeble or obtuse mind as to restore the wasted and languishing body. We hear, for instance, in the year 1605, of a noble youth of angelic disposition and most innocent life, but of extremely limited capacity, who was receiving his education in the Roman Seminary. Such a one must have been singularly dear to the heart of our saint; also the youth himself was very devout to Aloysius. Mortified and confounded at his repeated failures, he ran one day to his patron's tomb, and besought him with many tears to obtain for him at least so much intellect as might make him something better than a dry straw upon which his master wasted his breath. He persevered in prayer for ten days, when light seemed to dawn upon the boy's mind, and to the satisfaction of his master and the surprise of all, he was now able to keep his place with his fellow scholars. In gratitude for this signal benefit, he suspended an *ex-voto*, with a commemorative inscription, at his benefactor's tomb. Other similar cases are recorded, but this one may suffice as a specimen, and as an encouragement to studious youth.

We cannot, however, omit to notice the blessed effects which devotion to the saint and imitation of his virtues have produced in schools and seminaries. Indeed, it would be difficult, nay imposible, to reckon up the number of persons of every age and every condition who have been converted from evil ways or moved to aspire after perfection by the sole perusal of his life; but these sanctifying influences have been peculiarly effective among the young. "It pleased God"—these are the words of the great Bellarmine—"to exalt this His servant, in order that the multitude of youths who either live in the Company or frequent its schools should be animated to aim at perfection, and should understand that for God no age is immature, and that youth also may attain every degree of holiness." These words were verified more and more as time went on, and not the youth of the Company alone, but all the rising generation of the Universal Church were taught to look up to Aloysius as alike the patron and their pattern. Yet the fruits of his intercession were always specially abundant among the students of the Roman College; which will not surprise us when we reflect that not only had they a special claim on his love, but that here above all places was he devoutly honoured. During the triduo celebrated annually at his festival, there had always been a harvest of grace; but in the years immediately succeeding his canonization, the marvellous fruits of his patronage and the peculiarly sanctifying results which had been the constant accompaniment of devotion to him became more than ever striking and abundant. Speaking of the triduo of 1728, a narrator says, "How many general confessions, fastings, even on bread and water, the keeping of the eyes bent to earth during the whole time, in honour of the saint's humility and mortification, and other such-like practices might I record!" Modesty silence, contrition, increased fervour of spirit, and love of angelic purity, such were the virtues the exercise of which characterized and followed upon the homage paid to Aloysius by his youthful clients; while conversions, bearing those special marks which entitle them to be ranked as miraculous, were of frequent occurrence both amongst the students in the schools of the Company and amongst the concourse of worshippers from without who thronged to join in celebrating the saint's annual festivity.

Numerous miracles for the relief of corporal necessities or sufferings attest the saint's continual desire to make them minister, as they always ought to do, to the soul's good, for this, indeed, may be said to constitute their real value. He had graceful ways of insinuating perfection while healing infirmities. Witness what he said to a young girl who was suffering from an acute and painful malady, and invoked Aloysius as she lay on her sleepless couch. At midnight she heard herself called by her name: "Who is there?" she asked; "Your protector," was the reply; and immediately with her bodily eyes, for she was wide awake, the sick girl saw Aloysius before her resplendent with beauty and invested with sun-like glory. He wore the cotta, and had his crucifix in his hand; indeed, we cannot imagine him without it, for it seems part of himself. Having instantaneously cured her, he would not depart without leaving her a greater boon, by teaching her the contempt of female frivolity; so he gently touched her hair, which lay in luxuriant tresses on her pillow: "These," he said, "you will carry to the foot of the crucifix, for it is He and not I that has cured you." This young daughter of Eve made her thank-offering of that which she haply prized most dearly. So may it have been also with Magdalen in the days of her vanity and sin; and hence the first grateful expression of her penitent love was to bring to her Saviour's feet what she had cherished as the proudest ornament of her beauty. Thus it is that we so continually find Aloysius, while healing the body or relieving temporal distresses, now enjoining some act of sacrifice or self-renunciation, now some religious exercise or mortification, now the daily repetition of some prayer, amongst which may be specially noticed five Paters and five Aves to the Sacred Wounds of Jesus a devotion to which he had himself been tenderly attached and had practised from his very childhood.

The poor were especially favoured by this great lover of poverty. Amongst them we find renewed, along with bodily cures, those payments of debts, those restorations of lost or damaged property, those miraculous multiplications of oil, wine, flour, &c., for which this saint has been so famous; reminding us forcibly of the widow's barrel of meal and cruise of oil, and the poisoned pottage and lost axe of the sons of the prophets,* wonders worked in God's Israel of old, and the type of so many modern miracles which the proud sceptic is wont to contemn as unworthy of the exertion of divine power, or as a derogation from those laws of nature which in their minds usurp the place of God, or rather constitute a rigid and fantalistic deity of their own creation.

Although we have frequently alluded to the favours of a spiritual character granted to our saint's intercession, we have given detailed examples only from the temporal order, which are confessedly of subordinate importance. The subject would have carried us to too great a length had we attempted to illustrate both classes of the miraculous aid of which St. Aloysius has been so bountiful. Forced therefore to choose, and our object being to demonstrate Aloysius's power in Heaven, we have selected in preference miracles worked for the relief of the body, for the following reason. Temporal favours, bodily cures, and the like, are from their nature patent, and admit of a species of demonstration which is not applicable to spiritual marvels, however incontestably certain these may be; besides, miracles of the class in question have been ever chosen by God as the attestation of saintliness, and often as the evidence of divine revelation. Our Lord Himself went about doing mighty works of this nature, to which He appealed as to a testimony which His Father gave Him of His truth; and the Church, in which the Spirit of God abides, and which is moved by His inspiration, selects miracles of healing as part,

* III. Kings, xvii.; IV. Kings, iv., vi.

and an integral part, of the evidence which establishes the claims of a servant of God to the honours of beatification. We may add that it is impossible to be convinced of the interest which these favourites of Heaven can and will exercise in behalf of our bodily needs and temporal necessities, without being led to seek through their intercession those better things of which material benefits are but the shadows and symbols, and which, when granted through the prayers of God's saints, are intended as helps and means to the attainment of spiritual health and heavenly blessings. Yet we cannot quit the subject without giving one instance of miraculous conversion of which the saint was the instrument, particularly as it exhibits him acting in concert with the Blessed Mother of God.

We have seen Aloysius working miracles of healing in company with other glorious saints like himself; we shall now see him associated with the Queen of Saints in bringing a misbeliever into the fold of Christ. In the year 1767, a Turkish woman of the name of Bruca a native of Tripoli, having embarked with her husband and four brothers in a ship bound to Constantinople, had been taken by one of the galleys of the Knights of Malta. On their arrival in the island, the captives were, as usual, sold as slaves. All the four brothers having asked for baptism, were set at liberty, and lived ever after as good Christians. The husband, an obstinate Mahometan, contrived to make his escape. His wife bore a son after her arrival in Malta, who was baptized; but the mother still clung to her errors. She was, however, a simple, docile, and gentle creature, and the master with whom she lived for ten years, had every reason to be satisfied with her, save in this one respect, that she would not hearken to a word on the subject of religion: she had been born a Turk, and would die a Turk. Yet she was not a fanatic, but was possessed with the notion which the devil fosters in so many hearts, that eternal life being the reward of a good life, it matters little what doctrines we believe; with good works to show (so argued Bruca), Turks and Christians would alike be saved; if guilty of bad actions, both would alike be condemned. She did not, however, live without prayer, but asked of God the strength always to act virtuously, and gave herself no further anxiety about her soul. The Turks, misbelievers though they be, reverence Mary as the mother of a great prophet, which they allow Jesus to have been, while denying His Divinity. Bruca's master, who earnestly desired her conversion, unable to persuade her to examine into the truth of Christianity, prevailed upon her at least often to invoke the Blessed Virgin. She consented, and it was not long before she experienced the happy effects. One night as she lay in bed, the room was suddenly filled with a light intensely brilliant, in the midst of which she beheld a lady of surpassing beauty and of a countenance ineffably benign, who giving her a gentle stroke on her left cheek, said, "Become a Christian, and take the name of Marianna." This she repeated three times, and then the vision disappeared, leaving Bruca so changed in heart, that she ran forthwith to awaken her master and beg to be baptized immediately. He was greatly rejoiced and consoled, bade her go and thank our Lady, and promised that she should be baptized as soon as she had been duly instructed. Bruca passed the whole night in prayer before an image of Mary, and the next day followed with much fervour the instructions given her. Twenty days were spent in this work, and then the devil, who saw his prey escaping him, again laid siege to her heart, suggesting to her that the vision was an illusion. Bruca, yielded, and again intrenched herself in her old position: good works were the principle of salvation; she was born a Turk and would die a Turk. She persevered in this determination to the September of the year 1777, when her master, despairing, it may be supposed, of her conversion, sold her to a Roman. In the house of Signor Carlo Giorgi, her new owner, she again became the object of pressing solicitations to embrace the true faith; but her obstinacy appeared to be only the more confirmed by her rejection of the favour which had been shown her, making it too probable that she would now be left to the mere ordinary and sufficient movements of grace. She had slighted the invitation of the Mother of Mercy—what could be looked for more? Yet had that compassionate mother still those merciful eyes of hers turned upon her erring child, although she had reserved the glory of this ultimate conquest of grace to her son Aloysius. On the night of the 21st of February, 1778, Bruca was roused from sleep by a voice calling her by name. Again, as on the former occasion, her room was filled with a blaze of light, and by her bed there stood a youth apparelled in a robe of dazzling whiteness. Bruca was seized with mingled fear and reverence at the sight, but taking courage, she asked his name. "I am Luigi Gonzga," he replied; and then pointing to a lady of exceeding beauty who was standing at a distance, "look there," he added, "that is Mary the Mother of God, who will not approach you because you are not a Christian." Bruca was speechless at these words, but at once surrendered her heart to this fresh invitation of divine love. Being made acquainted with her determination, her master sent her the next day, accompanied by one of his servants, to the Roman College, and no sooner did she catch a sight of the basso-relievo likeness of Aloysius, than she joyfully exclaimed, "That is the youth who appeared and spoke to me last night." On the 9th of June following she was baptized, taking the name of Marianna Aloisia de' Giorgi, in gratitude to the Mother of God and to our saint, and in memory of the house where her happy conversion was effected.

To this day Aloysius continues to work wonders of healing and of grace in the land of his earthly sojourn; and so late as the year 1863 the little village of Colle d'Avendita witnessed the miraculous cure of a young maiden as marvellous as any we have related, followed by a consecration of her recovered health to God in religion according to the saint's injunction:* but here we must conclude. The world, which is ever disposed to cavil where it is a question of the supernatural, will, we know, be ready to say, "How comes it that Italy is so favoured with miracles? Show us some amongst Catholics at home. Why do we hear of none in our own country and in our own neighbourhood?" To this it may be replied that, while allowing that Catholic lands have been more abundantly favoured in this respect, yet, were there a sincere

* This miracle was juridically tested at Rome.

desire to ascertain the true facts, it might be found that there is scarcely perhaps a Catholic family even in this Protestant land which could not record some supernatural aid, some testimony, personal or traditional, that our little English flock has not been forgotten by the saints of God—or rather we might say that the saints have not been forgotton by us, for they are ever ready to assist. But these miraculous favours are family matters; we live amongst those who are aliens to the faith; who, dear as they are to us, in a thousand ways, and bound to us by so many ties, cannot share or sympathize in these secrets of God's household. Yet, undoubtedly (as we have said), Catholic lands have been more abundantly blessed with manifestations of God's glory in His saints and with the more striking effects of their patronage. And why so? It is because foreign Catholics are better than we? Be this as it may, it is certainly not the true answer. We see how many weak or imperfect persons have been the subject of these miraculous interpositions, and our compassionate Lord came specially to heal the sick, the afflicted and the infirm in soul as well as body. But we *do* think that, as a general rule, the Catholic who has not lived surrounded by an atmosphere of unbelief has habitually a simpler and more confiding faith. He expects more · he reckons on more; and this is quite enough to account for his obtaining more; for our good God will never disappoint his children. We are told in the Gospels that our Lord *could not* do any miracles amongst His own countrymen because of their unbelief.* It is faith which unlocks the treasure-house and opens wide the hand of God's liberality. The prophet Eliseus reproved king Joas because, at his command to strike, he had smitten the ground but three times, whereas had he repeated the blow five or six or seven times he would have smitten syria even to utter destruction.† Of course the adversaries of the Church have another and a very different reply to give: Italians are credulous, and believe that every mercy is a miracle. If by credulous be meant ready to expect a miracle, this may be freely granted. The prejudice—if such it must be called—amongst the devout population is all in favour of the supernatural: but what of this? The miracles here recorded do not rest on hearsay reports; they are not the reproductions of popular beliefs or impressions: they are facts, which have borne a thorough, searching legal scrutiny at the hands of those whose solicitude was, not to establish their truth, but to sift them severely and minutely in order to discover whether they were true.

And now our task, however imperfectly executed, is done. As far as our unequal ability has permitted, we have set the saint before our readers in his heroic conflicts with and in the world, in his perfection in the religious life, and in the riches and glory of his beatified state. Centuries have rolled on since angels sang in the room whence Aloysius rose to his throne in Heaven, and the numerous branches of the Gonzaga family which flourished in that day on the soil of Northern Italy have one by one, become extinct.

* Matt. xiii. 58; Mark vi. 5.

† IV. Kings, xiii.

Their stately splendour and even their princely names would have been by this time well-nigh forgotten, or known only to the patient historian to be classed with scant notice along with so many others, potent and celebrated in their time, but for one gentle youth of their race who, despising the empty honours of this world, trod under foot his earthly crown, and made himself poor and of no account that he might merit the favour of the King of kings. And now he wears a diadem in Heaven, and his name shall pass down with blessing, reverence, and honour to every Catholic generation.

One word in conclusion. Some may complain that we have begun by setting before them to perfect a saint: who (it may be said) can aspire to imitate Aloysius's heroic sanctity? But perfection in some sense is clearly set before all, since it is to all alike that our Lord gave the command, "Be you perfect, as also your Heavenly Father is perfect."* If God's perfection be our pattern, no saint can be too exalted to be our model. Perfection, in fact, is set before all as the object of their aim, but not the same perfection. The perfection to which we are all without exception commanded to aspire, is perfection in our calling; and if the character of Aloysius's perfection be above our aims, the exactness, at least, with which he followed his grace has a claim on the imitation of all. Nor can we do better than conclude with quoting the words he spoke to the careless Domenica,, words which embody the saint's own constant rule and practise:—"The good we do, ought to be well done."

* Matt. v. 48.

Prayer to St. Aloysius Gonzaga.

O holy Aloysius, beautiful for thy angelic virtues, I, thy most unworthy client, recommend to thee, in a particular manner, the purity of my soul and body. I beseech thee, by thy angelic chastity, to recommend me to the Immaculate Lamb, Christ Jesus, and to His Most Holy Mother, the Virgin of Virgins, and to preserve me from all sin. Never permit me to be defiled by any stain of impurity, but when thou seest me exposed to temptation and the danger of sin, remove far from my heart all impure thoughts and affections, and, renewing in me the remembrance of eternity, and of Jesus crucified, imprint deeply in my soul the fear of God, and enkindle within me the fire of divine love, that, imitating thee on earth, I may be worthy to have God for my possession with thee in Heaven. *Amen.*

To the above prayer is attached an indulgence of 100 days, to be gained once a day, applicable to the dead.

CATHOLIC BOOKS

PUBLISHED BY

PETER F. CUNNINGHAM,

216 South Third Street, Philadelphia.

☞ The attention of the Public is respectfully called to the following CATALOGUE of popular Catholic Works.

☞ In consequence of the variation in the price of materials for book-making, the following prices are liable to change as occasion requires.

Besides his own publications, the subscriber keeps constantly on hand a full stock of all other Catholic publications, which he is prepared to supply at publishers' lowest rates. All new books received as soon as published, and supplied wholesale and retail, at publishers' prices.

The Year of Mary; or, The True Servant of the Blessed Virgin.

Translated from the French of Rev. M. D'Arville, Apostolic Prothonotary, and published with the approbation of the *Right Rev. Bishop of Philadelphia*, the *Most Rev. Archbishop of Baltimore*, and the *Most Rev. Archbishop of New York.* 1 neat 12mo volume.

Price—In cloth.. $1.50
In gilt edges.. 2.00

This is a delightful book; brimful of sweet flowers; a lovely garland in honor of Mary our Mother and powerful intercessor before the throne of her Son.

Well has the *Magnificat* said, "all generations shall call me blessed;" all times, and in all lands, wherever the symbol, upon which her Divine Son ransomed a wicked and undeserving world with his excruciating sufferings and death, has a votary, her name, spotless and beautiful, shall be pronounced with reverence, and her protection implored.

The tome before us is a collection of the honors paid to Mary by the great and good of all lands; by those who, with the diadem of earthly grandeur adorning their brows, and vexed political commonwealths to guard and pacify, found time to honor the daughter of St. Anne, the beloved Mother of our Lord and Saviour.

Buy the book. Read one or two pages We promise a feast, a desire to read the whole, a determination to do so.—*Catholic Telegraph.*

This work is divided into seventy-two Exercises, corresponding with the number of years which the Blessed Virgin passed on earth, with a consecration to Mary of the twelve months of the year, in reference to her virtues; also a method of using certain of the Exercises by a way of devotion for the "Month of Mary," a Novena in honor of the Immaculate Conception, and other matters both interesting and advantageous to the true servant of Mary, and those who would become so.

"BALTIMORE, *April* 6, 1865.

"We willingly unite with the Ordinary of Philadelphia and the Metropolitan of New York in approving 'The Year of Mary,' republished by Peter F. Cunningham, of Philadelphia.

"M. J. SPALDING,
"*Archbishop of Baltimore.*"

A work presented to the Catholics with such recommendations does not need any word of encouragement from us.—*Pilot.*

This work meets a want long ungratified. The devotional Exercises which make up the book are ingeniously arranged in reference, 1st, to each year of the Blessed Virgin's long residence on earth; 2d, to every Sunday and festival throughout the year. The Exercises are therefore seventy-two in number, corresponding to the generally received belief of the duration of her terrestrial life.
The First Exercise is thus appropriated to the Immaculate Conception, and may be used both for the 8th of December and for the first day of the year. The seventy-second celebrates the Assumption, and may be profitably read on the 15th of August, and on the last day of the year.
Each Instruction is prefaced by a text from holy writ, and followed by an example, a historical fact, a practice and a prayer.
The Approbations are:
1st. By the Roman Theological Censor.
2d. By a favorable letter from his Holiness Gregory XVI.
3d. By the recommendatory signatures of the Archbishops of Baltimore and New York, and the Bishop of Philadelphia.
This Devotional is a deeply interesting and practical manual, and Mrs. Sadlier, who has very skilfully reduced the originally free translation into graceful conformity to the original, has rendered the Christian public a most essential service. We wish it the widest circulation.—*N. Y. Tablet.*

"The Year of Mary" is one of the most beautiful tributes to the Mother of God that a Catholic family could desire to have. We are free, however, to confess our partiality in noticing any book that treats of the pre-eminent glory of her whom God exalted above all created beings.
But, independently of this consideration, the present volume can be recommended on its own special merits. Besides being replete with spiritual instruction, it presents a detailed account of the life of the Blessed Virgin from the Conception to the Assumption, and views her under every possible aspect, both as regards herself and her relations with man. It lays down the rules by which we are to be guided in our practical devotions towards her; displays its genuine characteristics, and indicates the sublime sentiments by which we ought to be actuated when we pay her our homage, or invoke her assistance.
"The Year of Mary" contains seventy-two Exercises, in accordance with the received opinion of the Church that the Blessed Virgin lived that number of years on earth. In these instructions, the reader shall learn her life, her prerogatives, her glory in Heaven, and her boundless goodness to mankind. We would like to see this book in every Catholic family in the country. It is impossible for us to honor the Mother of God sufficiently well. But in reading this book, or any like it, we must ever bear in mind that acts, not mere professions of piety, should be the distinctive marks of "the true servant of the Blessed Virgin," and that she is really honored, only in so far as we imitate her virtues for the sake of Him through whom alone we can hope for eternal life.
The name of Mrs. Sadlier is familiar to the public; her talents as an authoress are too well known to need any eulogy here; she is an accomplished lady, and has faithfully done her part. As to the publisher, Mr. Cunningham, we say, without flattery, that he has done a *good* work in presenting this excellent book to his fellow-Catholics, and with all our heart we wish him the fullest measure of success to which this noble enterprise entitles him.—*The Monthly.*

Meditations of St. Ignatius; or, "The Spiritual Exercises" expounded,

By Father Siniscalchi, of the Society of Jesus.

Published with the approbation of the *Right Rev. Bishop of Philadelphia.* 1 vol. 12mo.

Price—Neatly bound in cloth, gilt back................................$1.50

The fame of the great founder of the Society of Jesus, would itself insure the character of the above book of meditations, as one of the most meritorious kind. But the greater part of Catholics of all nations have been made familiar with the nature, object, and efficiency of these meditations in the Spiritual Retreats conducted by the Fathers of this Society, in every language, in every country, and almost every town of Christendom. We are glad to see this valuable work published in our country and tongue, and feel assured it will be heartily welcomed by the multitudes who are familiar with it, if in no other way, at least from the free use which is made of it in the Jesuit Missions, forming, as it does, the basis of all those inspiriting exercises which constitute a spiritual retreat.—*Catholic Mirror.*

This is the first American edition of this celebrated work, which has been translated into nearly all the European languages. It supplies a want long felt in America. It is an excellent book of Meditations for the family, but it is particularly adapted for those attending Retreats or Missions, especially those given by the Jesuits, whose method this is. We cannot too strongly recommend this book to the Catholic public.—*New York Tablet.*

This is a timely publication of the Meditations of St. Ignatius, and the Catholic community are indebted to the Philadelphia publisher for bringing the work within their reach. In Europe, where it is well known, it would be superfluous to do more than call attention to the fact of a new edition being published; but inasmuch as American Catholics have not had an opportunity of becoming very familiar with the work, it may not be out of place to say a few words concerning it.

The Meditations are twenty-two in number, each divided into three parts, and in each division the subject is viewed, as it were, from a different point of view, the last being always the most striking. Death, Judgment, Hell, and Heaven, the Mysteries of the Saviour's Life, and the Happiness of Divine Love—these are the subjects of the Saint's meditations, and every consideration germain to such topics calculated to excite the feelings or influence the judgment, is brought before the reader in simple, forcible language, or impressed on the mind by means of a striking anecdote or opposite illustration. The volume is thickly strewn with quotations from sacred and patristic writings, and the whole range of profane history is laid under contribution to furnish material wherewith to point a moral or enforce a truth.

No Catholic family should be without this book, and no Catholic library should be depending on one copy. It is a noble edition to the ever-increasing stock of Catholic devotional literature, and we hope the publisher's judicious venture will be successful. We must not omit to mention that the publication has received the official sanction of the Right Rev. Bishop of Philadelphia.—*Metropolitan Record.*

Sacerdos Sanctificatus; or, Discourses on the Mass and Office,

With a Preparation and Thanksgiving before and after Mass for every day in the week Translated from the Italian of St. Alphonsus Ligouri,

By the Rev. James Jones

1 vol. 18mo.

Price—Neatly bound in cloth, ... 80 ts.

The Life of St. Teresa.

Written by herself.

Translated from the Spanish, by Rev. Canon Dalton, and published with the approbation of the *Right Rev. Bishop of Philadelphia.* 1 vol. 12mo., neatly bound in cloth.

Price—In cloth..$1.50
In cloth, gilt edge..2.00

The Life of St. Catherine of Sienna.

By Blessed Raymond of Capua, her Confessor.

Translated from the French, by the Ladies of the Sacred Heart. With the approbation of the *Right Rev. Bishop of Philadelphia.* 1 vol. 12mo., neatly bound in cloth.

Price—In cloth..$1.50
In cloth, gilt edge..2.00

Life of St. Margaret of Cortona.

Translated from the Italian, by John Gilmary Shea, and published with the approbation of the *Right Rev. Bishop of Philadelphia.* 1 vol. 16mo., neatly bound in cloth, gilt backs.

Price..80 cents.

The Life of St. Angela Merici of Brescia, Foundress of the Order of St. Ursula.

By the Abbe Parenty.

With a History of the Order in Ireland, Canada and the United States, by John Gilmary Shea. Published with the approbation of the *Right Rev. Bishop of Philadelphia.* 1 vol. 16mo., cloth, gilt back.

Price..80 cents.

The Life of Blessed Mary Ann of Jesus,

de Parades y Flores. "The Lily of Quito."

By Father Joseph Boero, S. J.

Translated from the Italian by a Father of the Society of Jesus, and published with the approbation of the *Right Rev. Bishop of Philadelphia.* 1 vol. 16mo., neatly bound in cloth, gilt back.

Price..80 cents.

The Life of St. Rose of Lima.

Edited by the Rev Frederick William Faber, D. D., and published with the approbation of the *Right Rev. Bishop of Philadelphia.* 1 vol., large 16mo., neatly bound in cloth, gilt back.

Price—Only...80 cents.

The Life of St. Cecilia, Virgin and Martyr.

Translated from the French of Father Gueranger, and published with the approbation of the *Right Rev. Bishop of Philadelphia.*
1 vol. 12mo.

Price—In cloth..$1 50
In cloth, gilt edge.. 2.00

The above is one of the most interesting works which has been issued for some time from the Catholic press in this country. The life and martyrdom of Saint Cecilia, is itself, one of the most beautiful chapters in the history of the Church. The account of it by Gueranger is most touching. It combines all the sprightliness of romance, with the solid truth of history. The author is one of the most learned archæologists that has appeared in this century, and is well known for many learned works. In connection with the life of St. Cecilia, he gives a graphic account of the state of the Church at the time of the persecutions under the Roman Emperors. There is a beautiful description of the catacombs and of the usages of the Christains in paying honor to the martyrs. In reading his work we seem to be transferred to their days. The character of St. Cecilia is drawn out in the most vivid colors, though the account is almost entirely taken from the ancient Acts, the authenticity of which is ably vindicated by the learned author. He then gives an account of the Church, built at her own request on the spot where she suffered. This goes over a period of over sixteen hundred years. It has been, during all that time, one of the most clearly cherished sanctuaries of Rome. The incidental accounts of various matters connected with the history of the Saint and her Church, are themselves sufficient to give great interest to the volume. we hardly know which to admire most in this work—the information imparted on many most interesting topics, the healthy tone of the work, so well calculated to enliven faith, and cherish a devout spirit, or the beauty of the style of the author who has weaved the whole into so interesting a narrative, that no romance can vie with this truthful account of the patroness of song.—*Baltimore Catholic Mirror.*

We are glad to see that the American public have been favored with this very interesting work. While the name of the author is a guarantee for historical accuracy, and learned research, the period of which it treats is one of great interest to the Catholic. In these pages one can learn the manners and customs of the early Christians, and their sufferings, and gain no little insight into their daily life. The devotion to the Saints is becoming daily more practical, and we are glad to see revived the memory of the ancient heroes and heroines whom the Church has honored in a special manner. The mechanical execution of the American edition is very good.—*Catholic Standard.*

We cannot sufficiently admire and commend to the attention of our readers, young and old, this delightful work. The tenderness and exquisite refinement and purity which surround, like a veil, the character of the lovely St. Cecilia, serve to throw into stronger relief the unfaltering courage by which she won the crown of martyrdom. The author has made use of all the authentic and important details connected with the life and death of the Saint, following the most approved authorities. The discoveries of her tomb in the ninth and sixteenth centuries form not the least interesting portion of the work, and the description of the church, which was once her dwelling and the witness of her sufferings and triumphs, brings those scenes so vividly before us that Cecilia seems to belong as much to our own day as to the period when young, beautiful, wealthy and accomplished. the virgin bride of the noble Valerian laid down her life for the martyr's crown of faith.—*N. Y. Tablet.*

Mr. Cunningham, of Philadelphia, has earned a new claim on our gratitude by publishing the LIFE OF SAINT CECILIA, VIRGIN AND MARTYR. The Acts of her martyrdom are a monument of the wonderful ways of God, and a most sweet record of Christian heroism, heavenly love, and prodigious constancy. Her very name has inspired Christianity for fifteen centuries, with courage, and the noblest aspirations. The work is a translation from the French of *Prosper Gueranger*. We have had only time to read the title, preface, and a few pages before going to press. But we can say this much, that it was a very happy thought to undertake this translation, and we know of no other book we should like to see in the hands of Catholics so much as the LIFE OF SAINT CECILIA VIRGIN AND MARTYR.—*Boston Pilot.*

Mr. Peter F. Cunningham has just brought out, in very admirable style, the "Life of St. Cecilia," from the French of the celebrated Dom. Gueranger. It is difficult to find a more delightful volume than this. Its subject is one of the most attractive in all the annals of the Church; and its author one of the most pious and gifted of modern French writers: the result is one of the most charming contributions ever made to Catholic literature. As intimated, the publisher has done his part in printing, in paper, and in binding. We return him thanks for a copy.—*Philadelphia Universe, Oct.* 6.

This is a most interesting volume, truer than history and stranger than fiction. The author does not confine himself to the details of the Saint's life and martyrdom, but describes, with the faithfulness and minuteness of an antiquary, the wonders of Imperial and Christian Rome--the catacombs, the basilicas, the manners of the times, the persecutions of the Christians, etc. The book is handsomely got up, and enriched with a portrait of St. Cecilia seated at her harp.—*N. Y. Met. Record.*

We have received this beautiful and very interesting life of one of the most beautiful Saints of the Church. The reading public ought to be much obliged to the Publisher for giving them such a work. It abounds in the sublimest sentiments of divine love and human devotion, such as Catholics would expect from the life of such a Saint; and at the same time portrays the combat of rising Christianity and decaying paganism in the liveliest colors. Such works as this form the proper staple of reading for all who desire to become acquainted with the period to which it refers, and who cannot afford to purchase or peruse the more profound works of our Historians.—*Western N. Y. Catholic.*

The name of the learned and religious Abbot of Solesmes, Dom. Gueranger, was long since made familiar and pleasant to us, in the pages of Chevalier Bonnetty's learned periodical, the *Annales de Philosophie Chretienne*, published in Paris. In the pages of his "Life of St. Cecilia"—which we have not met with in the French,--we have the same high talent devoted to other than liturgic themes. This is an admirable volume, well translated. The quiet style in which the story is told of the great honor with which Catholic ages have crowned St. Cecilia, is charming.—*N. Y. Freeman's Journal.*

Life of St. Agnes of Rome, Virgin and Martyr.

Published with the approbation of the *Right Rev. Bishop of Philadelphia.* 1 vol. 18mo, neatly bound in cloth, with a beautiful steel plate Portrait of the "Youthful Martyr of Rome."

Price..45 cents.

Man's Contract with God in Baptism.

Translated from the French by Rev. J. M. Cullen. 1 vol., 18mo.

Price..30 cents.

Life of St. Aloysius Gonzaga, Of the Society of Jesus.

Edited by Edward Healy Thompson. Published with the approbation of the *Rt. Rev Bishop of Philadelphia.* 1 vol., 12mo., neat cloth, beveled, $1.50. Cloth, Gilt, $2.00.

☞ This is the best life of the Saint yet published in the English language, and should be read by both the young and old.

The Life of Blessed John Berchmans of the Society of Jesus.

Translated from the French. With an appendix, giving an account of the miracles after death, which have been approved by the Holy See. From the Italian of Father Borgo, S. J. Published with the approbation of the *Right Rev. Bishop of Philadelphia.* 1 vol. 12mo.

Price—In cloth $1.25
In cloth, gilt edge 1.75

We have read with delight this charming life of the humble and holy youth whose simple and unaffected piety, and strict fulfilment of the duties of his vocation, have raised him to such a height of eminence. Next to the life of St. Aloysius and St. Stanislaus Kostka no story could be more interesting, no example more striking to the young, from the very fact that it was by obedience in little and commonplace matters as well as in those of graver importance that he attained his perfection. We hope that so bright an example of heroic virtue will not be lost. The book, which is well gotten up, has a beautiful portrait of the Blessed Berchmans. We ask for it a wide circulation among our Catholic youth.—*N. Y. Tablet.*

The Society of Jesus, laboring in all things for the "Greater glory of God," has accomplished, if not more, as much, towards that pious object, as ever did any Institution of our holy religion. Actuated by that sublime and single motive, it has given the world as brilliant scholars, historians and men of science in all departments, as have ever yet adorned its annals. Nor is this by any means its greatest boast; it is what has been achieved by the Society in the advancement of Catholicity and sanctity, that makes the brightest gem in its coronet. It is in that, that it is most precious in the sight of the angels of God; it is for that its children will sing with them a new canticle on high. It has peopled heaven with a host of sainted choristers, many of them endowed with a world-wide fame for sanctity, and many, like Blessed Berchmans, known to but few beyond the pale of her order. This saintly youth, like St. Aloysius and St. Stanislaus, died young, but a model of that true wisdom which never loses sight of the end for which man is created. The work before us beautifully describes the virtues, and the exemplary life and practices of this pious youth, and is richly entitled to a place in every Catholic library.—*Catholic Mirror.*

Mr. P. F. Cunningham, of Philadelphia, may well rejoice, in his Catholic heart, for having given us this work, the perusal of which must needs be the source of immense good. No better work can be placed in the hands of Religious novices Perhaps no other book has fired those privileged souls with more fervid aspirations towards attaining the perfection proper of their religious professions A perfect pattern is placed before them, and whilst the heart is drawn towards it with admiring love, the reader cannot allege any honest cause whereby to excuse himself from following the noble example placed before him. BLESSED BERCHMANS teaches, by his own life, that perfection is to be attained in the faithful and conscientious discharge of the duties of one's daily life, whatever its circumstances may be. An excellent, most excellent book this will also prove for sodalists.—*Boston Pilot.*

This is the fullest and best life published of this remarkable servant of God. John Berchmans lived at the beginning of the seventeenth century. He died at Rome, in his twenty-third year—a model of purity and devotion. We cannot better notice this volume than by copying the opening words of the Brief of his Beatification, pronounced by the Holy Father, last year:

"As youth is the foundation of manhood, and men do not readily in after life turn from the path they have trod from earliest years; that there be no excuse on plea of age or strength, for swerving from the ways of virtue, the All-wise Providence has ordered it that there should bloom, from time to time, in the Church, one and another *youth* eminent for sanctity, realizing the eulogium: 'Made perfect in a short space, be fulfilled a long time.'"

As such an one, the life of Blessed John Berchmans commends itself to the study especially of pious youth.—*N. Y. Freeman's Journal.*

It is unnecessary for us to say anything in recommendation of a life of the Blessed Berchmans. The devotion so long entertained for him, now solemnly approved by the Church, will cause many to read with delight and spiritual profit, this authentic account of his life and virtues. The Bishops of Belgium expressed their ardent wishes for the beatification of blessed John, hoping that through his intercession the great works of the Christian education of youth, which they are so nobly carrying on, might be furthered and made more and more successful. In the United States there is a similar work to be done, and we hope and pray that the blessed Berchmans will not forget our wants in his supplications to the Father of Mercies.

We recommend the work before us to the young especially, among whom it should be widely circulated.—*Catholic Standard.*

We have received from Mr. Cunningham, a very handsome and a very delightful new book—THE LIFE OF BLESSED JOHN BERCHMANS OF THE SOCIETY OF JESUS. This is an exquisite biography, which every college professor should place in the hands of his pupils, and every parent in the hands of his children. It is quite as charming a contribution to sacred letters as the life of St. Aloysius himself. The publisher has brought it out very becomingly and tastefully. We understand that he will soon have published *The Life of St. Cecelia, from the French of Gueranger.* Gueranger wrote a fascinating life of the Patroness of Church music. We hope it has been gracefully and accurately translated.—*Philadelphia Universe.*

The Sodalist's Friend. A Beautiful Collection of Meditations and Prayers.

Compiled and translated from approved sources, for the use of members and leaders of confraternities. 1 vol. 18mo., neatly bound.

Price—In cloth........................80 cents.
Roan embossed........................$1.00
Embossed gilt........................1.50
Full gilt edges and sides........................2.00
Turkey, superior extra........................3.00

The Month of the Sacred Heart.

Arranged for each day of the month of June. Containing also the Arch Confraternity of Sacred Heart, and Father Borgo's Novena to the Sacred Heart of Jesus. With the approbation of the *Right Rev. Bishop of Philadelphia.* 1 neat vol. 24mo. Cloth, gilt back.

Price........................50 cents.

The Month of St. Joseph.

Arranged for each day of the month of March. From the French of the Rev. Father Huguet, of the "Society of St. Mary." Published with the approbation of the *Right Rev. Bishop of Philadelphia.* 1 neat vol. 18mo. Cloth, gilt back.

Price..50 cents.

An attentive perusal of this little work will prove, with a sincere utterance of the prayers contained therein, a powerful means to reform one's life. Let us secure the friendship and intercession of St. Joseph. He is the foster-father of our Saviour. He can say a good word for us, indeed. O, the beauty of Catholic devotions! how its practices, when in direct connection with the life and teachings of Jesus Christ, fill the soul with happiness and hope!—*Boston Pilot.*

This will be found to be an interesting book to all the children of Mary, and the lovers of her pure, saintly, and glorious spouse, St. Joseph. It is a good companion to the lovely "Month of May."—*New York Tablet.*

The Little Offices.

Translated from the French by the Ladies of the Sacred Heart. Containing the Little Offices of the Sacred Heart, Holy Ghost, Immaculate Conception, Our Lady of Seven Dolours, Most Holy Heart of Mary, Holy Angel Guardian, St. Joseph, St. Louis de Gonzaga, St. Stanislaus, St. Jude, Apostle. To which is added a Devout Method of Hearing Mass. Published with the approbation of the *Right Rev. Bishop of Philadelphia.* 1 vol. 18mo. Neatly bound.

Price..50 cents.

The Religious Soul Elevated to Perfection, by the Exercises of an Interior Life.

From the French of the Abbé Baudrand, author of "The Elevation of Soul." 1 vol. 18mo.

Price..60 cents.

La Mère de Dieu.

A beautiful and very edifying work on the Glories and Virtues of the Blessed Virgin Mary, Mother of God; from the Italian of Father Alphonse Capecelatro, of the Oratory of Naples, with an Introductory Letter of Father Gratry, of the Paris Oratory. Published with the approbation of the *Right Rev. Bishop of Philadelphia.* 1 neat vol. 18mo. Cloth.

Price..50 cents.

The Roman Catacombs; or, Some account of the Burial Places of the Early Christians in Rome.

By Rev. J. Spencer Northcoate, M. A, with Maps and various Illustrations. Published with the approbation of the *Right Rev. Bishop of Philadelphia.*
1 vol., 16mo., neatly bound in cloth, gilt back.

Price..80 cents.

Charity and Truth; or, Catholics not uncharitable in saying that None are Saved out of the Catholic Church.

By the Rev. Edward Hawarden.

Published with the approbation of the *Right Rev. Bishop of Philadelphia.*
1 vol. 12mo.

Price—Neatly bound in cloth..$1.00

In this book, the learned and earnest author discusses a question of vital importance to all, viz.: Is there salvation out of the Catholic Communion? At the present moment, when the strongest proof of Christianity, in the popular opinion, is a belief that every road leads to heaven, and that every man who lives a moral life is sure to be saved, the very title of this book will grate harshly on many ears. To such we would say—Read the work, and learn that "a charitable judgment may be very unfavorable, and a favorable judgment may be very uncharitable" "Charity and Truth" is the work of one of the ablest controversialists and most learned theologians of the Catholic Church in England. The method adopted in "Charity and Truth" is the catechetical, and to help the memory the questions are set in large characters at the top of each page. In the preface, the Reverend reviewer takes up and disposes of six vulgar errors,—1st. That it is charity to suppose all men saved whose life is morally honest. 2d. That the infinite goodness of God will not suffer the greater part of mankind to perish. 3d. That it is charity to believe the Jews and Turks are saved. 4th. That if I judge more favorably of the salvation of another man than he does of mine, I am the more charitable of the two. 5th. That, setting all other considerations apart, if Protestants judge more favorably of the salvation of Catholics than Catholics do of theirs, Protestants are on the more charitable side. 6th. That he is uncharitable whoever supposes that none are saved in any other religion unless they are excused by invincible ignorance. —*Met Record.*

We owe Mr. Cunningham an apology for not having noticed this work ere this; and we should have done it more readily, as we hail with utmost pleasure the republication of one of those works written by the uncompromising champions of the Church during the hottest days of persecution and Catholic disabilities in England. We have often wished that some of the learned professors of the illustrious College of Georgetown would select from among the numerous collection they have of books written by English missionaries during the first two centuries of persecution in England, some such work as "Charity and Truth," and republish them in this country. These works will not please, of course, our milk and water Catholics. But, after all, they are the real kind of works we need. It is high time that we should take the aggressive. We have put up long enough with Protestant attacks. We owe nothing to Protestants. We have allowed them to say all kind of things to us. We have received with thanks the benign condescension with which they grant us the merit of there being some good people among the Catholics, and that some bishops and priests are clever, in spite of their being Catholics. We have bowed so low as to kiss the right hand that has patted us on the head, while the left was lifting its thumb to the nose of the smiling but double-hearted caresser. It is high time, we say, that we should do away with this sycophancy. It is high time that war was carried to the heart of the enemy's country. Hence we are thankful to the American editor of this work. Let Catholics buy it, read it, and then give it to their Protestant acquaintances.—*Boston Pilot.*

This is the republication of a standard Catholic book, written and published for the first time in the early part of the last century. It is a work of great ability, being the production of one of the most eminent theologians and controvertists of his day. Its tone is temperate and conciliatory, its style simple and flowing. The subject is important, ably reasoned, and presented in a striking and captivating manner.—*Baltimore Catholic Mirror.*

CATHOLIC TALES.

Grace Morton; or, The Inheritance.

new and beautiful Catholic tale, written by Miss Meaney of Philadelphia.
1 vol., large 18mo., neatly bound in cloth.
Price.. ....80 cents.

This is a pleasing story, instructive as well as amusing, and worth an especial place in the library of youthful Catholics. It depicts with rare skill the trials and sacrifices which attend the profession of the true Faith, and which are so often exacted of us by the fostering solicitude of our Mother the Church. —*Catholic Mirror.*

Mr. Cunningham, of Philadelphia, has just published "Grace Morton; or, The Inheritance," a Catholic Tale. None the worse for that the author sets herself down on the title page as M. L. M. The scene is laid in Pennsylvania, and as far as we have read it, we should judge it to be a really interesting and well-told tale of Catholic life.—*New York Tablet.*

A chastely written Catholic tale of American life, which is most pleasantly narrated; and conveys much that is instructive and elevating.—*Irish American.*

The Knout; a Tale of Poland.

Translated from the French by Mrs. J. Sadlier.
1 vol., large 18mo., neatly bound in cloth, gilt back, with frontispiece.
Price.. ....80 cents.

Laura and Anna; or, The Effect of Faith on the Character.

A beautiful tale, translated from the French by a young lady, a Graduate of St. Joseph's, Emmittsburg.
1 vol. 18mo., neatly bound in cloth.
Price. ....60 cents

The Confessors of Connaught; or, The Tenants of a Lord Bishop.

A tale of Evictions in Ireland. By Miss Meaney, author of "Grace Morton."
Small 12mo., cloth.
Price...................................... ....80 cents.

This is at once a historical and political tale of our times, founded on the sad incidents in Irish life, which, on one side, illustrate the horrible misgovernment and proselytizing efforts of England and Ireland, and on the other, the virtue and constancy with which the people of the Green Isle cling to their ancient faith and traditions. It is specially of Connaught that our author treats; and, therefore, we have pictures and portraitures of the inhuman and bigoted Lord Plunkett and his Souper minions, and of their zealous and saintly opponent, Father Lavelle. The tale is spiritedly told, and shows that its writer has a tender heart to feel and a graceful pen to record, the virtues and woes of poor Ireland.—*Irish American.*

Read this book and you will have a feeling knowledge of the sufferings of our brethren in the Isle of Saints.—*Boston Pilot.*

This is a story of Irish evictions, founded upon well-known facts. The deplorable infatuation of Lord Plunkett, Protestant Bishop of Tuam and landlord of a great portion of the town of Partry and its vicinity, is perhaps still fresh in the memory of our readers.

That a man not deficient in intellectual attainments, and really anxious to stand well with his tenantry, should have turned a deaf ear to all generous remonstrances, and should have persisted in believing that in this nineteenth century the dispossession of a multitude of helpless tenants at will in the midst of winter, was on the whole a good expedient for making the evictor's "religion popular among the victims," is one of the most impressive illustrations we have ever met with of the incurableness of judicial blindness, when contracted in opposing the Catholic Church.

This is the reflection forced upon the reader of the "Confessors of Connaught," a tale put together with remarkable skill.—*Tablet.*

We have read this work with great satisfaction. What pleases us most is to find that those noble Irish peasantry who, for the sake of their religion, were willing to endure the loss of homes, food and raiment, and all earthly comforts, have found a worthy champion to perpetuate the memory of their noble sacrifices. God bless the noble and accomplished lady who has undertaken this glorious task.—*Baltimore Catholic Mirror.*

The Young Catholic's Library.

In neat 18mo. vols., cloth. Each..50 cents.

The following volumes are now ready:

THE YOUNG CATHOLIC'S LIBRARY.

1. ***Cottage Evening Tales*** for Young People. Six Charming Tales; one for each day of the week. 1 vol. 18mo. Neat Cloth, 50 cts.
2. ***Children of the Valley;*** or, The Ghost of the Ruins. A beautiful Catholic Tale, from the French. 1 vol. 18mo Neat Cloth, 50 cts.
3. ***May Carleton's Story;*** or, The Catholic Maiden's Cross. And, The Miller's Daughter; or, The Charms of Virtue. Two lovely Tales in 1 vol. 18mo. Neat Cloth, 50 cts.
4. ***Philip Hartley;*** or, A Boy's Trials and Triumphs. A Tale by the author of "Grace Morton," etc. 1 vol. 18mo. Neat Cloth, 50 cts.
5. ***Count Leslie;*** or, The Triumph of Filial Piety. A Catholic Tale of great interest. 1 vol. 18mo. Neat Cloth, 50 cts.
6. ***A Father's Tales,*** of the French Revolution. Delightful Stories for Catholic Youth. *First series.* 1 vol. 18mo. Neat Cloth, 50 cts.
7. ***Ralph Berrien,*** and other Tales of the French Revolution. *Second series.* 1 vol. 18mo 50 cts.
8. ***Silver Grange.*** A charming American Catholic Tale. And, Philippine; or, The Captive Bride. Both in 1 vol. 18mo. 50 cts.
9. ***Helena Butler,*** a Story of the Rosary. 1 vol. 18mo. 50 cts.
10. ***Charles and Frederick.*** A beautiful Story, by Rev. John P. Donnellon. 1 vol. 18mo. 50 cts.
11. ***The Beauforts,*** a Story of the Alleghanies. 1 vol. 18mo. 50 cts.
12. ***Lauretta and the Fables.*** A charming little Book for Young People. 1 vol. 18mo. 50 cts.
13. ***Conrad and Gertrude,*** the Little Wanderers. A lovely Swiss Tale. 1 vol. 18mo. 50 cts.
14. ***Three Petitions,*** a Tale of Poland. 1 vol. 18mo. 50 cts.
15. ***Alice;*** or, The Rose of the Black Forest. A German Story. 1 vol. 18mo. 50 cts.
16. **Caroline**; or, Self-Conquest. 1 vol., 18mo. 50 cts.
17. **Tales of the Commandments.** 1 vol., 18mo. 50 cts.
18. **The Seven Corporal Works of Mercy.** 1 vol., 18mo.
19. **Elinor Johnson.** Founded on Facts, and a beautiful Catholic Tale. 1 vol., 18mo. Cloth. 50 cts.

☞ Other volumes of this series are preparing for publication.

☞ **Other volumes of this series are preparing for publication.**

These little volumes are admirably suited for the reading of Catholic children. Without being what is called "religious," the stories are thoroughly Catholic in their style and conception, and are extremely interesting.—*N. Y. Tablet.*

Excellent books which cannot fail to prove very acceptable to our little folk. —*Pilot.*

Printed in Poland
by Amazon Fulfillment
Poland Sp. z o.o., Wrocław